Success with
Rhododendrons and Azaleas

Success with Rhododendrons and Azaleas

by
H. Edward Reiley

TIMBER PRESS
Portland, Oregon

Neither Timber Press, Inc., nor H. Edward Reiley is liable for injury or damage resulting from the use of materials mentioned in this book. Readers are urged to follow all label precautions when handling garden chemicals.

Cover photograph courtesy of the author.

Drawings on pp. 25, 98, 130, 154, and 194 by Micheline S. Ronningen, based on material provided by the author.

Reprint corrections are listed on page 285.

Paperback reprint 1995, 1998, 2002

Printed in Hong Kong

TIMBER PRESS, INC.
The Haseltine Building
133 S.W. Second Avenue, Suite 450
Portland, Oregon 97204, U. S. A.

Library of Congress Cataloging-in-Publication Data

Reiley, H. Edward.
    Success with rhododendrons and azaleas / by H. Edward Reiley.
        p. cm.
    Includes bibliographical references and indexes.
    ISBN 0-88192-331-1 (paperback)
    1. Rhododendron. 2. Azalea. I. Title.
SB413.R47R35   1992
635.9'3362—dc20   91-23249
                                CIP

Contents

Preface   9

Acknowledgments   10

ONE: *History*   13
  Taxonomy and Origins   13
  Plant Introductions   17
  Azaleas   20

TWO: *Site Selection and Growing Requirements*   23
  Soil pH   24
  Soil Drainage and Moisture   28
  Light   31
  Organic Matter and Mulches   33
  Minerals: N–P–K   36
  Wind Damage and Air Drainage   37
  Air Temperature   38

THREE: *Selection of Rhododendron Species/Cultivars*   41
  Climate   42
  What Plants and Where to Purchase Them   46
  The Good Doer Lists   47

FOUR: *Use in the Landscape*   83
  Color Guidelines   84
  Specific Uses in the Landscape   85
    Specimen Plants/Accent Plants   85
    Group Plantings of *Rhododendron*   86
    Border Plantings, Screens, and Hedges   87
    Woodland Plantings   87
    Container Growing and Bonsai   89
    Foundation Plantings and Companion Plants   90

FIVE: *Transplanting to the Landscape*   93
  Preparing to Plant   94
  Planting   97
  Aftercare   100
  Transplanting Large *Rhododendron*   102

SIX: *Care in the Landscape*   105
  Watering   105
  Mulching   107
  Nutritional Needs   108
  Weeds   112
  Pruning   113

SEVEN: *Plant Disorders*   119
  Fungus Diseases   120
  Insects   126
  Physiological Problems   132

EIGHT: *Propagation*   135
  Cutting Basics   136
  Evergreen Azaleas   143
  Deciduous Azaleas   146
  Rhododendrons   149
  Other Methods   157

NINE: *Nursery Growing*   165
  Field Growing   165
    Transplanting Liners   166
    Second Year Field Management   173
  Container Growing   177

TEN: *Hybridizing*   187
  Introduction   187
  Azaleas   190
  Rhododendrons   192
  Making a Cross   194
  The Seedlings   198

ELEVEN: *The Flower Show*   201
  Organizing   201
  Preparing Trusses for Judging   204
  Show Classes and Rules for Entry   206

APPENDIX A: *Good Doer Tables*   211

APPENDIX B: *Plant Listing by Flower Color*   258

APPENDIX C: *Cold Tolerant Plants*   265

Glossary   266

Further Reading   269

Plant Index: Rhododendrons   271

Plant Index: Azaleas   277

Subject Index   283

Color illustrations:

Figs. 9–64 follow page 64

Figs. 65–81 follow page 88

Figs. 82–88 follow page 92

Figs. 128–134 follow page 208

Preface

Rhododendrons and azaleas are more exacting in their cultural requirements than many commonly grown plants and so will not readily grow in every garden. On the other hand the genus *Rhododendron* is so diverse that with some modification of site and the correct selection of species or cultivar most garden sites can be modified to meet their requirements.

Wherever successfully grown they are without equal as landscape plants. The evergreen forms are beautiful year-round, the deciduous azaleas have beautiful winter stems, bark and buds, and offer some of the brightest colors of yellow and orange when in flower. As a group they surpass any other plant in the landscape in their beauty.

This book is written out of years of practical knowledge of propagating and growing rhododendrons and azaleas in the garden, nursery, and landscape. It will not simply advise the reader on what needs to be done to successfully grow these plants, but gives specific details on how this can be accomplished. This is not intended for experts interested in a source of scientific knowledge but rather represents the personal experience and successful techniques used over many years of growing these beautiful plants. Technical information on diseases and insects is derived from a number of state university experimental stations.

I am of the belief that the information presented here is sufficient to lead the beginner to success in growing these plants and will assist current growers to grow them more successfully.

A word of caution is in order, however. By becoming a successful grower the reader will be exposed to a contagion for which there is no cure. Once infected with an appreciation of rhododendrons and azaleas most gardeners spend a lifetime collecting these most beautiful of all plants.

Acknowledgments

To my wife Mary for the many hours at the typewriter; to Richard Abel for his patience and editorial skill; and to all these listed below who provided pictures, information, direction, and encouragement.

Allen, Mrs. Melvin	Santa Cruz, California
Arsen, Frank	Lindenhurst, New York
Ayers, Jack, Dr.	Oakton, Virginia
Baird, Marjorie	Bellevue, Washington
Beasley, Mrs. George, Sr.	Lavonia, Georgia
Beaudry, Norman and Jean	Bethesda, Maryland
Bedwell, William	Richmond, Virginia
Behrendt, Walter	St. Louis, Missouri
Bosley, Paul R., Jr.	Mentor, Ohio
Brooks, Richard	Concord, Massachusetts
Cathey, Henry, Dr.	Washington, D.C.
Chaiken, Richard, Dr.	Falmouth, Massachusetts
Clark, Elinor	Ashfield, Massachusetts
Day, Norma	Smithburg, Maryland
Deckert, Emile	Hampstead, Maryland
Donovan, Ian E.	Newton, Massachusetts
Dyer, Russell	Southampton, Hampshire, U.K.
Dzurick, Ernie	Bellevue, Washington
Eaton, Mr. and Mrs. Lesley	Australia
Egan, Ed	Tigard, Oregon
Fox, Stephen and Anne	Manchester, U.K.
French, Betty (Hon. Sect.)	R.H.S., U.K.
Galle, Fred C.	Hamilton, Georgia

Goodrich, Col. and Mrs. R. H.	Vienna, Virginia
Gouin, Francis R., Dr.	College Park, Maryland
Greer, Harold	Eugene, Oregon
Hall, Barbara	Gloucester, Virginia
Hattery, Suzanne	Seattle, Washington
Heller, Virginia	Detroit, Michigan
Hixson, John	Watsonville, California
James, Paul S.	Boones Mill, Virginia
Jones, Adele	Lake Oswego, Oregon
Jurgens, Michael	Berkshire, U.K.
Justice, Clive L.	British Columbia, Canada
Kehr, August E., Dr.	Hendersonvill, North Carolina
Kennell, Austin	Waynesboro, Virginia
Layman, Daniel (Betts)	Wynnewood, Pennsylvania
Leach, David G., Dr.	North Madison, Ohio
McDonald, Kenneth, Jr.	Hampton, Virginia
McDonald, Sandra, Dr.	Hampton, Virginia
McNees, Pete	Tuscumbia, Alabama
Myers, Helen	Westminster, Maryland
Neal, John W., Jr., Dr.	Beltsville, Maryland
Parks, Joe B.	Dover, New Hampshire
Paschall, Eugene	Palos Heights, Illinois
Pierce, Lawrence J.	Seattle, Washington
Ring, George W., III	Fairfax, Virginia
Ring, Thomas L., Dr.	Bellaire, Ohio
Robinson, C. E.	Auburn, Alabama
Salley, Homer, Dr.	Grand Rapids, Ohio
Sandifur, Mrs. J. J.	Aberdeen, Washington
Schram, Brian	Fenwick, Ontario, Canada
Schroeder, Steven	Evansville, Indiana
Smith, Clarence	Gaston, Oregon
Spady, Herbert A., Dr.	Salem, Oregon
Sproul, Hugh B., Jr.	Staunton, Virginia
Thornton, John T., Dr.	Franklinton, Louisiana
VanVeen, Ted	Portland, Oregon
Voss, Donald H.	Vienna, Virginia
Watts, Mrs. Lynden M.	Bellevue, Washington
Weiskittel, Harry	Chase, Maryland
Wood, Edward G., Dr.	Crestwood, Missouri

ONE: *History*

TAXONOMY AND ORIGINS

The genus *Rhododendron* is a member of the Heath family of plants, which is an offshoot of the Magnolia family. The taxonomy is as follows:

Division: Magnoliophyta
Class: Magnoliopsida
Subclass: Dilleniidae
Order: Ericales
Family: Ericaceae or Heath
Genus: *Rhododendron*

The genus *Rhododendron* is one of the largest in the plant kingdom, made up of nearly 1,000 species, ranging in size from the alpines which are a couple of inches (5 cm) tall to tree size plants up to eighty feet (24 m) tall. They bear flowers in nearly every color other than true blue, and some, especially those producing lighter colored flowers, are fragrant.

I have no intention of overwhelming the novice rhododendron grower with classification and listing of all of the rhododendron species. For present purposes we need only note that all rhododendron species can be assigned to one of two divisions: Elepidote and Lepidote.

The Elepidote rhododendron species are non-scaly, large-leaved forms which generally grow to be large plants at maturity. Scaly refers to the presence or absence of small, almost microscopic scales on the underside of the plant leaves. The Lepidote species are scaly, small-leaved forms which generally mature at a smaller size. The two groups differ sufficiently in their genetic makeup that cross-breeding or hybridizing between them is virtually impossible. Most growers' catalogs as well as other materials describing rhododendrons maintain this differentiation.

The huge number of species in the genus *Rhododendron* are not only diverse in size, shape, and color but also in the growing conditions they require. Up and down Asian mountain slopes they are found growing as epiphytes in the tops of trees in rainforests and as terrestrials under trees, along river beds and on rocks on bare cliffs, on crumbled rocky sites, on ledges and in ravines, and in open grassland. Light conditions vary from full sun to complete shade. They so dominate the terrain in some areas that entire mountain slopes are completely covered, yet in other cases they may appear as single trees. Very few plant groups show as much variability as the genus *Rhododendron*.

In *Plant Hunters Paradise* (Jonathan Cape Ltd., 1938) Kingdon-Ward observed that rhododendrons simply change their growth form as they adapt to different altitudes, a characteristic shared by no other genus. He found them growing from sea level to 15,000 ft. (4,572 m) in the Himalayas in what he described as "three broad belts." The first from sea level to 5,000 ft. (1,524 m) dominated by small, often epiphytic shrubs, the second belt from 5,000 to 10,000 ft. (1,524–3,048 m) as trees and shrubs, and the third belt from 10,000 to 15,000 ft. (3,048 to 4,572 m) with shrubs becoming increasingly more dwarf at the higher elevations.

Rhododendrons are believed to have originated in Asia, for it is here that the greatest number of species exist in the wild. The center of origin seems to be at about where Burma, Yunnan, and Tibet meet because the widest variety of species is found in this area. The region is marked by high humidity, the atmosphere is always wet and misty since the rains persist all summer, and deep snow covers the ground in winter. From this area they continued to spread around the world to wherever soil and climate allowed growth. Figs. 1 and 2 show the distribution in the wild in North America, Europe, and Asia respectively. Their distribution is, with a few minor exceptions, confined to the Northern Hemisphere. Dr. David G. Leach in his *Rhododendrons of the World* (Charles Scribner's Sons, New York, 1961, p. 19) writes, "They reach their southernmost limit in northern Australia which has one species, possibly an immigrant from a secondary concentration of about 200 species in New Guinea."

Rhododendrons have existed for approximately fifty million years in essentially the same form as found in Asia today.

A look at their native habitat indicates that *Rhododendron* generally inhabit mountains. The climatic and soil conditions of mountainous areas appears most congenial to their growth and can be characterized by cooler temperatures and more precipitation. These same climatic conditions readily evolve acidic soil and a buildup of organic matter on top of the soil. Furthermore mountain soils are largely

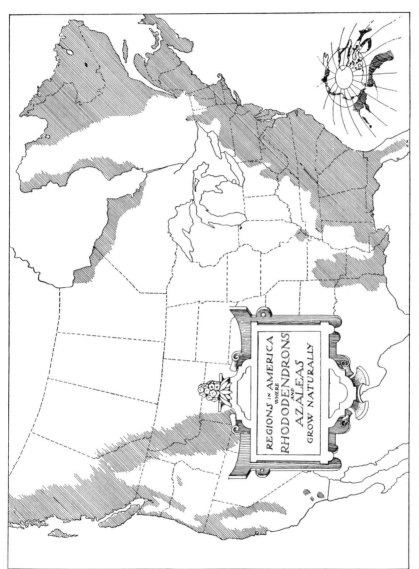

Fig. 1. Regions in North America where rhododendrons and azaleas grow naturally. From *Rhododendrons of the World* by David G. Leach, published by Charles Scribner's Sons, New York, 1961, p. 20. Reprinted by permission.

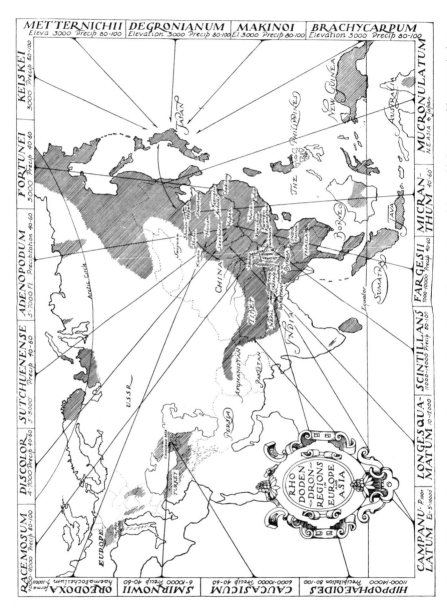

Fig. 2. Rhododendron regions in Europe and Asia. From *Rhododendrons of the World*. Reprinted by permission.

formed by erosion of bed rock, resulting in a coarse, well drained soil. Cooler summer temperatures, continued high humidity, and good snow cover in winter found in most mountain areas round out the environment in which rhododendrons evolved and to which they are adapted.

In all situations in which soil, site, and climatic conditions are favorable, rhododendrons are capable of dominating the landscape. The huge numbers of seeds produced each year, some of which are winged for better distribution by the wind, often results in solid masses of seedlings which quickly cover the ground and smother out all competition. Being social plants capable of growing in dense clumps, they successfully crowd out other species and in effect produce their own wind protection and shade. Plant collector Kingdon-Ward described, in *RHS-Rhododendron Yearbook 1947*, "The rocks glowing with a bright red crest of *R. simsii*," as the entire surface was covered with and dominated by rhododendron.

PLANT INTRODUCTIONS

It is difficult to convey the anticipation and eagerness with which the introduction of a new species or hybrid from the wild is greeted by rhododendron collectors. Not only the collectors but hybridizers become inextricably bound up in the excitement of a new find offering a new color, disease resistance, outstanding foliage, compact plant habit, or any one of a number of new and potentially outstanding characteristics. Being among the first to grow a new introduction or use it in a breeding program bestows a definite prestige on the grower.

This kind of excitement filled the minds and hearts of the early plant explorers, motivating them to risk life and limb in inhospitable settings to discover and return to the gardening world yet another example of the superb plants found in *Rhododendron.*

The new species were collected and sent in increasing numbers primarily to Britain and also to Germany, Holland, or wherever discerning horticulturists were prepared to spend the money to support the collectors in the field. Only in the 20th century were North Americans prepared to join the ranks of their European counterparts. One can imagine the excitement these new, heretofore unheard of, species provoked and the extraordinary competition among collectors to be among the first to own each new treasure. Early introductions include

1653	*Rhododendron hirsutum* from the Alps
1734–36	*Rhododendron canescens, R. nudiflorum* (now *periclymenoides*), *R. viscosum,* and *R. maximum* from North America
1752	*Rhododendron ferrugineum* from the Alps
1763	*Rhododendron ponticum* from Gibraltar
1780–96	German naturalist Pallas described *Rhododendron dauricum, R. flavum,* and *R. chrysanthum* from eastern Europe and Asia
1800	Still only twelve species known in cultivation
1803	*Rhododendron caucasicum, R. obtusum,* and *R. minus* from North America
1809	*Rhododendron catawbiense* from North America
1823	*Rhododendron molle* from China
1832	*Rhododendron zeylanicum* from Ceylon
1835	*Rhododendron campanulatum* from the Himalayas of Sikkim and Nepal
1840	*Rhododendron barbatum* from the Himalayas of Nepal and Sikkim

One of the first explorers was Sir Charles Hooker who in 1850 introduced forty-five species from Sikkim in the Himalayas. Introductions included the luminous, yellow-flowered *Rhododendron campylocarpum* and *R. wightii,* the red *R. thompsonii,* the epiphytes *R. dalhonsiae* and *R. maddenii,* and the treelike *R. falconeri, R. grande,* and *R. hodgsonii.*

Robert Fortune sent seeds of *R. fortunei* from China to England in 1850. This species proves to be one of the most valuable parents in breeding large-flowered, fragrant hybrids which are also widely adaptable and cold hardy. Also in the 19th century Dr. Augustine Henny introduced the blue flowering *R. augustinii.*

One can only imagine the breathtaking sights unfolding before the early plant explorers as they encountered entire mountainsides radiating in full color or their anticipation of what lay over the next hill or hidden in the valley below.

20th-Century Explorers

By the beginning of the 20th century 300 species were known to botanists and about thirty-five were in cultivation. Meanwhile enthusiasm for the genus was growing and led to increasing support among plant collectors eager to send explorers into the wilderness to search out new and exciting plants. Some of the most notable of these 20th-century explorers include

E. H. Wilson, 1899. Wilson sent back forty new species of *Rhododendron* among hundreds of other plants during his first two years in China. Many of his finds are cold hardy and widely adaptable and include *Rhododendron discolor* with its large, fragrant, white blossoms and *R. williamsianum,* a low growing, dense species with nodding, pink bells. Both these species contributed to the interest and enthusiasm for *Rhododendron,* encouraging others to join the race of discovery and return to Europe and North American gardens a seemingly inexhaustible array of exotic wonders.

George Forest, 1904. Forest was sent to China to explore south of the area E. H. Wilson explored. He introduced 260 species ranging from the 3 in. (7.5 cm) tall, scarlet-flowered *Rhododendron forrestii* to the treelike *R. sino-grande,* 30 ft. (9 m) tall with leaves 1 ft. (30 cm) wide by 3 ft. (90 cm) long. Wilson's introductions were hardier than those made by Forest but Forest sent back a higher number of species. One of the best of Forest's introductions is *R. croceum.*

F. Kingdon-Ward, 1911. Kingdon-Ward introduced nearly 100 species from China, Tibet, Burma, and Assam. Most notable among his introductions is *Rhododendron wardii,* the classic yellow. Other introductions include *R. macabeanum, R. elliottii, R. pemakoense,* and *R. leucaspis.*

While far from complete, this brief account of the major plant explorers and their collections does give some sense of the fascination rhododendrons have held for gardeners for nearly 200 years.

At present very little plant exploration is going on. The huge costs involved in mounting such expeditions and limited access to China and other Asian countries have greatly reduced the search for new plants. Much remains to be explored and certainly when circumstances permit many new and exciting species will be found. Today's 20th-century gardener and hybridizer must for the most part rely on the gene pool now available.

Species and Hybrids in the Wild

Species rhododendrons are plants that have pretty much evolved in isolation. Plants in isolated groups tend to become more alike and each such group evolves uniform characteristics. Such uniformity of character is the result of inbreeding within the species over great lengths of time. Plants inheriting characteristics unsuited to local growing conditions do not survive. Consequently a uniform race of plants adapted to a specific area results, and movement of plants into areas widely divergent results in less than favorable plant response.

Species tend to propagate "true" from seed with very little variability among seedlings.

Hybrids in the wild result from the cross-pollination between populations of two different species. The resulting seedlings are genetically more heterogeneous than their parents, exhibit more variation among themselves, and differ from either parent. Hybrids are often more vigorous and adapt more readily to a wider variety of growing conditions than their parents.

It is initially difficult to determine whether a plant newly discovered in the wild is a species or a natural hybrid. Much hybridization spontaneously occurs whenever populations of species come together; this can lead to much debate regarding whether such plants as *R. yakushimanum* Mist Maiden, for example, are species or hybrid. The significant thing to most gardeners fortunate enough to own one of these gems is that they can be beautiful, exciting plants and a great addition to the garden regardless of whether they are species or hybrid.

Hybridizing

In 1810 the Englishman Michael Waterer made the first artificial cross of rhododendron species using the North American *Rhododendron maximum* and *R. catawbiense*. His success led to further hybridizing activity using the newly discovered Asian species to improve flower size and color. The first hybrids introduced into commerce were those of Anthony Waterer, Knap Hill Nursery, in the 1860s. Some of these hybrids are so outstanding that they remain standard commercial hybrids in the eastern U.S.A. and in other areas of extreme cold. They are commonly known as the "Ironclads" due to their cold hardiness and ease of cultivation.

Hybridizing is an ongoing activity pursued by horticulturists and professional geneticists as well as hobbyists. Numerous new hybrids, and a handful of very exciting hybrids, are released to the world each year. A few of these introductions are genuine improvement upon previous cultivars.

AZALEAS

Azaleas are members of the genus *Rhododendron* and the binomial system for identifying azaleas uses for example *Rhododendron* (genus) *kaempferi* (species). But because most gardeners and nurseries continue to separate azaleas from the rest of the genus *Rhododendron*, I refer to them as "azaleas" in this book, using *Rhododendron* for the balance of the genus.

There are two distinct and separate groups of azaleas: the deciduous azaleas, which lose their leaves in winter, and the evergreen azaleas, which hold some of their leaves year-round. These two groups are not sufficiently related genetically to readily cross-breed although there are a few cases where a viable hybrid has resulted.

Azaleas are not as widely distributed over the earth's surface as are the other rhododendrons. The wild azalea species are found in eastern North America and eastern Asia, China, Taiwan, Japan, Korea, the Philippines, and central Vietnam. One species is found in the Caucasus Mountains (the Pontic azalea or *R. flavum*), and one in the Pacific Northwest (*R. occidentale*). The largest number of the deciduous species are found in North America.

The evergreen azaleas are found growing naturally in Japan, Taiwan, the Philippines, Korea, southeastern China, and central Vietnam.

The Asian evergreen species are further grouped into two subseries, Obtusum and Tashiroi. The Tashiroi subseries contains only one species (*R. tashiroi*) from Japan. The Obtusum subseries contains over forty species* from the following geographic areas:

CHINA
R. microphyton
R. simsii

JAPAN
R. indicum
R. kaempferi
R. komiyamae
R. kiusianum
R. macrosepalum
R. mucronatum
R. obtusum
R. otakumii
R. repense
R. sataense
R. scabrum
R. serpyllifolium
R. serpyllifolium var. albiflorum
R. tamurae
R. tosaense
R. tschonoskii
R. tsusiophyllum

KOREA
R. yedoense
R. yedoense var. poukhanense

TAIWAN
R. nakaharai
R. oldhamii
R. rubropilosum

---

*plus 33 uncommon species from Vietnam (2), China (21), Japan (2), Taiwan (7), and Korea (1).

Deciduous azalea species are native to China, Europe, Japan, and North America as follows:

CHINA
R. farrerae
R. mariesii
R. molle

EUROPE
R. luteum

JAPAN
R. albrechtii
R. amogianum
R. japonicum
R. nipponicum
R. nudipes
R. pentaphyllum
R. quinquefolium
R. reticulatum
R. sanctum

NORTH AMERICA
R. alabamense
R. arborescens
R. atlanticum
R. austrinum
R. bakeri
R. calendulaceum
R. canadense
R. canescens
R. coryi
R. flammeum
R. oblongifolium
R. occidentale
R. periclymenoides (R. nudiflorum)
R. prinophyllum (R. roseum)
R. prunifolium
R. serrulatum
R. vaseyi
R. viscosum

Azaleas prefer the same soil and climatic conditions as rhododendrons—namely a cool, moist atmosphere, an acid soil with good internal drainage, and some protection from strong winds. They tolerate more sun than the larger leaved rhododendrons. The natural distribution of azaleas is generally in mountainous regions providing these conditions.

To date no yellow-flowered or deep blue-flowered evergreen azaleas have been discovered. However, the deciduous azaleas present some beautiful yellows and oranges as well as white, pink, red, yet again no blue.

I hope this brief discussion, aimed at providing some idea of where these exciting plants come from and how they reached modern gardens, has fostered some interest in the genus *Rhododendron*.

TWO: *Site Selection and Growing Requirements*

Site selection, and if necessary modification, is one of the most important elements in successfully growing rhododendrons and azaleas. As they prefer an acid soil their requirements differ markedly from most landscape plants. Rhododendron growers having a naturally satisfactory site are fortunate since these plants could be grown with very little effort. As with most plant species a poor site yields poor growth; it is in these cases that modification of the site becomes necessary. Fortunately a few minor adjustments can often transform a poor site into a very satisfactory one.

As noted earlier, rhododendrons generally grow most luxuriously and in greater numbers and variety of species in mountainous areas. So it follows that success is dependent upon duplicating such conditions as nearly as possible. Some of the specific conditions rhododendrons and azaleas need to flourish are:

1. An acid soil—pH between 4.5 and 5.5.

2. Good soil drainage, (especially refers to the structural drainage of the soil) and cool soil temperature.

3. Light shade—as a rule of thumb the larger the plant leaves the more shade is required.

4. A high percentage of organic matter in the soil especially near the surface and a loose porous mulch.

5. Adequate light for flower bud formation.

6. Protection from wind and air drainage with no frost pockets.

7. Air temperature of −20°F (−28°C) to 90°F (32°C).

Regardless of which landscape use is intended, the above conditions must be met for rhododendrons to flourish. If most of these conditions are present in the garden, little or no modification will be needed. But as existing conditions diverge from these characteristics, an increasing number of modifications are required.

SOIL pH

Azaleas and rhododendrons grow best in a soil with a pH in the range of 4.5–5.5. A pH above 7 indicates an alkaline or sweet soil, while a pH below 7 indicates an acidic or sour soil (see Fig. 3). pH measurements are logarithmic, meaning that each pH unit is 10 times as acidic or alkaline as the unit before or after it. Thus a soil pH of 5.5 is 10 times more acid than a soil pH of 6.5 and 100 times more acid than a pH of 7.5.

— 0.0—	
— 1.0—	ACID RANGE
— 2.0—	
— 3.0—	
— 4.0—	
— 5.0—	Best Range for Azaleas and Rhododendrons
— 6.0—	
— 7.0—	—————————— NEUTRAL ——————————
— 8.0—	
— 9.0—	
—10.0—	ALKALINE RANGE
—11.0—	
—12.0—	
—13.0—	
—14.0—	

Fig. 3.   pH scale. A pH of 7.0 is neutral, pH 1.0 is extremely acidic, and pH 14.0 would represent the most alkaline soil. Each unit on the scale is ten times more acid or alkaline than the one next to it. Thus a pH of 4.5 is ten times as acid as a pH of 5.5 and 100 times as acid as pH 6.5.

The reason rhododendrons and azaleas need a soil pH of 4.5–5.5 is that those soil minerals most needed by plants of this genus for good growth are in soluble form in this pH range. Soil pH also affects the pH of plant cell sap. Departures from proper acidity cause elements of plant food to become insoluble in the cell sap and thus unavailable to the plant. As soil pH changes, the availability of various plant food elements in the soil solution changes. Fig. 4 shows the availability of plant nutrients at various pH levels. Iron availability for example, essential to *Rhododendron* for the manufacture of chlorophyll, starts decreasing at about 5.5. Acid-loving plants would be unable to manufacture sufficient chlorophyll under such soil conditions of pH above 5.5. Lack of chlorophyll production leads to

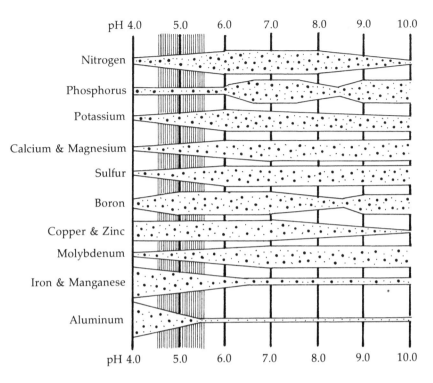

Fig. 4.   Nutrient availability by soil pH. Different mineral elements vary in availability to plants by soil pH. In the illustration above, the wider the bar the more available is that particular element. Rhododendron soil pH preference is 4.5 to 5.5. Notice how much more iron and manganese are available in acid (below 7.0) soils. Also of note is how aluminum, which is toxic to plants, increases at pH below 5.0 (From Truog, USDA Yearbook of Agriculture 1943–47).

the yellowing of foliage; the resulting chlorosis can result in plant death if the soil pH is not amended to the proper range.

Conversely, at a pH range of 5.5–6.5 available calcium and magnesium begin to increase. Rhododendrons and azaleas are adversely affected by high soil levels of free calcium and magnesium, and so not only are needed elements unavailable above pH 5.5 but other elements are available at toxic levels.

The only way to accurately determine soil pH is by taking a soil test. The do-it-yourself pH test is very simple and can be done by the gardener with equipment such as a pH meter or with chemicals available in soil test kits. However, particularly if you suspect a problem, it is best to resort to the more accurate tests made by local soil testing laboratories including those at state agricultural colleges.

If soil pH is not within the proper range the following guidelines can be used to correct it.

a. **Soil Too Acid.** If the soil tests indicate a pH below 4.5 some correction is necessary. The most effective material to use in raising soil pH is dolomitic limestone which contains more of the essential plant food element magnesium than do other forms of lime. Since lime moves through the soil very slowly the material needs to be incorporated into the soil before planting. To raise pH one unit, approximately 7–8 pounds (3.0–3.6 kg) of ground limestone per 100 sq. ft. (10 m²) is required for loam soils. Heavy soils, those with high clay content, need slightly more, 9–10 pounds (5 kg); sandy soils require only 6 pounds (3 kg) to change the pH one unit. These differences are due to the higher cation exchange capacity of clay that allows it to hold more hydrogen ions (elemental hydrogen). These must be replaced by calcium ions in order to change soil pH. The soil needs to be re-tested a month after the lime application to again determine the actual pH. If additional lime is needed it can be broadcast on the soil surface after planting and will move down through the soil at the rate of about 0.5–1 inch (1.3–2.5 cm) per year. Since limestone is finely ground stone there is no danger of root burning in mixing limestone in the soil at planting time. Applying too much calcium, by an overly heavy lime application, can however produce toxic levels of calcium.

b. **Acidity in the Proper Range.** If soil pH tests between 4.5 and 5.5, which fortunately is the case in many soils, no need exists to modify it. The pH of any acidic soil amendments used, such as sphagnum peat moss, should be checked if the soil pH is near 4.5 because their addition may lower soil pH below the satisfactory range. To cancel out this effect 1.5 pounds (0.7 kg) of dolomitic limestone per 4 cu. ft. bag of sphagnum peat moss raises the pH of the moss from 3.5 to 5.7. This matter is discussed in greater detail under soil amendments.

c. **Soil Not Acid Enough.** In some areas the soil is too alkaline for the best growth of rhododendrons. High pH readings are usually the outcome of one of two processes. One is that calcium and/or sodium ions build up in the soil in regions of low rainfall. These ions replace hydrogen ions, which are the acidifiers, and soil pH goes up. The other common cause is soil formed from limestone which again results in excess calcium ions in the soil. In either case a soil pH above 5.5 requires modification.

   Either of two materials is recommended to lower soil pH or acidify the soil. The first is iron or ferrous sulfate, a fast-acting material which changes pH immediately upon watering into the soil. The sulfate portion combines with calcium to form soluble calcium sulfate which leaches from the soil and removes the calcium. The treatment of soil of limestone origin is frequently a temporary measure since further weathering of the limestone moves the pH up again. Additional soil tests, about every six months, are advised to monitor the condition. Since iron sulfate is a salt it can severely damage plant roots to the point of toxicity, even in wet soils, if too much is applied at once. Reverse osmosis occurs when the soil salt content is higher than the salt content of the root cells; water then moves out of the plant cells and into the surrounding soil, leading to dehydration of the roots. To avoid a salt buildup use several light applications of ferrous sulfate at one pound (0.45 kg) per 100 sq. ft. (10 m²) of area at one week intervals. Water in thoroughly with about 1 in. (2.5 cm) of water. Each application will change soil pH about 0.2 pH units. In preparing new beds the entire quantity of ferrous sulfate needed to bring about the desired pH change can be applied in a single application. (See Fig. 5 for amount to use.) Wait at least one week after treatment before planting.

To Change pH from	Pounds of Ferrous Sulphate Needed Per 100 Square Feet	Metric Equivalent (kg)
7.5 to 7.0	8.2	3.7
7.5 to 6.5	9.4	4.3
7.5 to 6.0	16.5	7.2
7.5 to 5.5	23.5	10.5
7.5 to 5.0	30.6	13.7
7.0 to 6.5	7.1	3.2
7.0 to 6.0	9.4	4.3
7.0 to 5.5	16.5	7.2
7.0 to 5.0	23.5	10.5
6.5 to 6.0	7.1	3.2
6.5 to 5.5	11.8	5.4
6.5 to 5.0	18.8	8.6
6.0 to 5.5	7.1	3.2
6.0 to 5.0	14.1	6.2
5.5 to 5.0	7.1	3.2

Fig. 5.   Adjusting soil pH. From *Rhododendrons of the World,* p. 281. Metric equivalents added; pH readings of 8.0 omitted. Note that one-fifth as much sulfur is required to yield the same results as iron sulfate (ferrous sulphate).

The other material used to lower soil pH is sulfur. It is much slower in its action but the acidifying effect lasts much longer. It is slower because elemental sulfur first forms sulfuric acid. Sulfates then develop which combine with calcium and remove calcium ions from the soil. The more finely ground the sulfur the faster it will react to remove calcium. Sulfur must be physically incorporated into the soil since it is not soluble in water. The change in pH caused by sulfur begins slowly, gradually gathering speed as the soil becomes more acid. A re-test of soil pH should be delayed for a year to best determine the effect of the sulfur application.

Aluminum sulfate is often recommended as a soil acidifier and while very effective, it is not recommended for rhododendrons. *Rhododendron* is quite easily damaged by excess aluminum in the soil. As soil pH drops below 5.0 more aluminum ions become available in increasing numbers.

Rhododendrons do not grow well in alkaline soils, including those of limestone parent material. This need not be cause for despair, however, since *Rhododendron* plantings can still be very successful. The gardener need only incorporate large amounts of organic matter into the soil or place acid soil atop existing soil or employ a combination of these two methods to assure success. The important point is to raise the plant roots up out of the native alkaline soil and allow them to grow into an amended or replaced medium of a proper pH. More detail on this alternative is given in Chapter Five.

Proper soil pH is especially important when plants are forcibly grown under heavy fertilization to promote maximum growth. The higher the concentration of soluble salts in the soil, resulting from heavy fertilization, the more sensitive the plant will be to soil pH. Rhododendrons grow much more satisfactorily, and over a wider range of pH, in woodland soils that are very low in soluble plant food elements than in the well fertilized landscape or nursery. This difference may reflect an imbalance of minor plant food elements such as iron or magnesium in relation to the major elements of nitrogen, phosphorus and potassium available to the plant. This hypothesis is supported by recent research which shows that when sphagnum peat moss is used along with heavy applications of fertilizer, pH tolerance is widened. It is thought that the peat moss supplies minor elements responsible for the difference. Similar effects result from the addition of minor elements to major element fertilizers in the absence of peat moss. Peat moss also has a high ion exchange capacity and thus can buffer the effect of excess calcium.

pH tolerance does vary among rhododendron species and cultivars. For example, the cultivar 'Cunninghams White' tolerates a higher soil pH than most other rhododendrons. This is one of the reasons 'Cunninghams White' is commonly used as a rootstock in grafting plants for the alkaline regions of Europe.

SOIL DRAINAGE AND MOISTURE

Rhododendrons and azaleas, being mostly represented as broadleaved evergreens, require ample moisture year-round. In addition they require high levels of oxygen around their roots. The consequence of these requirements points to the need for a well drained yet moisture retentive soil. Such a medium may seem a contradiction but is not; moist is quite different from wet.

Soils are made up of a collection of solid particles with pore spaces between the particles. These pore spaces are largest in sandy soils, with their characteristic large soil particles, and smallest in clay soils which are composed of small, tightly packed, soil particles. The pore space in soils fills with water and air in varying percentages; these percentages constantly vary. The pore spaces of a poorly drained soil contain a much higher percentage of water than air. The heavier water simply replaces the air in the pore space and thereby excludes soil oxygen. In a well drained soil water moves through the pores and on down into the subsoil and oxygen-rich air is pulled in behind the water. Well drained soil, except for sandy soils, retains enough moisture and plant food elements in a film around the soil particles to allow plant roots rapid growth. Optimum growing conditions exist when soil pore space is filled with approximately 50% air and 50% water. Plants grow over a wide range of soil moisture/air conditions, but rhododendrons and azaleas require more oxygen around the roots than do most.

Soils are classified according to texture or size of soil particles. Sandy soils have large soil particles and are classified as light. Clay soils have small soil particles and are classified as heavy. Soil texture or particle size determine to a large extent how much water a soil will retain. Small particles collectively present a greater soil surface area. As each particle holds a thin film of water around it by the forces of adhesion and cohesion, much more water can then be held than in soils composed of large particles. Smaller pore spaces also better act as capillary tubes to pull up and hold water. Light or sandy soils with larger soil particles and less surface area thus hold less water than silt and clay soils.

Soil amendments can be used to modify the moisture-holding capacity of soils. Sandy soils lose water and soluble fertilizer elements rapidly. The best way to improve a sandy soil is to add organic matter such as coarse sphagnum peat moss, bark, sawdust, compost, or other materials that will remain in the soil as long as possible before total decay. As much as 50% of the growing medium by volume for *Rhododendron* should consist of organic matter. Sphagnum peat moss holds more water than most organic amendments, and if coarse sphagnum moss is used, it will last a reasonable length of time. Pine bark will last even longer in the soil, but it will not retain as much moisture. Hardwood barks have a high cellulose content and will decompose quickly in the soil, so they are not recommended as amendments. Sandy soils benefit greatly from the moisture retentive qualities of sphagnum moss. Use about 50% sphagnum moss in the organic amendments incorporated into sandy soils.

Clay soils on the other hand tend to be too wet. Organic amendments are again recommended since their incorporation will always
result in improved soil drainage. Bark or sawdust may be more effective than peat moss in clay soils since they will not hold as much moisture. In my opinion however, there is no substitute for the advantages of coarse sphagnum peat moss. Even for clay soils it could comprise at least 25% of the total organic amendment. Recent research
may have discouraged use of organic amendments in clay soils, but I
think any problem is more with how the plantings are made than with
any use of amendments. This will be discussed in detail in Chapter
Five. A year or two after adding organic materials, clay soil particles
start to flocculate or stick together like bread crumbs. In effect larger
soil particles form and the increasing pore size improves internal
(structural) drainage.

The texture and drainage of loam soils is intermediate between
that of clay and sandy soils. It is the best soil texture for rhododendrons and azaleas. Loams are classified as sandy loam, silt loam,
and clay loam depending on the percent of sand, silt, and clay
present.

It is easy to check soil drainage. Dig a hole 12 in. (30.5 cm) deep
and fill it with water. If water remains in the hole for more than two
hours, there is a drainage problem which can be corrected by amending the soil as outlined above. If water remains for twenty-four hours
or more, there is a serious drainage problem that cannot ordinarily be
corrected simply by adding organic matter. In this situation all
plantings need to be made on top of the soil in raised beds about 18 in.
(45.7 cm) above the existing soil level. Rainwater puddling and
remaining on top of the soil for more than a few hours after the rain
stops also indicates poor drainage and a need to grow in raised
beds.

A well drained soil is a must for rhododendrons and azaleas. If the
native soil in the planting site drains poorly the planting site must be
modified.

Rhododendrons and azaleas grow best if their roots have a cool,
moist environment. Soil moisture will not be lost as quickly from a
cool soil and will be available longer to the plant. Furthermore the
major root-rot diseases need high soil temperatures as well as wet
conditions to become pathogenic. When plants have an adequate
supply of moisture and healthy roots, good plant growth will not be
interrupted.

The most effective way to keep the soil cool is by shading the soil
surface. Shade can be provided naturally by trees or smaller plants or
with a loose, organic mulch. A mulch also provides other advantages
to be discussed later. Lath houses or planting in the shade cast by

buildings is equally effective, especially for smaller plants in nursery beds.

LIGHT

The various species and cultivars of rhododendron and azalea display a rather wide tolerance to sunlight, which illustrates their strong ability to adapt. Most rhododendron species evolved in a wet, misty atmosphere under a canopy of trees or in the open in the cool temperatures and high humidity of mountaintops, yet others have evolved in sunnier and drier conditions.

The amount of sun a particular species or cultivar of rhododendron can tolerate is often difficult to learn in advance. Azaleas seem to be better understood in this regard. The amount of sunlight will have pronounced effects on a variety of plant responses, including—the profusion of flowers, the compactness of plant growth, cold hardiness, color quality of foliage, and so forth.

So how can the grower determine the amount of sun or shade a particular species requires? Several criteria can be used to answer this question. The first general rule of thumb is that the larger the leaves, the more shade required. Further species that evolved in full sun such as *R. catawbiense*, which grows on the mountaintops of the Blue Ridge Mountains in North America, tolerate more sun than species from the deeply shaded rainforests.

Other factors that influence sun tolerance are humidity, amount and seasonal distribution of precipitation, summer high temperatures, and number of cloudy days. Full exposure on mountaintops where humidity is high is not nearly as harsh as full exposure in a dry, low humidity site. The west coast of North America has about 65% more cloudy days than the east coast, so full sun in these locations is not the same in terms of heat and subsequent drying of foliage. Misty, cloudy conditions, such as are prevalent in England, will permit the use of a wider selection of species and cultivars.

It is probably best to plant in as much sun as a specimen can tolerate without adverse effect. Plants will grow more compactly in sun, their stems seem to be tougher and more cold hardy, and they certainly set more flower buds. Conversely, plants in too much shade bloom sparingly and tend to grow tall and produce leggy flushes of growth with fewer branches.

The foliage of a plant getting too much sun will turn lighter green to yellow. As sun damage progresses the color change becomes more pronounced until edges or spots brown from completely dead tissue. The yellowing is a result of the rapid destruction of chlorophyll, a green pigment found in plant cells, due to heat buildup. The same heat buildup also causes the leaf to transpire faster and thus lose moisture more rapidly. When moisture is lost from the leaves faster than the roots can replenish it, the leaf tissue dries out and the tissue dies, turning brown. This problem is often worse in the winter because roots in frozen soil are unable to pick up moisture to replace that lost from the leaves.

Many of the small-leaved rhododendron and azaleas grow very well in full sun except in climates where temperatures stay above 90°F (32°C) week after week and the humidity is low. A single afternoon with temperatures of 95°F (35°C) and a relative humidity of 40% or lower can grievously injure virtually every species of rhododendron and azalea. To reduce or eliminate damage, site plants so they receive shade from other plants or buildings during the afternoon hours of greatest heat. Planting under trees is particularly recommended since the moisture transpired from the tree leaves raises humidity and lowers the temperature in the immediate vicinity. Buildings may offer enough shade, particularly for a north and east side planting site. If other plants or buildings are not available, lath houses may be constructed to provide shade.

Most rhododendrons growing in unmanaged woodlands do not receive enough sunlight to form compact plants or to flower at their maximum. When *Rhododendron* are planted as a primary landscape feature, many trees may have to be removed and others trimmed up to allow the best results. In the author's experience enough trees had to be removed prior to planting to provide open areas of sunlight at least two times the width of the crowns of the remaining trees—a spacing of 75–100 ft. (23–30 m)—and all lower branches had to be removed up to at least 20 ft. (6 m) above the ground level. The trees had to be removed before any planting was done to prevent possible damage to plants from falling limbs. Fig. 6 illustrates this forest area clearing for rhododendrons.

Remember that sun tolerance and heat tolerance are not the same. Plants can flourish in full sun under lower temperatures, but in temperatures above 90°F (32°C) more shade is required.

A plant will display its need for more light or shade by how compactly it grows, whether the foliage is green, or yellow and brown, and whether it sets flower buds profusely. It is not always necessary to learn this through trial and error; contact experienced growers in the local gardening area for suggestions.

Fig. 6.   Notice the wide spacing of large oak trees to allow sufficient light for good growth of rhododendrons. Large evergreens in the background provide a windbreak. Author's garden, Woodsboro, Maryland. Photo by the author.

ORGANIC MATTER AND MULCHES

There is currently much controversy over the need to amend soils for rhododendrons and azaleas with organic matter. Field grown (grown in the soil), landscape size plants may, in my experience, be planted directly into a good loam soil of proper pH without the need to add organic matter. Growth rate, however, may not be as fast as in amended soil.

Continer grown plants present quite a different situation. They are usually grown in a coarse soilless mix composed of varying combinations of peat moss, perlite, bark, vermiculite, and other materials. The texture of soilless mixes is so different from actual soil that plant roots do not readily move out of this medium and venture into the soil. Outer roots must be pulled free of such media for a distance of approximately 2 in. (5.0 cm) so they can be directly incorporated in the soil at time of planting. Amending the soil with 50% organic matter will result in more vigorous root extension since the soil texture will more closely resemble the accustomed medium. Whenever finer textured soil and coarse soilless mixes come together, the differing particle sizes cause a moisture transfer problem. The larger particles in the soilless mix dry out quickly while the finer textured soil remains moist. Furthermore moisture does not transfer from the finer soil into the coarsely textured soilless medium. The soilless medium then dries out and shrinks away from the surrounding soil. This in turn prevents any root extension into the surrounding soil. The plant roots may never grow beyond the original root ball, especially in heavy soils, and will dry out and die.

If the planting soil needs to be amended, prepare an area wide enough to accommodate 2–3 years of additional root growth. This usually means a minimum of 3–4 ft. (0.9–1.2 m) in diameter. If the plants are planted in beds, amend the entire bed with organic matter.

Organic matter does several things. As noted earlier, it greatly improves the soil's ability to hold water and nutrients. Yet the greatest benefit is that organic matter will improve soil structure and aeration and adds plant food elements to the soil. As organic materials decompose, the soil particles flocculate into bread crumb size forms and thereby improve soil structure.

When incorporating fresh non-composted bark, sawdust, and similar materials into the soil, a nitrogen fertilizer, preferably a slow release form, such as urea formaldehyde (38% nitrogen), should be dug in with the material prior to planting. This must be done as early as possible. The decomposition of the organic material requires nitrogen, and the organisms responsible for decomposition are more efficient in using soil nitrogen than are plants, resulting in a possible nitrogen deficiency in the plants. Nitrogen is later released and made available to plants as the soil organisms die and their bodies decompose. Sphagnum peat moss and composted organic materials withdraw very little nitrogen from the soil.

Coarse sphagnum peat moss is different from the finely ground peat moss usually found in garden centers. While the finely ground peat moss will improve soil structure and water holding capacity, it does not do this as effectively nor last as long in the soil as the coarse moss. Since rhododendrons are usually long-term plantings, it is preferable to use the coarse cut sphagnum peat moss.

Other materials may be dug into the soil to add organic matter, but nothing is as safe and uniform in results as sphagnum peat moss or composted bark. Leaves, leaf mold, wood chips, and sawdust may be used but leaves and leaf mold do not persist in a landscape planting. Chips and sawdust adversely affect nitrogen availability unless nitrogen is added and the material composted before digging into the soil. Nitrogen reduction is not as severe with pine, fir, or redwood sawdust. Hardwood bark should not be used as a soil amendment because of its high cellulose content. Severe nitrogen withdrawal occurs as the cellulose is quickly broken down by soil organisms. The net effect is that hardwood bark is an organic matter soil amendment that disappears rapidly while creating a critical nitrogen deficiency.

To maintain soil organic matter, loose organic mulch needs to be added each year, late in the season, just after the soil freezes or growth has hardened off. This late application of mulch will also help control stem bark split. As the organic mulch rots over the years, earthworm activity carries it down through the soil to maintain a higher level of soil organic matter. The rotting mulch also builds a layer of humus on top of the soil which benefits the plant roots and is much like the conditions many *Rhododendron* enjoyed in their native regions. This buildup of a humus layer on top of the soil is probably far more important for larger plants in the landscape over the long term than is organic matter dug into the soil. Rhododendrons and azaleas in nature grow in soils with most of the organic matter in the top 2–3 in. (5–8 cm) of soil. For example, woodland soils, the habitat of may ericaceous plants, have a layer of humus on top but very little organic matter in the soil as compared to grass-covered soils. A mulch that slowly rots down over the years and is replenished each year duplicates natural conditions and is very beneficial.

Mulches are used for several reasons, some of these are touched on in the preceding paragraph. They will also provide good weed control and, by keeping the soil cooler, conserve moisture and help prevent root rot. An effective organic mulch provides plant food as it rots or is broken down by soil organisms. It also builds a layer of beneficial humus on top of the soil.

In winter mulches can prevent soil from freezing deeply, thus permitting at least some plant roots to pick up moisture. By keeping moisture available to the plant, mulch goes a long way in offering winter protection. In the woodland leaves from deciduous trees serve to mulch plants growing nearby. This loose, airy mulch is ideal, providing shade and insulating the soil against freezing while at the same time allowing air movement to the roots. Woodland soils freeze less deeply in winter, if at all, while open grass areas freeze much more deeply.

When selecting a mulch look for coarse, light materials which will not pack tightly and so exclude air from the roots.

MINERALS: N–P–K

The only way to positively determine the need for fertilizer in a new planting area is to test the soil and then apply the amounts of nutrient elements recommended. Any phosphorus (P) and potassium (K) needed can be dug in prior to planting as these elements will remain for long periods in the soil. If these elements are supplied by chemical fertilizers such as superphosphate or muriate of potash, they should be dug in at least a month before planting. Organic sources of the same elements, such as rock phosphate, may be dug in at time of planting. Sandy soils with their low nutrient-holding capacity need more of these fertilizers applied more often than is needed for heavier soils. Organic forms of phosphorus and potassium remain in sandy soils longer than chemical forms.

Since nitrogen (N) is lost from all soils rather quickly, it is necessary not only to dig this element in at the time the site is prepared but to add it as a top dressing from time to time after planting. Nitrogen will leach down through the soil and so is effective as a top dressing. An excellent form of nitrogen is urea formaldehyde. Since it is an organic material containing 38% nitrogen, the nitrogen is released slowly, (as urea and ammonium ions) over a period of six to eight months and will not burn or damage roots. Dig urea formaldehyde in at the rate of 15 pounds (6.5 kg) per 1,000 sq. ft. (93 m^2). Nitrogen release from urea formaldehyde is slow to nonexistent in cold soils and speeds up as soils warm in the spring, which provides the nitrogen when plants are actively growing and need it. The slow release nature of this form is also significant because nitrogen can leach from soil rapidly. Nitrogen in the nitrate form, such as nitrate of soda, can damage ericaceous plants and also leaches rapidly and cannot be recommended.

There are many other organic forms of fertilizer which are entirely safe in use. They are usually recommended for small plantings as in larger plantings they may be too expensive. Materials such as cottonseed meal (7% nitrogen, 3% phosphorus, and 2% potash) and soybean meal are excellent organic sources when used at the rate of 4–5 pounds (1.8–2.3 kg) per 100 sq. ft. (9 m^2). They are complete fertilizers containing all three of the major plant food elements (N–P–K) as well as trace elements. Rock phosphate, a very safe form of phosphorus, and granite meal, a safe source of potash, can be used as organic sources for these two elements.

Rhododendron require a number of minor elements, yet for the most part these are seldom in short supply in the average soil. Sandy soils may have shortages severe enough to slow plant growth, but if organic soil amendments such as sphagnum peat moss are used and a good, organic mulch is maintained, enough minor elements are usually added to insure satisfactory growth. Nurserymen pushing plants for maximum growth rate and using large amounts of fertilizers need to test for minor elements from time to time. A soil testing laboratory can advise on the specific tests needed to define amount needed.

Rhododendrons and azaleas do not require much fertilizer but do respond well to appropriate application.

WIND DAMAGE AND AIR DRAINAGE

Rhododendrons and azaleas cannot tolerate strong winds and on windy sites would benefit greatly from a good windbreak. This is because reduced wind speed reduces both moisture loss from leaves and leaf damage. Preventing moisture loss is important in the summer and perhaps even more important in below-freezing temperatures. Since most rhododendron species have broad leaves, moisture loss is high, and if moisture is lost through the leaves faster than the roots can absorb it, plant leaves wilt and burn on the margins and may eventually die if the situation is not corrected. Deciduous azaleas are able to survive windy winter locations better because they lose their leaves in winter and thus do not have moisture needs as great as their evergreen releatives.

Whenever possible I think living windbreaks, such as hedges, shrubs, or trees, should be used since their beauty can add to the overall landscape effect. Evergreen trees or evergreen shrubs tall enough to break the wind are ideal. Even deciduous trees in large numbers will reduce wind velocity considerably. Use deep-rooted trees for windbreaks as they do not compete so vigorously with plantings for nutrients and moisture; definitely do not use maples. If possible plant *Rhododendron* far enough away from windbreaks to eliminate root competition.

Structural windbreaks such as picket fences are also excellent. One advantage is that plantings may be made close to them with no concern about root competition.

The corners of buildings are especially windy spots as wind velocity increases as the wind whips around a corner. Planting a needled evergreen such as pine or an upright yew provides an excellent windbreak at such corners and will greatly benefit plants on the lee side. Small microclimate alterations such as creating a windbreak often make the difference between a successful or failed planting and can be created quite easily.

A windbreak is generally considered to affect an area to a horizontal distance of about seven times its height.

Air drainage refers to the downward movement of heavier cold air and the rising of lighter warm air. It is not the same thing as wind movement but rather is the slow, steady movement of cold air into low-lying areas or into physical barriers which dam air movement. The accumulation of cold air reduces the temperature in these areas and is usually observed on still nights with little or no wind to mix the cold and warm air. Such cold air pockets should be avoided in planting rhododendrons for two reasons. First temperatures fall below freezing earlier in the fall, damaging plants that have not yet hardened off. Second, frost occurs later in the spring, resulting in damage to early flowering plants.

AIR TEMPERATURE

As mentioned earlier, azaleas and rhododendrons grow best in moderate temperatures. This moderate range encompasses U.S.D.A. plant hardiness zones 5 through 8. When temperatures drop below −15°F (−26°C) the flower buds of many rhododendron and azalea species and cultivars are blasted. Prolonged temperatures above 90°F (31°C) damage virtually all rhododendrons and azaleas planted in full sun. Chapter Three presents lists of species and cultivars adapted to specific U.S.D.A. cold hardiness zones.

Not as much work has been done to sort out cold hardiness in azaleas, but the lists in Chapter Three will help in selecting cold hardy azaleas. Most deciduous azalea hybrids, being derived from cool climate species, are not as heat tolerant as the evergreen sorts, although considerable breeding work is now being done to develop increased heat tolerance in deciduous azalea cultivars. There are species deciduous azaleas growing naturally in hardiness zone 10. Conversely, most deciduous azalea hybrids are cold hardy to −20°F (−29°C) with some hardy to −35°F (−37°C).

An unmentioned consideration in site selection is visibility. Select sites so that plants can be viewed from a window or can enhance frequently used areas outside the house.

In summary, it is important when growing rhododendrons and azaleas to select or modify the planting site so that it provides an acid soil pH, 4.5–5.5; good internal drainage; sufficient light, sun or bright indirect light 50% or more of the day to induce good flower bud formation; the regular replenishment of a porous mulch to keep the soil cool; soil high in organic matter, 25–50%; protection from wind; good air drainage; and adequate soil fertility.

THREE: *Selection of Rhododendron Species/Cultivars*

Selecting the best plant for a particular region and site is at the heart of creating a fine garden. When one sees a huge, beautiful, old rhododendron thriving without help, one can be certain that is a species/cultivar well adapted to local conditions and clearly a form for the local gardener to consider. On the other hand, a poorly adapted species/cultivar will require continual attention and never become a magnificent specimen. Proper selection can greatly reduce the number and extent of cultural problems encountered. Only after developing some expertise can the gardener risk planting marginally adapted species/cultivars (or new untested cultivars) with any hope for success.

The surest and safest way to select plants suitable to a particular region is to choose from those included here in the Good Doer lists. Thousands of rhododendrons have been tested in an expensive, time-consuming process of elimination, resulting in these lists. The lists specify those species/cultivars which have survived the test of time in a particular geographic area and have performed well for a number of growers in the region.

Another useful criterion in selecting rhododendrons is the quality of the plant as established by the American Rhododendron Society quality rating system. This rating system evaluates the quality of both the flower and the plant. The rating scale ranges from 1 to 5, with 1 the poorest and 5 the best. The quality rating is written 5/4, the first number referring to flower quality and the second to plant quality. The rating 5/4 designates a species/cultivar with a superb flower and above average plant. Sometimes an evaluation of the entire plant in terms of how it performs in the garden is added. This performance character is then designated using a third number, based on the 1–5 scale as used for the flower and plant, and in this example would be written 5/4/4.

A wide variety of sources for further assistance in plant selection are available, some of course more reliable than others. I would recommend the books *Azaleas* by Galle, *Rhododendron Species* by Davidian, *Rhododendron Hybrids* by Sally and Greer, *Rhododendrons in America* by VanVeen, and *Greer's Guidebook to Available Rhododendrons.* Local gardeners and nurseries can be good sources of information. If you join the local chapter of the American Rhododendron Society, enthusiastic, willing help can always be found among its members.

Following the general discussion of major factors involved in the selection of rhododendrons, the bulk of this chapter is devoted to the Good Doer lists. These were compiled with the generous help of a number of leading rhododendron gardeners in this country and abroad, including members of various chapters of the American Rhododendron Society (ARS). I offer my deep appreciation to them for their contribution. The criteria used for inclusion as a Good Doer rhododendron or azalea adapted to a particular area were

1. Disease resistance
2. Cold hardiness
3. Heat tolerance
4. Capacity to produce good root systems (vigor)
5. Drought tolerance
6. Insect resistance
7. Consistently heavy blooms
8. Good plant form

CLIMATE

Climate is the foremost consideration when selecting plants for a garden. The effects of climate (minimum temperature, maximum temperature, duration of high and low temperatures, timing and amount of rainfall, direction and velocity of winds, etc.) combine to absolutely define the plants which, assuming reasonably satisfactory cultivation, can or cannot be grown. If one has not lived in a region long enough to have gathered a good sense of local climate, one can gain much by consulting the local extension or agricultural college office.

Average cold temperatures are outlined on the U.S.D.A. Plant Hardiness Zone Map of North America (Fig. 7). This is a primary reference tool for every gardener who must then only consider microclimate effects—the specific situations of higher or lower temperatures always found within the larger zones. An example of its use: U.S.D.A. Zone 6 represents regions in which the average annual minimum temperature is −10°F to 0°F (−23.3 to −17.8°C). This indicates that only plants known to be cold hardy to this temperature should be selected for planting in U.S.D.A. Zone 6.

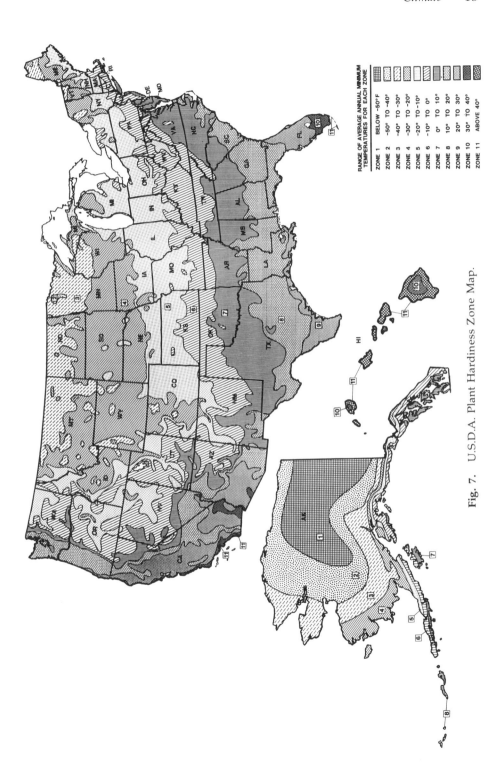

Fig. 7. U.S.D.A. Plant Hardiness Zone Map.

In addition to minimum temperatures, rapid temperature changes must be taken into account. Sudden temperature drops, especially in the fall or early winter before plants have hardened off, can be devastating. In such zones use only plants known to harden off early. This can be considered in light of cultural practices during the growing season which will affect fall plant hardiness. If moisture is readily available and nitrogen fertilizer is applied late in the summer, plants may remain in active growth. They will then be subject to damage by sudden drops in temperatures to below freezing in the early fall. Some species/cultivars are more sensitive to these cultural practices than others.

Late spring frosts represent a different kind of temperature hazard; obviously early flowering species/cultivars need to be avoided in regions experiencing such frosts with any regularity.

Maximum temperatures affect the selection of plants as surely as do minimum temperatures. Heat tolerant forms are those able to endure temperatures above 90°F (32°C) and up to 100°F (38°C) for short periods of time. At high temperatures afternoon shade is required even for heat tolerant species/cultivars. All rhododendrons and azaleas will suffer severely from prolonged periods of 100°F (38°C) temperatures in full sun. Extreme heat is especially harmful to flowers and tender new growth, both of which can be severely damaged in one such afternoon. All rhododendrons and azaleas grow better at maximum temperatures of 80°F (28°C) or less.

While to my knowledge no effort has been made to establish maximum temperature zones, the Good Doer lists will provide first-class guidelines to plants adapted to regions experiencing high temperatures.

A general review of the regions in which rhododendrons naturally evolved shows that some species are native to the tropics, and such species should succeed in warm climates. A closer review shows that most species are from mountain ranges where higher elevations and cool mountain mists greatly reduce maximum summer temperature and provide high humidity. The mountain environment is quite different from that typical of the southerly latitudes. Thus many rhododendron species/cultivars find the climatic conditions of England and the west coast of the U.S.A. and Canada particularly favorable to their well-being.

Another kind of temperature problem is encountered in regions in which warm periods regularly occur during late winter and early spring and are interrupted by days of freezing temperatures. Some species/cultivars lose dormancy quickly after seven to ten consecutive days of temperatures above 50°F (10°C) and are easily damaged by temperatures which they readily tolerate when completely dormant. Rhododendrons typically complete dormancy following a period of approximately 320 hours spent at temperatures above 28°F (−2°C) but below 43°F (6°C), and day length reaches ten hours.

Additional problems associated with high temperature appear in the forms of increased insect damage and disease attacks, particularly the fungus causing root rot.

The average rainfall of the various regions is provided in the following Good Doer lists and is also readily available from local weather stations. Even if a review of rainfall data for a region indicates a fairly uniform annual distribution, the heat of summer results in faster moisture loss from the soil and so creates a relatively drier condition than found in spring, fall, or winter. While some rhododendron species/cultivars are more drought tolerant than others, none does well in dry conditions. The early flowering forms adapt better to areas with dry summers since flowering and active vegetative growth, both of which require a good supply of moisture, occur early in the season ahead of such droughts.

Factors other than annual rainfall also contribute to the amount of soil moisture available to the plant—the amount of rainfall during the growing season, the capacity of the soil to absorb and retain moisture, soil temperatures, and the presence or absence of competitive plants. Of course, the gardener can do nothing about the total amount of rainfall but can affect all other factors determining the amount of water available to plants.

An open, porous soil absorbs more water faster than a compacted soil; the former readily absorbs a greater quantity of water from rain or irrigation. A loam soil fortified with organic matter will store more water, for a longer period of time, than a sandy soil or a compacted, clay soil. Further, a loose mulch on top of the soil not only prevents soil compaction (allowing more water to enter the soil) but also lowers soil temperatures resulting in less moisture loss. Thus an open, porous, loam soil, fortified with organic matter, and properly mulched, provides better utilization of available water.

Any plant species grows best in the area in which it evolved or in other parts of the world having similar growing conditions. For example, Japanese azaleas do well along the eastern seaboard of North America where the climate is similar to Japan's. For the same reason the natives of temperate Asia do well in England and the Pacific Northwest of North America because these areas have climates similar to that in which the plants evolved. Thus the origin of a species, or in the case of a cultivar, the origin of its parents, has much to do with growing success in a particular region. There are of course exceptions to this rule of thumb as a few *Rhododendron* are suitable to a wide range of conditions.

In summary, adaptability to all factors which together describe climate, not simply cold hardiness, must be considered in plant selection.

WHAT PLANTS AND WHERE TO PURCHASE THEM

Only nursery grown plants should be purchased, not plants collected in the wild. This recommendation is given for several reasons. Collected plants are seedlings which will exhibit all the variation in plant characteristics associated with sexual reproduction. They seldom have the compact form of top or root system associated with well-grown nursery plants and so do not transplant and grow on as well. And finally, plants should not be dug from the wild in the interest of plant conservation. I do not believe gardeners should encourage this practice by purchasing collected plants.

In addition to the matter of selecting species/cultivars based on particulars of a given region and site, the gardener must also consider the size of the selected plant to be purchased/planted. For example, one gardener may wish to have an instant landscape and will need to buy good-sized plants. Another gardener with an established landscape may prefer a small plant which will be grown along to ultimately replace a plant no longer wanted.

Plants in the 2–3 ft. (0.6–1.0 m) size probably best survive transplanting into the landscape. Mature size must also be a selection factor. Where growing space is limited, as in small lots or foundation plantings, dwarf or low growing forms are most suitable.

There is also the question of species versus cultivar which is endlessly argued by rhododendron fanciers. Cultivars are typically larger and easier to grow, with larger, more spectacular flowers. A majority of gardeners seem to prefer cultivars, yet there is a growing body of collectors dedicated to growing species. The latter may argue that the plant habit is more satisfying and that the plant and its flowers are more proportionate. Each gardener is urged to develop his or her opinion on this matter based on personal landscape aesthetics.

The gardener is well advised to purchase only named cultivars or selected species which are asexually propagated. Such plants are consistent in their characteristics since each is a clone of a parent plant of known character and will be identical to the parent. This will eliminate future surprises or disappointments in the landscape.

It cannot be assumed that a local retailer sells only locally adapted plants. Plant availability from growers or wholesalers, who may be located hundreds of miles away, often determines which species/cultivars are offered for sale. Genetic makeup of the plant will determine performance to a large extent and purchase of a species/cultivar not adapted to the local area cannot be rectified through good cultural practices. Another essential matter when purchasing plants is to consider only fresh material. Plants that exhibit wilting due to improper care should be avoided, regardless of price.

Local growers who sell retail are excellent plant sources since they grow locally adapted plants, understand cultural requirements, and are better able to advise the gardener on proper plant care. Additionally, if the local nursery person grows plants in the field, in local soil, there could be a further advantage. Plants transplanted into a medium of similar texture will extend roots into the surrounding soil faster after transplanting than plants growing in a medium of different texture.

Reputable mail order nurseries are another source of healthy plants, but it might be wise to determine adapted species/cultivars before opening the catalogs. The beautiful pictures and poetic descriptions can redirect purchases to plants not locally adapted.

Acclimation is a factor often considered in purchasing plants with the assumption that northern grown plants are more cold hardy. The area the plants are grown in does not affect genetic cold hardiness; thus a 'Nova Zembla' rhododendron purchased in Maine, for example, has no more hardiness potential than one purchased in North Carolina or Oregon. The maturity or dormancy of the plant, however, does affect survival of a fall planted plant, but is not a consideration in spring planting. Plants grown in southern areas, with longer growing seasons, and not yet dormant and hardened off, will be damaged if moved north and fall planted where temperatures below freezing are encountered prior to hardening off. The southern grown plant is thus more tender because of differences it has experienced in the current growing season between the two geographic locations.

Selection of a specific species/cultivar adapted to the local area, a Good Doer, is vital to the successful culture of rhododendrons and azaleas. There are many outstanding *Rhododendron* available which have been tested by experienced growers in specific regions and under specific conditions of climate. The local gardener is wise to take advantage of this extensive testing and selection process.

THE GOOD DOER LISTS

The remainder of this chapter is devoted to the Good Doer lists, arranged alphabetically by state in the U.S.A. followed by information from Australia, the British Isles, and Canada. The lists include those species/cultivars recommended by committed, knowledgeable rhododendron growers in each region. The person or persons supplying the lists are identified; in some cases lists and information have been taken from the 1980 ARS publication *American Rhododendron Hybrids* and are so noted. Tabulated information, arranged alphabetically by species, can be located in Appendix A.

Climatic data for the U.S.A. is based on records of the National Climatic Data Center, NESDIS, NOAH, U.S. Department of Commerce. The average and extremes of temperature are for the thirty-year period beginning in 1951. Data are necessarily recorded for the major city in a particular region, and the reader in local areas must compensate for his or her particular conditions. The recently published U.S.D.A. Hardiness Zone Map was in turn used to assign the average low temperature (see Fig. 7). More specific zone information is included for most cities participating in the Good Doer lists and is derived from the more detailed U.S.D.A. color zone map. However, such zone details are unavailable for most of the foreign cities. A comparison table follows which summarizes the a b zone temperature distinctions (Fig. 8).

The lists are presented as guides and should not be construed to include all the species/cultivars which can be grown in a region. Rather the lists represent plants which are widely grown in and well adapted to that particular geographic area.

The letters E and L following rhododendron species plant names refer to (E) elepidote and (L) lepidote. Elepidote species are non-scaly, large-leaved forms; lepidote species are scaly, small-leaved forms which are generally smaller at maturity. Rhododendron hybrid listings (cultivars) have been separated by elepidote and lepidote. Azaleas follow in order by deciduous species, deciduous hybrid, evergreen species, and evergreen hybrid. Examples of each type will be found in Figs. 9–64 (color photos).

U.S.D.A. Average Annual Minimum Temperatures

	Degrees F	Degrees C
Zone 1	below –50	–45.6 and below
Zone 2	–50 to –40	–45.6 to –40
Zone 2a	–45 to –50	–42.8 to –45.5
Zone 2b	–40 to –45	–40.0 to –42.7
Zone 3	–40 to –30	–40.0 to –34.5
Zone 3a	–35 to –40	–37.3 to –40.0
Zone 3b	–30 to –35	–34.5 to –37.2
Zone 4	–30 to –20	–34.5 to –28.9
Zone 4a	–25 to –30	–31.7 to –34.4
Zone 4b	–20 to –25	–28.9 to –31.6
Zone 5	–20 to –10	–28.9 to –23.3
Zone 5a	–15 to –20	–26.2 to –28.8
Zone 5b	–10 to –15	–23.4 to –26.1
Zone 6	–10 to 0	–23.3 to –17.8
Zone 6a	– 5 to –10	–20.6 to –23.3
Zone 6b	0 to –5	–17.8 to –20.5
Zone 7	0 to 10	–17.8 to –12.3
Zone 7a	5 to 0	–15.0 to –17.7
Zone 7b	10 to 5	–12.3 to –15.0
Zone 8	10 to 20	–12.3 to –6.6
Zone 8a	15 to 10	– 9.5 to –12.2
Zone 8b	20 to 15	– 6.7 to –9.4
Zone 9	20 to 30	– 6.6 to –1.1
Zone 9a	25 to 20	– 3.9 to –6.6
Zone 9b	30 to 25	– 1.2 to –3.8
Zone 10	30 to 40	– 1.1 to 4.4
Zone 10a	35 to 30	1.6 to –1.1
Zone 10b	40 to 35	4.4 to 1.7
Zone 11	40 and above	4.5 and above

Fig. 8.   Zone Designations

Alabama: Zones 7–8

Weather Data: Birmingham, Zone 7b.

TEMPERATURE EXTREMES	AVERAGE TEMPERATURES
Max. 106°F (41°C)	Jan. 36–57°F (2–14°C)
Min. −2°F (−19°C)	July 71–93°F (22–34°C)

Average Rainfall: 52 in. (103 cm), evenly distributed throughout the year.

99 clear, 111 partly cloudy, 155 cloudy, 117 days with precipitation.

65% of days are sunny from May–August.

This list is provided by Pete McNees of Tuscumbia, Alabama.

RHODODENDRON SPECIES
R. *catawbiense* E
R. *maximum* E
R. *minus* L
R. *yakushimanum* K. Wada E
R. *yakushimanum* Ken Janeck E

RHODODENDRON HYBRIDS—ELEPIDOTE
'Catawbiense Boursault'
'Champayne'
'County of York'
'Cynthia'
'Gi Gi'
'Gomer Waterer'
'Ice Cube'
'Janet Blair'
'Kate Waterer'
'Maximum Roseum'
'Mrs. Furnival'

RHODODENDRON HYBRIDS—LEPIDOTE
'Blue Ridge'
'Early Bird'
'Lannys Pride'
'Mary Fleming'
'Pioneer'
'Windbeam'

DECIDUOUS AZALEA SPECIES
R. *alabamense*
R. *arborescens*
R. *atlanticum*
R. *austrinum*
R. *bakeri*
R. *canescens*
R. *prunifolium*
R. *serrulatum*
R. *speciosum (flammeum)*
R. *viscosum*

EVERGREEN AZALEA HYBRIDS
'Ben Morrison'
'Delaware Valley White'
'Dorothy Clark'
'Fascination'
'George L. Tabor'
'H. H. Hume'
'Margaret Douglas'
'Mrs. G. G. Gerbing'
'Pink Ruffles'
'Sherwood Red'

Weather Data: Montgomery, Zone 8a.

TEMPERATURE EXTREMES
Max. 105°F (41°C
Min. 0°F (−18°C)

AVERAGE TEMPERATURES
Jan. 36–57°F (2–14°C)
July 72–92°F (22–33°C)

Average Rainfall: 49.16 in. (123 cm), even distributed throughout the year.

107 clear, 109 partly cloudy, 149 cloudy, 108 days with precipitation.

65% of days are sunny from May–August.

This list is provided by C. E. Robinson of Auburn, Alabama.

RHODODENDRON SPECIES
R. *fortunei* E
R. *maximum* E
R. *minus* L

RHODODENDRON HYBRIDS—ELEPIDOTE
'A. Bedford'
'America'
'Anah Kruschke'
'Anna Rose Whitney'
'Belle Heller'
'Caroline'

'Gomer Waterer'
'Grierosplendour'
'Nova Zembla'
'Scintillation'
'Trude Webster'
'Vulcan'

DECIDUOUS AZALEA SPECIES
R. *alabamense*
R. *arborescens*
R. *austrinum*
R. *bakeri*

R. *calendulaceum*
R. *canescens*
R. *prunifolium*
R. *speciosum (flammeum)*
R. *vaseyi*

DECIDUOUS AZALEA HYBRIDS
'Gibraltar'
'Ilam Red Letter'
'Klondyke'
'Orangeade'

EVERGREEN AZALEA HYBRIDS
'Coral Bells' ('Kirin')
'Fashion'
'Festive'
'George L. Tabor'
'Hinode Giri'
'Margaret Douglas'
'Pink Pearl'
'Pink Ruffles'
'Red Ruffles'
'Snow'

California: Zones 7–10

Weather Data: Santa Cruz, Zone 9b. Plant listing for Monterey Bay (Zones 9b–10a) follows.

TEMPERATURE EXTREMES	AVERAGE TEMPERATURES
Max. 107°F (42°C)	Jan. 38–59°F (3–15°C)
Min. 22°F (−6°C)	July 48–74°F (9–24°C)

Average Rainfall: 55 in. (140 cm), extremely dry from May–September.

162 clear, 98 partly cloudy, 105 cloudy, and 63 days of precipitation.

The Santa Cruz list is provided by Mrs. Melvin C. Allen of Santa Cruz, California.

RHODODENDRON SPECIES
R. *aberconwayii* E
R. *augustinii* L
R. *burmanicum* L
R. *davidsonianum* L
R. *dichroanthum* E
    ssp. *scyphocalyx*
R. *ponticum* E
R. *racemosum* L
R. *yakushimanum* E
R. *zeylanicum* E

RHODODENDRON HYBRIDS—ELEPIDOTE
'Anah Kruschke'
'Jean Marie de Montague'
'Lems Cameo'
'Loder's White'
'Markeeta's Flame'
'Mrs. G. W. Leak'
'Pink Pearl'
'Purple Splendour'
'Trilby'

'Trude Webster'
'Unique'

RHODODENDRON HYBRIDS—LEPIDOTE
'California Blue'
'Fragrantissimum'
'Lemon Mist'
'Mi Amor'
'Myrtifolium'
'Pink Snowflakes'
'P. J. M.'
'Ramapo'
'Saffron Queen'

DECIDUOUS AZALEA HYBRIDS
'Betty Oliver'
'Cecile'
'Corringe'
'Gibraltar'
'Homebush'
'Klondyke'
'Life'

'Princess Royal'
'Renne'
'Sun Chariot'

EVERGREEN AZALEA SPECIES
R. kiusianum

EVERGREEN AZALEA HYBRIDS
'Cloud Nine'
'Coral Bells' ('Kirin')

'Glamour'
'Gumpo'
'Iveryana'
'John Haerens'
'Refrain'
'Sherwood Orchid'
'Sherwood Red'
'Starlight' (Kerrigan)

The Monterey Bay list is provided by John Hixson of Watsonville, California.

RHODODENDRON SPECIES
R. augustinii L
R. bureavii L
R. burmanicum L
R. davidsonianum L
R. lutescens L
R. moupinense L
R. ponticum E
R. smithii E
R. veitchianum L
R. yunnanense L

RHODODENDRON HYBRIDS—ELEPIDOTE
'Anah Kruschke'
'Antoon van Welie'
'Gomer Waterer'

'Halfdan Lem'
'Jean Marie de Montague'
'Markeeta's Flame'
'Markeeta's Prize'
'Pink Walloper'
'Queen Nefertite'
'Ruby Bowman'

RHODODENDRON HYBRIDS—LEPIDOTE
'Bric-a-brac'
'Elsie Frye'
'Forsterianum'
'Frangrantissimum'
'Lemon Mist'
'Ramapo'
'Snow Lady'

Georgia: Zones 7–8

Weather Data: Atlanta, Zones 7a–7b.

TEMPERATURE EXTREMES	AVERAGE TEMPERATURES
Max. 105°F (41°C)	Jan. 33–51°F (1–11°C)
Min. 8°F (−13°C)	July 69–88°F (21–31°C

Average Rainfall: 49 in. (124 cm), evenly distributed save for slightly more in April–October.

140 clear, 138 partly cloudy, 123 cloudy, and 104 days of precipitation.

This list is provided by Mrs. George Beasly, Sr. of Lavonia, Georgia.

RHODODENDRON SPECIES
R. carolinianum L
R. catawbiense E
R. fortunei E

R. makinoi E
R. mucronulatum L
R. yakushimanum E

RHODODENDRON HYBRIDS—ELEPIDOTE
'A. Bedford'
'Anna Rose Whitney'
'Janet Blair'
'Mr. W. R. Coe'
'Nova Zembla'
'Sappho'
'Scintillation'
'Tom Everett'
'Wheatley'

RHODODENDRON HYBRIDS—LEPIDOTE
'Donna Totten'
'Dora Amateis'
'Ginnie Gee'
'Laurie'
'Mary Fleming'
'Olga Mezitt'
'Pikeland'
'P. J. M.'
'Tom Koenig'
'Windbeam'

DECIDUOUS AZALEA SPECIES
R. alabamense
R. austrinum
R. bakeri
R. calendulaceum
R. canescans
R. flammeum
R. periclymenoides (nudiflorum)
R. prinophylum (roseum)

R. prunifolium
R. viscosum

DECIDUOUS AZALEA HYBRIDS
'Buzzard'
'Chetco'
'Gibraltar'
'Klondyke'
'My Mary'
'Old Gold'
'Orangeade'
'Peachy Keen'
'Primrose'
'Windsor Buttercup'

EVERGREEN AZALEA SPECIES
R. macrosepalum
R. nakaharae
R. oldhamii
R. serpyllifolium

EVERGREEN AZALEA HYBRIDS
'Adelaide Pope'
'Anna Kehr'
'Debonnaire'
'Easter Parade'
'Glacier'
'Hardy Gardenia'
'Mrs. G. G. Gerbing'
'Nancy of Robin Hill'
'Parfait'
'Sunglow'

The Great Lakes Chapter ARS: Zones 5–6

The area covered includes the area near Cleveland, Ohio, and the southern and eastern shores of Lake Erie of Pennsylvania and New York state, and parts of West Virginia.

Weather Data: Cleveland, Ohio, Zone 6a.

TEMPERATURE EXTREMES	AVERAGE TEMPERATURES
Max. 104°F (40°C)	Jan. 19–33°F (−7–1°C)
Min. −19°F (−28°C)	July 61–82°F (16–28°C)

Average Rainfall: 35.4 in. (89 cm), evenly distributed throughout the year.

62 clear, 105 partly cloudy, 198 cloudy, 158 days of rain, and 26 of snow.

This list is compiled from the Great Lakes Chapter List in the ARS *American Rhododendron Hybrids 1980* edited by Meldon Kraxberger.

RHODODENDRON SPECIES
R. *brachycarpum* E
R. *carolinianum* L
R. *catawbiense* E
R. *dauricum* L
R. *hippophaeoides* L
R. *impeditum* L
R. *yakushimanum* E

RHODODENDRON HYBRIDS—ELEPIDOTE
'Albert Close'
'America'
'Besse Howells'
'Boule de Neige'
'Brown Eyes'
'Caroline'
'Dexter's Pink' ('Apple Blossom')
'English Roseum'
'Ice Cube'
'Janet Blair'
'Lee's Dark Purple'
'Nova Zembla'
'Newburyport Belle' ('Fowle 19')
'Parker's Pink'

RHODODENDRON HYBRIDS—LEPIDOTE
'Dora Amateis'
'Mucram'
'Windbeam'

DECIDUOUS AZALEA SPECIES
R. *arborescens*
R. *bakeri*
R. *calendulaceum*
R. *canadense*
R. *periclymenoides (nudiflorum)*
R. *vaseyi*

EVERGREEN AZALEA SPECIES
R. *kiusianum*

EVERGREEN AZALEA HYBRIDS
'Cascade' (Shammarello)
'Corsage'
'Fedora'
'Geraldine'
'Herbert'
'Marjorie'
'Nadine'
'Springtime'

Weather Data: Johnstown, Pennsylvania, Zones 5b–6a.

TEMPERATURE EXTREMES	AVERAGE TEMPERATURES
Max. 104°F (40°C)	Jan. 19–37°F (−7– −3°C
Min. −20°F (−29°C	July 68–81°F (20–27°C)

Average Rainfall: 46 in. (117 cm), evenly distributed throughout the year.

Weather Data: Akron, Ohio, Zone 5b.

TEMPERATURE EXTREMES	AVERAGE TEMPERATURES
Max. 100°F (38°C)	Jan. −22–33°F (−30–1°C)
Min. −22°F (−30°C)	July 61–82°F (16–28°C)

Average Rainfall: 36 in. (91 cm), evenly distributed throughout the year.
68 clear, 100 partly cloudy, 197 cloudy, 153 days of precipitation, and 15 of snow.

Weather Data: Wheeling, West Virginia, Zone 6a.

TEMPERATURE EXTREMES	AVERAGE TEMPERATURES
Max. 103°F (39°C)	Jan. 21–38°F (−7–4°C)
Min. −18°F (−28°C)	July 62–85°F (17–29°C)

Average Rainfall: 38 in. (96 cm), heaviest March–September.

This list is provided by Dr. Thomas L. Ring, Bellaire, Ohio; Great Lakes Chapter ARS.

RHODODENDRON SPECIES
R. *carolinianum* L
R. *catawbiense* E
R. *fortunei* E
R. *maximum* E
R. *yakushimanum* E

RHODODENDRON HYBRIDS—ELEPIDOTE
'Albert Close'
'Ben Mosely'
'Besse Howells'
'Calsap'
'Catawbiense Album'
'English Roseum'
'Ice Cube'
'Lee's Dark Purple'
'Newburyport Belle'
'Parker's Pink'

RHODODENDRON HYBRIDS—LEPIDOTE
'Carolina Rose'

Early bloomers are frequently caught by frost.

DECIDUOUS AZALEA SPECIES
R. *bakeri*
R. *calendulaceum*
R. *prunifolium*
R. *vaseyi*

DECIDUOUS AZALEA HYBRIDS
'Crimson Tide'
'Rufus'
'Yellow Pom Pom'

EVERGREEN AZALEA SPECIES
R. *kiusianum* Komo Kulshan

EVERGREEN AZALEA HYBRIDS
'Boudoir'
'Delaware Valley White'
'Fedora'
Pride Hybrids

Evergreen azaleas do not do well in this area.

Illinois: Zones 5–6

Weather Data: Chicago, Zones 5a–5b.

TEMPERATURE EXTREMES	AVERAGE TEMPERATURES
Max. 104°F (40°C)	Jan. 14–29°F (−10– −2°C)
Min. −27°F (−33°C)	July 63–83°F (17–28°C)

Average Rainfall: 33.3 in. (84 cm), the heaviest in the months of April–September.

109 clear, 120 partly cloudy, 136 cloudy, and 107 days of rain, with 9 days of snow.

This list is provided by Eugene Paschall of Palos Heights, Illinois.

RHODODENDRON SPECIES
R. *carolinianum* L
R. *catawbiense* E
R. *dauricum* L
R. *mucronulatum* L
R. *mucronulatum* Cornell Pink L
R. *yakushimanum* E

RHODODENDRON HYBRIDS—ELEPIDOTE
'America'
'Anna H. Hall'

'Bali'
'Besse Howells'
'Bravo'
'Catawbiense Album'
'Catawbiense Boursault'
'Edith Pride'
'English Roseum'
'Golden Gala'
'Holden'

'Ice Cube'
'Ignatius Sargent'
'Lee's Dark Purple'
'Lodestar'
'Maximum Roseum'
'Nova Zembla'
'Party Pink'
'Roseum Pink'
'Russell Harmon'
'Slippery Rock'
'Trinity'
'Vernus'

RHODODENDRON HYBRIDS—LEPIDOTE
'Alfred Wiacek'
'Alice Swift'
'Arctic' Pearl'
'Balta'
'Macopin'
'Molly Fordham'
'Olga Mezitt'
'Pink Diamond' ('Weston's Pink
  Diamond')
'Pioneer'
'P. J. M.'
'Ramapo'
'Shrimp Pink'
'Waltham'
'Weston's Pink Diamond'
'Windbeam'

DECIDUOUS AZALEA SPECIES
R. bakeri
R. periclymenoides (nudiflorum)
R. prinophyllum (roseum)
R. vaseyi

DECIDUOUS AZALEA HYBRIDS
'Aurora'
'Buttercup'
'Cecile'
'Fireball'
'Gibraltar'
'Homebush'
'Kathleen'
'Klondyke'
'Mt. St. Helens'
Northern Lights Hybrids
'Old Gold'
'Oxydol'
'Persil'
'Strawberry Ice'
'Tang'
'Tonga'
'White Swan'

EVERGREEN AZALEA SPECIES
R. poukhanense

EVERGREEN AZALEA HYBRIDS
'Border Gem'
'Boudoir'
'Elsie Lee'
'Helen Curtis'
'Hino Red'
'Hot Shot'
'Maybelle'
'Mother's Day'
'Purple Splendour'
'Red Red'
'Springtime'
'Yankee Doodle'

Indiana: Zones 5–6

Weather Data: Evansville, Zones 6a–6b.

TEMPERATURE EXTREMES	AVERAGE TEMPERATURES
Max. 105°F (41°C)	Jan. 22–29°F (−6– −2°C)
Min. −23°F (−31°C)	July 67–89°F (20–32°C)

Average Rainfall: 42 in. (105 cm), the least in July–October.

103 clear, 99 partly cloudy, 163 cloudy, 115 days of precipitation, and 4 of snow.

73% of days are sunny from May–August.

This list is provided by Stephen Schroeder, Evansville, Indiana; Great Lakes Chapter ARS.

RHODODENDRON SPECIES
R. *carolinianum* L
R. *catawbiense* E
R. *chapmanii* L
R. *fortunei* E
R. *keiskei* L
R. *lapponicum* L
R. *maximum* E
R. *micranthum* L
R. *minus* L
R. *mucronulatum* L

RHODODENDRON HYBRIDS—ELEPIDOTE
'America'
'Caroline'
'Catawbiense Album'
'Ice Cube'
'Janet Blair'
'Maximum Roseum'
'Roseum Elegans'
'Scintillation'
'Summer Rose'
'Yaku Prince'

RHODODENDRON HYBRIDS—LEPIDOTE
'Aglo'
'April Blush'
'Arctic Pearl'
'Early Bird'
'Hudson Bay'
'Laurie'
'Llenroc'
'Mary Fleming'
'Olga Mezitt'
'P. J. M.'

DECIDUOUS AZALEA SPECIES
R. *albamense*
R. *arborescens*

R. *atlanticum*
R. *austrinum*
R. *bakeri*
R. *calendulaceum*
R. *canescens*
R. *prinophyllum (roseum)*
R. *prunifolium*
R. *serrulatum*

DECIDUOUS AZALEA HYBRIDS
'Cannon's Double'
'Daviesi'
'Fireball'
'Gibraltar'
'Golden Peace'
'Homebush'
'Klondyke'
'Mt. St. Helens'
'Sun Chariot'
'Tunis'

EVERGREEN AZALEA SPECIES
R. *kaempferi*
R. *kiusianum*
R. *nakaharae*
R. *obtusum*

EVERGREEN AZALEA HYBRIDS
'Dr. Henry Schroeder'
'Dr. James Dippel'
'Eliza Hyatt'
'Elsie Lee'
'Helen Curtis'
'Hino Pink'
'Hino Red'
'Mrs. Henry Schroeder'
'Mrs. Nancy Dipple'
'Stewartstonian'

Louisiana: Zones 8–9

Weather Data: New Orleans, Zone 9b.

TEMPERATURE EXTREMES	AVERAGE TEMPERATURES
Max. 107°F (42°C)	Jan. 20–38°F (−7–4°C)
Min. −18°F (−28°C)	July 69–89°F (21–32°C)

Average Rainfall: 59.7 in. (152 cm), the heaviest in the months of April–October.

104 clear, 120 partly cloudy, 141 cloudy, and 117 days of precipitation.

This list is provided by John T. Thornton of C & T Nursery, Franklinton, Louisiana.

RHODODENDRON SPECIES
R. *adenopodum* E
R. *chapmanii* L
R. *fortunei* E
R. *hyperythrum* (Creech's Narrowleaf Form) E
R. *makinoi* E
R. *maximum* E
R. *minus* L
R. *pseudochrysanthum* (Nelson's Form) E

RHODODENDRON HYBRIDS—ELEPIDOTE
'Albert Close'
'Anna Rose Whitney'
'Caroline'
'Damozel'
'Grierosplendour'
'Janet Blair'

RHODODENDRON HYBRIDS—LEPIDOTE
'P. J. M.'

Flowers of all species/cultivars suffer in the heat, although R. *makinoi* is sun tolerant.

Maryland: Zone 7

Weather Data: Hagerstown, Zones 6a–6b.

TEMPERATURE EXTREMES	AVERAGE TEMPERATURES
Max. 104°F (40°C)	Jan. 22–38°F (−6–4°C)
Min. −17°F (−27°C)	July 63–87°F (17–31°C)

Average Rainfall: 39 in. (99 cm), evenly distributed throughout the year.

Weather Data: Oakland, Zone 5b.

TEMPERATURE EXTREMES	AVERAGE TEMPERATURES
Max. 95°F (35°C)	Jan. 16–36°F (−9–2°C)
Min. −27°F (−33°C)	July 56–79°F (13–26°C)

Average Rainfall: 47 in. (119 cm), the heaviest in the months of March–August.

This list is provided by the author.

RHODODENDRON SPECIES
R. *carolinianum* L
R. *catawbiense* E
R. *chapmanii* L
R. *dauricum* L
R. *keiskei* L
R. *maximum* E
R. *metternichii* E
R. *yakushimanum* E

RHODODENDRON HYBRIDS—ELEPIDOTE
'Anna H. Hall'
'Blue Ensign'
'Boule de Neige'
'Caroline'
'Catawbiense Album'
'Chionoides'
'Ice Cube'
'Janet Blair'

'Lodestar'
'Nova Zembla'
'Roseum Elegans'
'Scintillation'
'Spring Parade'

RHODODENDRON HYBRIDS—LEPIDOTE
'Conewago'
'Dora Amateis'
'Mary Fleming'
'Olga Mezitt'
'P. J. M.'
'Windbeam'

DECIDUOUS AZALEA SPECIES
R. bakeri
R. calendulaceum
R. periclymenoides (nudiflorum)
R. prunifolium
R. schlippenbachii

DECIDUOUS AZALEA HYBRIDS
'Brazil'
'Cecile'
'Gibraltar'
'Homebush'
'Kathleen'

'Klondyke'
'Narcissaflora'
'Old Gold'
'Strawberry Ice'
'Toucan'

EVERGREEN AZALEA SPECIES
R. kaempferi
R. kiusianum
R. poukhanense

EVERGREEN AZALEA HYBRIDS
'Delaware Valley White'
'Girard Border Gem
'Girard Chiara'
'Girard Fuschia'
'Helen Curtis'
'Herbert'
'Hino Red'
'James Gable'
'Louise Gable'
'Maybelle'
'Rose Greeley'
'Rosebud'
'Springtime'
'Stewartstonian'

Massachusetts: Zones 5–7

Weather Data: Boston, Zones 6a–6b

TEMPERATURE EXTREMES	AVERAGE TEMPERATURES
Max. 102°F (39°C)	Jan. 23–36°F (−5–2°C)
Min. −12°F (−24°C)	July 65–82°F (18–28°C)

Average Rainfall: 43.8 in. (112 cm), evenly distributed throughout the year.

Average Snowfall: 42 in. (107 cm) annually.

95 clear, 115 partly cloudy, 165 cloudy, 119 days of rain, and 7 days of snow.

This list, from a 1980 survey by the Massachusetts Chapter ARS, is provided by A. Richard Brooks of Concord, Mass.

RHODODENDRON SPECIES
R. brachycarpum E
R. carolinianum L
R. dauricum L
R. ferrugineum L
R. fortunei E
R. hippophaeoides L

R. impeditum L
R. mucronulatum Cornell Pink L
R. racemosum L
R. russatum L
R. yakushimanum E
R. yakushimanum K. Wada E
R. yakushimanum Ken Janeck E

RHODODENDRON HYBRIDS—ELEPIDOTE
'Anna H. Hall'
'Besse Howells'
'Boule de Neige'
'Cadis'
'Catawbiense Album'
'English Roseum'
'Janet Blair'
'Jean Marie de Montague'
'Mary Belle'
'Mrs. C. S. Sargent'
'Mrs. Furnival'
'Nova Zembla'
'Scintillation'
'Wheatly'

RHODODENDRON HYBRIDS—LEPIDOTE
'Balta'
'Dora Amateis'
'Laurie'
'Llenroc'
'Mary Fleming'
'Olga Mezitt'
'Pioneer'
'P. J. M.'
'Ramapo'
'Windbeam'

DECIDUOUS AZALEA SPECIES
R. calendulaceum
R. japonicum
R. prinophyllum (roseum)
R. schlippenbachii

R. vaseyi
R. viscosum

DECIDUOUS AZALEA HYBRIDS
'Cecile'
'Daviesi'
'Gibraltar'
'Golden Oriole'
'Homebush'
Jane Abbott Hybrids
'Klondyke'

EVERGREEN AZALEA SPECIES
R. kaempferi
R. kiusianum (including var. *album*)
R. nakaharae
R. poukhanense

EVERGREEN AZALEA HYBRIDS
'Boudoir'
'Buccaneer'
'Delaware Valley White'
'Fedora'
'Guy Yerkes'
'Herbert'
'Hino Crimson'
'Lorna'
'Mother's Day'
'Palestrina' ('Wilhelmina Vuyk')
'Rosebud'
'Springtime'
'Stewartstonian'

Weather Data: Edgartown, Zone 7a.

TEMPERATURE EXTREMES	AVERAGE TEMPERATURES
Max. 79°F (26°C)	Jan. −5–65°F (−21–18°C)
Min. −9°F (−23°C)	July 58–91°F (14–33°C)

Average Rainfall: 45.5 in. (115 cm), the least in June–July.
122 days of precipitation.

This list is provided by Dr. Richard Chaiken of Falmount, Massachusetts; Cape Cod and Islands Chapter ARS.

RHODODENDRON SPECIES
R. bureavii E
R. calophytum E.
R. carolinianum L
R. degronianum E
R. fastigiatum L
R. ferrugineum L
R. fortunei E
R. impeditum L

R. keiskei 'Yaku Fairy' L
R. makinoi E
R. pachysanthum E
R. pseudochrysanthum E
R. racemosum L
R. russatum L
R. smirnowii E
R. yakushimanum E

RHODODENDRON HYBRIDS—ELEPIDOTE
'Anna H. Hall'
'Atroflo'
'Baden Baden'
'Bonnie Maid'
'Buttermint'
'Catawbiense Album'
'Chikor'
'Chionoides'
'David Gable'
Dexter's Hybrids
'Golden Star'
'Gomer Waterer'
'Hello Dolly'
'Janet Blair'
'Mary Belle'
'Melanie Shaw'
'Olin O. Dobbs'
'Parker's Pink'
'Platinum Pearl'
'Purple Splendour'
'Scintillation'
'Taurus'
'Unique'
'Vulcan'
'Vulcan's Flame'

RHODODENDRON HYBRIDS—LEPIDOTE
'April Gem'
'Conewago'
'Dora Ameteis'
'Laurie'
'Llenroc'
'Mary Fleming'
'Molly Fordham'
'Olga Mezitt'
'Patty Bee'
'Pioneer'

'P. J. M.'
'Purple Gem'
'Rose Marie'
'Starry Night'
'Tiffany'
'Weston's Pink Diamond'
'White Surprise'

DECIDUOUS AZALEA SPECIES
R. arborescens
R. bakeri
R. calendulaceum
R. prunifolium
R. schlippenbachii
R. vaseyi
R. vaseyi var. *alba*

DECIDUOUS AZALEA HYBRIDS
'George Reynolds'
'Mt. St. Helens'
'My Mary'
'Persian Melon'
'Windsor Appleblossom'
'Windsor Buttercup'

EVERGREEN AZALEA SPECIES
R. kiusianum white
R. kiusianum pink
R. kiusianum SH-RBF

EVERGREEN AZALEA HYBRIDS
'Conversation Piece'
'Desiree'
'Eureka'
'Girard Hot Shot'
'Girard Rose'
'Louise Gable'
'Mary Dalton'
'Nancy of Robin Hill'
'Surprise'

Michigan: Zones 4–6

Weather Data: Detroit, Zones 6a–6b.

TEMPERATURE EXTREMES	AVERAGE TEMPERATURES
Max. 102°F (39°C)	Jan. 16–31°F (−9– −1°C)
Min. −18°F (−28°C)	July 61–83°F (16–28°C)

Average Rainfall: 31 in. (79 cm), evenly distributed throughout the year.

76 clear, 107 partly cloudy, 182 cloudy, 133 days of precipitation, and 13 of snow.

66% of days are sunny from May–August.

This list is provided by Mrs. Virginia L. Heller of Detroit, Michigan.

RHODODENDRON HYBRIDS—ELEPIDOTE
'Album Elegans'
'Calsap'
'Chionoides'
'Hong Kong'
'Janet Blair'
'Lemon Ice'
'Mrs. Tom Lowinsky'
'Pink Twins'
'Sham's Candy'
'Spring Parade'
'Summer Summit'

RHODODENDRON HYBRIDS—LEPIDOTE
'Ambie'
'Dora Amateis'
'Mary Fleming'
'Molly Fordham'
'Towhead'

DECIDUOUS AZALEA HYBRIDS
'Brazil'
'Gibraltar'
'Ginger'
'Golden Eagle'
'Klondyke'
'Mt. St. Helens'

Missouri: Zones 5–6

Weather Data: St. Louis, Zones 6a–5b.

TEMPERATURE EXTREMES	AVERAGE TEMPERATURES
Max. 107°F (42°C)	Jan. 20–38°F (−7–4°C)
Min. −18°F (−28°C)	July 69–89°F (21–32°C)

Average Rainfall; 33.9 in. (82 cm), the heaviest in the months of April–October.

135 clear, 100 partly cloudy, 130 cloudy, 88 days of rain, and 6 of snow.

This list is compiled from the fall 1989 *ARS Journal*, Missouri Botanical Garden, article by Walter Behrendt.

RHODODENDRON SPECIES
R. yakushimanum E

RHODODENDRON HYBRIDS—ELEPIDOTE
'Gen. Schmidt'
'Pink Sherbet'
'Yaku Duchess'
'Yaku King'
'Yaku Queen'

RHODODENDRON HYBRIDS—LEPIDOTE
'Alice Swift'
'Carolina Rose'

'Dora Amateis'
'Epoch'
'Ethel Mae'
'Ginny Gee'
'Jenny'
'P. J. M.'
'Spring Delight'
'Yellow Eye'

DECIDUOUS AZALEA SPECIES
R. prinophyllum (roseum)

EVERGREEN AZALEA HYBRIDS
'Amoenum'

'Atlanta'
'Boudoir'
'Cascade' (Shammarello)
'Corsage'
'Fedora'

'Gable's Tall Lavender'
'Hino Crimson'
'Palestrina'
'Sherwood Orchid'

This list is provided by Ed Wood, of the Great Rivers chapter ARS.

RHODODENDRON HYBRIDS—ELEPIDOTE
'Album Elegans'
'Apple Blossom'
'Blue Ensign'
'Bosley-Dexter 1009'
'Boule de Neige'
'Catawbiense Album'
'Francesca'
'Great Eastern'
'Ice Cube'
'Janet Blair'
'Lodestar'
'Maximum Roseum'

'Parson's Gloriosum'
'Purpureum Elegans'
'Roseum Pink'
'Russell Harmon'
'Scintillation'
'Shawme Lake'
Yakushimanum, species and hybrids

RHODODENDRON HYBRIDS—LEPIDOTE
'Conewago Improved'
'Olga Mezitt'
'P. J. M.'
'Windbeam'
'Wyanoki'

New Hampshire: Zones 4–5

Weather Data: Dover, Zone 5b.

TEMPERATURE EXTREMES	AVERAGE TEMPERATURES
Max. 102°F (39°C)	Jan. −30–68°F (−35–20°C)
Min. −37°F (−38°C)	July 35–102°F (2–39°C)

Average Rainfall: 36.53 in. (93 cm), evenly distributed throughout the year.

92 clear, 111 partly cloudy, 162 cloudy, 125 days of precipitation, and 18 of snow or sleet.

55% of days are sunny from May–August.

This list is provided by Joe B. Parks of Dover, New Hampshire.

RHODODENDRON SPECIES
R. carolinianum L
R. catalgla E
R. catawbiense E
R. dauricum L
R. impeditum L
R. maximum E
R. minus L
R. smirnowii E
R. yakushimanum (Exbury Form) E

R. yakushimanum Ken Janeck E
R. yakushimanum Mist Maiden E

RHODODENDRON HYBRIDS—ELEPIDOTE
'Anna H. Hall'
'Besse Howells'
'Boule de Neige'
'Henry's Red'
'Janet Blair'
'Mrs. C. S. Sargent'
'Sham's Candy'

RHODODENDRON HYBRIDS—LEPIDOTE
'Conewago'
'Llenroc'
'Olga Mezitt'
'P. J. M.'
'Ramapo'
'Waltham'
'Windbeam'

DECIDUOUS AZALEA SPECIES
R. *arborescens*
R. *canadense*
R. *mucronulatum* Cornell Pink
R. *prinophyllum (roseum)*
R. *prunifolium*
R. *schlippenbachii*
R. *vaseyi*
R. *viscosum*

DECIDUOUS AZALEA HYBRIDS
'Brazil'

'Gibraltar'
'Golden Oriole'
'Golden Sunset'
'Homebush'
'Lemon Drop'
'Queen Emma'
'Satan'
'Toucan'

EVERGREEN AZALEA SPECIES
R. *kaempferi*
R. *poukhanense*

EVERGREEN AZALEA HYBRIDS
Not adapted, act as
deciduous plants. Two
that flower are
'Pride's Pride'
'Pride's White'

New York Chapter ARS: Zones 3–6

Weather Data: New York City, Zone 6b.

TEMPERATURE EXTREMES	AVERAGE TEMPERATURES
Max. 104°F (40°C)	Jan. 25–37°F (−4–3°C
Min. −2°F (−19°C)	July 67–83°F (20–28°C)

Average Rainfall: 41.7 in. (106 cm), evenly distributed throughout the year.

98 clear, 116 partly cloudy, 151 cloudy, 117 days of precipitation, and 7 of snow.

This list is provided by Frank Arsen, Lindenhurst, New York.

RHODODENDRON SPECIES
R. *bureavii* E
R. *fortunei* E
R. *keiskei* L
R. *makinoi* E
R. *metternichii* E
R. *pseudochrysanthum* E
R. *racemosum* L
R. *roxieanum* E
R. *yakushimanum* E

RHODODENDRON HYBRIDS—ELEPIDOTE
'Boule de Neige'
'Dexter 974'
'Everestianum'
'Gi Gi'

'Janet Blair'
'Old Port'
'Parker's Pink'
'Scintillation'
'Tom Everett'
'Vulcan'

RHODODENDRON HYBRIDS—LEPIDOTE
'Fairy Mary'
'Ginny Gee'
Guyencourt Hybrids
'Mary Fleming'
'Patty Bee'
'P. J. M.'
'Springsong'
'Windbeam'

Fig. 9. *R. catawbiense.* Photo courtesy of the Rhododendron Species Foundation.

Fig. 10. *R. fortunei.* Photo by the author.

Fig. 11. *R. makinoi.* Photo by William Bedwell.

Fig. 12. *R. maximum.* Photo by Paul James.

Fig. 13. *R. yakushimanum* Ken Janek. Photo by the author.

Fig. 14. *R. strigillosum.* Photo courtesy of the Rhododendron Species Foundation.

Fig. 15. *R. augustinii.* Photo by William Bedwell.

Fig. 16. *R. viscosum.* Photo by William Bedwell.

Fig. 17. 'Anah Kruschke'. Photo by Harold Greer.

Fig. 18. 'Anna H. Hall'. Photo by the author.

Fig. 19. 'Anna Rose Whitney'. Photo by Harold Greer.

Fig. 20. 'Besse Howells'. Photo by the author.

Fig. 21. 'Caroline'. Photo by Harold Greer.

Fig. 22. 'Catawbiense Album'. Photo by Harold Greer.

Fig. 23. 'Catawbiense Boursault'. Photo by Harold Greer.

Fig. 24. 'County of York'. Photo by William Bedwell.

Fig. 25. 'English Roseum'. Photo by Emile Deckert.

Fig. 26. 'Gomer Waterer'. Photo by Harold Greer.

Fig. 27. 'Ice Cube'. Photo by Harold Greer.

Fig. 28. 'Janet Blair'. Photo by the author.

Fig. 29. 'Jean Marie de Montague'. Photo by William Bedwell.

Fig. 30. 'Nova Zembla'. Photo by Helen Myers.

Fig. 31. Rhododendron 'Purple Splendour'. Photo by William Bedwell.

Fig. 32. 'Roseum Pink'. Photo by the author.

Fig. 33. 'Scintillation'. Photo by Harold Greer.

Fig. 34. 'Bric-a-brac'.
Photo by Harold Greer.

Fig. 35. 'Dora Amateis'.
Photo by the author.

Fig. 36. 'Mary Fleming'.
Photo by the author.

Fig. 37. 'P. J. M.'. Photo by Harold Greer.

Fig. 38. 'Ramapo'. Photo by Harold Greer.

Fig. 39. 'Snow Lady'. Photo by Harold Greer.

Fig. 40. 'Windbeam'. Photo by the author.

Fig. 41. *R. albrechtii.* Photo courtesy of the Rhododendron Species Foundation.

Fig. 42. *R. bakeri.* Photo by Paul James.

Fig. 43. *R. calendulaceum.* Photo by Paul James.

Fig. 44. *R. luteum.* Photo by Don Hyatt.

Fig. 45. *R. periclymenoides.* Photo by Paul James.

Fig. 46. *R. schlippenbachii.* Photo by the author.

Fig. 47. *R. vaseyi.*
Photo by William Bedwell.

EVERGREEN AZALEA SPECIES

Fig. 48. *R. poukhanense.* Photo by Helen Myers.

Fig. 49. 'Cecile'. Photo by Don Hyatt.

Fig. 50. 'Fireball'.
Photo by Ed Egan.

Fig. 51. 'Gibraltar'. Photo by Don Hyatt.

Fig. 52. 'Homebush'. Photo by William Bedwell.

Fig. 53. 'Ben Morrison'.
Photo by William Bedwell.

Fig. 54. 'Coral Bells' ('Kirin'). Photo by Harold Greer.

Fig. 55. 'Delaware Valley White'. Photo by the author.

Fig. 56. 'Herbert'. Photo by Harold Greer.

Fig. 57. 'Hershey's Red'. Photo by the author.

Fig. 58. 'Hino Crimson'. Photo by Harold Greer.

Fig. 59. 'Louise Gable'. Photo by Harold Greer.

Fig. 60. Azalea 'Purple Splendour'. Photo by Harold Greer.

Fig. 61. 'Rosebud'. Photo by Harold Greer.

Fig. 62. 'Sherwood Red'. Photo by the author.

Fig. 63. 'Springtime'. Photo by the author.

Fig. 64. 'Stewartstonian'. Photo by Harold Greer.

DECIDUOUS AZALEA SPECIES
R. albrechtii
R. arborescens
R. bakeri
R. calendulaceum
R. luteum
R. pentaphyllum
R. periclymenoides (nudiflorum)
R. prunifolium
R. schlippenbachii
R. vaseyi

DECIDUOUS AZALEA HYBRIDS
'Coccinea Speciosa'
'Copper Cloud'
'Corneille'
'Fireball'
'Gibraltar'
'Homebush'
'Narcissiflora'

EVERGREEN AZALEA SPECIES
R. balsaminaeflorum
R. kaempferi
R. kiusianum
R. macrosepalum
R. nakaharae
R. serpyllifolium

EVERGREEN AZALEA HYBRIDS
'Ben Morrison'
'Dayspring'
'Delaware Valley White'
'Forest Fire'
'Margaret Douglas'
'Nancy of Robin Hill'
'Orange Beauty'
'Stewartstonian'
'Surprise'

North Carolina
Piedmont Chapter ARS: Zones 6–8

The Piedmont Chapter represents North Carolina, from the Smoky Mountains, past the piedmont and on toward the eastern shore.

Weather Data: Raleigh, Zones 7a–7b.

TEMPERATURE EXTREMES	AVERAGE TEMPERATURES
Max. 105°F (41°C)	Jan. 25–50°F (−4–10°C)
Min. −9°F (−23°C)	July 67–88°F (20–31°C)

Average Rainfall: 41.7 in. (105 cm), the heaviest in the months of July–August.

111 clear, 139 partly cloudy, 115 cloudy, 110 days of rain, and 1 of snow.

The list is compiled from the Piedmont Chapter list in the ARS *American Rhododendron Hybrids 1980* edited by Meldon Kraxberger.

RHODODENDRON SPECIES
R. catawbiense alba E
R. chapmanii L
R. maximum E
R. yakushimanum E

RHODODENDRON HYBRIDS—ELEPIDOTE
'Anna Rose Whitney'
'Cadis'

'Chionoides'
'Cynthia'
'Jean Marie de Montague'
'Nova Zembla'
'Roseum Elegans'
'Ruby Bowman'
'Scintillation'
'Vulcan'

RHODODENDRON HYBRIDS—LEPIDOTE
'Dora Amateis'
'Mary Fleming'
'Windbeam'

DECIDUOUS AZALEA SPECIES
R. atlanticum
R. calendulaceum
R. periclymenoides (nudiflorum)

DECIDUOUS AZALEA HYBRIDS
Exbury azaleas

EVERGREEN AZALEA SPECIES
R. macrantha

EVERGREEN AZALEA HYBRIDS
'Chinsoy'
'Delaware Valley White'
'Gumpo'
'Guy Yerkes'
'Modesty'
'Moonbeam'
'Pink Pearl'
'Vespers'
'Wakaebisu'

Oregon: Zones 5–9

Weather Data: Eugene, Zones 8a–8b.

TEMPERATURE EXTREMES	AVERAGE TEMPERATURE
Max. 83°F (28°C)	Jan. 34–40°F (1–5°C)
Min. −4°F (−20°C)	July 48–74°F (9–24°C)

Average Rainfall: 46 in. (117 cm), the least in July–August.
75 clear, 82 partly cloudy, 210 cloudy, 138 days of rain, and 2 of snow.

This list is provided by Harold Greer of Greer Gardens.

RHODODENDRON SPECIES
R. augustinii L
R. calophytum E
R. davidsonianum L
R. decorum E
R. fortunei E
R. haematodes E
R. hippophaeoides L
R. impeditum L
R. keiskei L
R. keleticum L
R. litangense L
R. metternichii E
R. mucronulatum L
R. pseudochrysanthum E
R. racemosum L
R. roxieanum E
R. sutchuenense E
R. williamsianum E
R. yakushimanum E
R. yungningense L

RHODODENDRON HYBRIDS—ELEPIDOTE
'Anah Kruschke'

'Autumn Gold'
'Grace Seabrook'
'Hallelujah'
'Jean Marie de Montague'
'Ring of Fire'
'September Song'
'Trude Webster'
'Unique'
'Van'

RHODODENDRON HYBRIDS—LEPIDOTE
'Blaney's Blue'
'Crater Lake'
'Dora Amateis'
'Ginny Gee'
'Mother Greer'
'Patty Bee'
'P. J. M.'
'Ramapo'
'Senoria Meldon'
'Wigeon'

DECIDUOUS AZALEA SPECIES
R. atlanticum

R. *canadense*
R. *japonicum*
R. *luteum*
R. *occidentale*
R. *periclymenoides (nudiflorum)*
R. *schlippenbachii*

DECIDUOUS AZALEA HYBRIDS
'Cecile'
'Gibraltar'
'Ginger'
'Homebush'
'Kathleen'
'Lhetco'
'Tangelo'
'Washington State Centennial'
'White Lights'

EVERGREEN AZALEA SPECIES
R. *indicum*
R. *kiusianum*
R. *nakaharae*
R. *obtusum*
R. *yedoense*

EVERGREEN AZALEA HYBRIDS
'Alexander'
'Gaiety'
'Glamour'
'Hershey's Red'
'Hino Crimson'
'Polypetalum'
'Purple Splendour'
'Sherwood Orchid'
'Stewartstonian'
'Vuyk's Scarlet'

Weather Data: Portland, Zones 8a–8b.

TEMPERATURE EXTREMES	AVERAGE TEMPERATURES
Max. 107°F (42°C)	Jan. 33–44°F (1–7°C)
Min. −3°F (−19°C)	July 56–79°F (13–26°C)

Average Rainfall: 37 in. (94 cm), the least in June–August.

69 clear, 69 partly cloudy, 227 cloudy, 154 days of precipitation, with 2 of snow.

60% of days are sunny from May–August.

This list is provided by Clarence Smith, past president of the Tualatin Valley Chapter ARS; compiled by the chapter membership.

RHODODENDRON SPECIES
R. *augustinii* L
R. *decorum* E
R. *fargesii* E
R. *fortunei* E
R. *mucronulatum* L
R. *oreodoxa* L
R. *oreotrephes* L
R. *racemosum* L
R. *russatum* L
R. *williamsianum* E
R. *yakushimanum* E

RHODODENDRON HYBRIDS—ELIPIDOTE
'Anna Rose Whitney'
'Golfer'
'Halfdan Lem'
'Helene Schiffner'
'Medusa'
'Mrs. Betty Robertson'

'Pink Walloper'
'Purple Splendour'
'Taurus'
'Unique'

RHODODENDRON HYBRIDS—LEPIDOTE
'Barto Alpine'
'Cilpinense'
'Dora Amateis'
'Olive'
'P. J. M.'
'Ramapo'
'Rose Elf'
'Sapphire'
'Seta'
'Small Gem'

DECIDUOUS AZALEA SPECIES
R. *albrechtii*
R. *arborescens*

R. atlanticum
R. bakeri
R. canadense
R. luteum
R. occidentale
R. periclymenoides (nudiflorum)
R. schlippenbachii
R. vaseyi

EVERGREEN AZALEA SPECIES
R. amoenum
R. indicum
R. kaempferi
R. kiusianum
R. nakaharae
R. obtusum
R. oldhamii
R. simsii

DECIDUOUS AZALEA HYBRIDS
'Chetco'
Exbury Hybrids
Ghent Hybrids
'Gibraltar'
'Homebush'
Knap Hill Hybrids
'Marina'
Mollis Hybrids
'Princess Royal'
'Renne'

EVERGREEN AZALEA HYBRIDS
'Blue Danube'
'Conversation Piece'
'Everest'
'Hino Crimson'
'Mildred Mae', Gable
'Mother's Day'
'Purple Splendour'
'Rosebud'
'Stewartstonian'
'Twenty Grand'

Pennsylvania: Zones 5–6

Weather Data: Philadelphia, Zone 6b.

TEMPERATURE EXTREMES	AVERAGE TEMPERATURES
Max. 104°F (40°C)	Jan. 24–39°F (−4–4°C)
Min. −7°F (−22°C)	July 67–86°F (20–30°C)

Average Rainfall: 41.4 in. (105 cm), evenly distributed throughout the year.

93 clear, 111 partly cloudy, 161 cloudy, 117 days of precipitation, and 6 of snow.

61% of days are sunny from May–August.

This list is provided by Daniel (Betts) Layman of Wynnewood, Pennsylvania; Philadelphia Chapter ARS. Plants marked with an asterisk are additions made by the author.

RHODODENDRON SPECIES
*R. carolinianum L
*R. catawbiense E
*R. fortunei E
*R. keiskei L
 R. maximum E
*R. minus L
*R. mucronulatum L
*R. yakushimanum E

RHODODENDRON HYBRIDS—ELEPIDOTE
*'Anna H. Hall'
 'Ballet'
*'Catawbiense Album'
 'Chesterland'
 'Dr. Edward Lufton'
*'Janet Blair'
 'Joseph Paterno'
*'Nova Zembla'

'Pink Bonnet'
'Pink Fondant'
'Pink Touch'
'Redder Yet'
*'Scintillation'
'Terrific'

*RHODODENDRON HYBRIDS—LEPIDOTE
'Conewago'
'Dora Amateis'
*'Ginny Gee'
'Mary Fleming'
'Olga Mezitt'
'P. J. M.

DECIDUOUS AZALEA SPECIES
R. bakeri
R. calendulaceum
R. luteum
R. periclymenoides (nudiflorum)
R. prunifolium
R. schlippenbachii
R. viscosum

DECIDUOUS AZALEA HYBRIDS
'Bouquet De Flore'
'Brazil'
'Cecile'
'Daviesi'
'Gibraltar'

'Golden Oriole'
'Homebush'
'Klondyke'
'Narcissiflora'
'Old Gold'
'Oxydol'
'Renne'
'Strawberry Ice'
'Toucan'

EVERGREEN AZALEA SPECIES
R. kaempferi
R. kiusianum
R. poukhanense

EVERGREEN AZALEA HYBRIDS
'Beni Kirishima'
'Big Joe'
'Delaware Valley White'
'Dream'
'Elizabeth Gable'
'Everest'
'Herbert'
'James Gable'
'Louise Gable'
'Polaris'
'Rosebud'
'Springtime'
'Stewartstonian'

Virginia: Zones 6–7

Weather Data; Richmond, Zones 7a–6b.

TEMPERATURE EXTREMES	AVERAGE TEMPERATURES
Max. 105°F (41°C)	Jan. 27–47°F (−3–8°C)
Min. −12°F (−24°C)	July 67–88°F (20–31°C

Average Rainfall: 44 in. (112 cm), the heaviest in the months of July–September.

102 clear, 105 partly cloudy, 158 cloudy, 113 days of rain, and 4 of snow.

66% of days are sunny from May–August.

Weather Data: Roanoke, Zones 6a–6b.

TEMPERATURE EXTREMES	AVERAGE TEMPERATURES
Max. 105°F (41°C)	Jan. 26–45°F (−3–7°C)
Min. −4°F (−20°C)	July 65–87°F (18–31°C)

Average Rainfall: 39 in. (99 cm), evenly distributed throughout the year.

103 clear, 112 partly cloudy, 150 cloudy, 120 days of precipitation, and 7 of snow.

This list is from a survey by Hugh B. Sproul, Jr., of Staunton, Virginia; Middle Atlantic Chapter ARS.

RHODODENDRON SPECIES
R. *carolinianum* L
R. *catawbiense* E
R. *chapmanii* L
R. *fortunei* E
R. *keiskei* L
R. *makinoi* E
R. *maximum* E
R. *metternichii* E
R. *racemosum* L
R. *yakushimanum* E

RHODODENDRON HYBRIDS—ELEPIDOTE
'A. Bedford'
'Caroline'
'Catawbiense Boursault'
'County of York'
'David Gable'
'Dr. H. C. Dresselhuys'
'English Roseum'
'Gomer Waterer'
'Jean Marie de Montague'
'Nova Zembla'
'Roseum Elegans'
'Scintillation'

RHODODENDRON HYBRIDS—LEPIDOTE
'Mary Fleming'

'P. J. M.'
'Windbeam'

DECIDUOUS AZALEA SPECIES
R. *bakeri*
R. *calendulaceum*
R. *periclymenoides (nudiflorum)*
R. *prinophyllum (roseum)*
R. *vaseyi*

DECIDUOUS AZALEA HYBRIDS
'Cecile'
'Gibraltar'
'Goldflakes'
'Klondyke'
'Toucan'

EVERGREEN AZALEA HYBRIDS
'Coral Bells' ('Kirin')
'Corsage'
'Delaware Valley White'
'Elsie Lee'
'Glacier'
'Herbert'
'Hershey's Red'
'Hino Crimson'
'Rosebud'
'Stewartstonian'

Weather Data: Norfolk, Zone 10b.

TEMPERATURE EXTREMES	AVERAGE TEMPERATURES
Max. 104°F (40°C)	Jan. 32–48°F (0–9°C)
Min. −3°F (−19°C)	July 70–90°F (21–32°C)

Average Rainfall: 45.2 in. (114 cm), the heaviest in the months of April–October.

104 clear, 119 partly cloudy, 142 cloudy, 119 days of precipitation, and 2 of snow.

This list is provided by Sandra McDonald of Hampton, Virginia, and based on a survey by Kenneth McDonald, Jr., of Hampton, Virginia; the Rhododendron Hybrids—Elepidote list is from the Mid-Atlantic Chapter list compiled by William Bedwell for all Mid-Atlantic Chapter Area, revised May 1990.

RHODODENDRON SPECIES
R. *carolinianum* L
R. *catawbiense* E
R. *chapmanii* L
R. *dauricum* L
R. *decorum* E
R. *fortunei* E
R. *makinoi* E
R. *maximum* E
R. *metternichii* E
R. *viscosum* L
R. *yakushimanum* E

RHODODENDRON HYBRIDS—ELEPIDOTE
'Albert Close'
'Anna Rose Whitney'
'Autumn Gold'
'Beaufort'
'Ben Mosely'
'Besse Howells'
'Catawbiense Album'
'Catawbiense Boursault'
'David Gable'
'Disca'
'English Roseum'
'Everestianum'
'Holden'
'Ice Cube'
'Janet Blair'
'Madame Masson'
'Maxecat'
'Maximum Roseum'
'Minnie'
'Roseum Pink'

'Tom Everett'
'Wheatley'

RHODODENDRON HYBRIDS—LEPIDOTE
'Early Bird'
'Mary Fleming'
'P. J. M.'
'Windbeam'

DECIDUOUS AZALEA HYBRIDS
'Berryrose'
'Brazil'
'Bullfinch'
'Gay'
'Gibraltar'
'Golden Crest'
'Golden Peace'
'Golden Sunset'
'Klondyke'
'Orient'
'Toucan'

EVERGREEN AZALEA HYBRIDS
'Cavalier'
'Coral Bells' ('Kirin')
'Elsie Lee'
'Flamingo'
'Glacier'
'Hampton Beauty'
'Helen Curtis'
'Hershey's Red'
'Hino Crimson'
'Peggy Ann'
'White Rosebud'

Washington, District of Columbia: Zones 6–7

Weather Data: Washington D.C., Zones 6b–7a.

TEMPERATURE EXTREMES	AVERAGE TEMPERATURES
Max. 102°F (39°C)	Jan. 28–42°F (−2–6°C)
Min. −12°F (−24°C)	July 70–88°F (21–31°C)

Average Rainfall: 39 in. (99 cm), the heaviest in the months of March–August.

93 clear, 119 partly cloudy, 153 cloudy, 107 days of precipitation, and 5 days of snow.

This list is updated by the author from the Potomac Valley list in the ARS *American Rhododendron Hybrids 1980* edited by Meldon Kraxberger.

RHODODENDRON SPECIES
R. *carolinianum* L
R. *houlstonii* E
R. *maximum* E
R. *metternichii* E
R. *minus* L
R. *mucronulatum* L
R. *ovatum* L
R. *vernicosum* E
R. *yakushimanum* E

RHODODENDRON HYBRIDS—ELEPIDOTE
'Anna H. Hall'
'Blue Peter'
'Boule de Neige'
'Cadis'
'Caroline'
'Catawbiense Album'
'Chionoides'
'County of York'
'Ice Cube'
'Janet Blair'
'Lodestar'
'Nova Zembla'
'Roseum Pink'
'Scintillation'
'Wheatly'
'Yaku Prince'
'Yaku Queen'

RHODODENDRON HYBRIDS—LEPIDOTE
'Ginny Gee'
'Mary Fleming'
'Olga Mezitt'
'P. J. M.'
'Windbeam'

DECIDUOUS AZALEA SPECIES
R. *bakeri*
R. *calendulaceum*
R. *prinophyllum (roseum)*
R. *schlippenbachii*
R. *vaseyi*

DECIDUOUS AZALEA HYBRIDS
'Brazil'
'Cecile'
'Gibraltar'
'Homebush'
'Klondyke'
'Narcissiflora'
'Oxydol'
'Red Velvet'
'Strawberry Ice'
'Toucan'

EVERGREEN AZALEA SPECIES
R. *kaempferi*
R. *poukhanense*

EVERGREEN AZALEA HYBRIDS
'Delaware Valley White'
'Dream'
'Elsie Lee'
'Girard Border Gem'
'Girard Chiara'
'Helen Curtis'
'Herbert'
'Hino Red'
'Red Red'
'Rose Greeley'
'Springtime'
'Stewartstonian'

Washington State: Zones 5–8

Weather Data: Aberdeen, Zone 8a.

TEMPERATURE EXTREMES	AVERAGE TEMPERATURES
Max. 100°F (38°C)	Jan. 34–45°F (1–7°C)
Min. 10°F (−12°C)	July 52–69°F (11–21°C)

Average Rainfall: 32 in. (81.28 cm), the least in May–September. 211 days of precipitation.

This list is provided by Mrs. J. J. Sandifur of Aberdeen, Washington; Lewis County Chapter ARS.

RHODODENDRON SPECIES
R. *augustinii* L
R. *campylogynum* E
R. *decorum* E
R. *degronianum* E
R. *discolor* E
R. *fortunei* E
R. *impeditum* L
R. *orbiculare* E
R. *wardii* E
R. *yakushimanum* E

RHODODENDRON HYBRIDS—ELEPIDOTE
'Anna Rose Whitney'
'Autumn Gold'
'Blue Ensign'
'Blue Peter'
'Bow Bells'
'Faggetter's Favorite'
'Gomer Waterer'
'Hello Dolly'
'Jean Marie de Montague'
'Virginia Richards'

RHODODENDRON HYBRIDS—LEPIDOTE
'Blue Diamond'
'P. J. M.'

DECIDUOUS AZALEA SPECIES
R. *atlanticum*
R. *bakeri*

R. *canescens*
R. *occidentale*
R. *schlippenbachii*

DECIDUOUS AZALEA HYBRIDS
'Beaulieu'
'Brazil'
'Chief Joseph'
'Gibraltar'
'Ginger'
'Homebush'
'Inspiration'
'Kathleen'

EVERGREEN AZALEA SPECIES
R. *indicum*
R. *kiusianum*
R. *nakaharae*

EVERGREEN AZALEA HYBRIDS
'Edna'
'Fedora'
'Glamour'
'Hino Crimson'
'James Gable'
'Louise Gable'
'Mother's Day'
'Pink Drift'
'Purple Splendour'
'Rosebud'

Weather Data: Seattle–Tacoma, Zones 8a–8b.

TEMPERATURE EXTREMES	AVERAGE TEMPERATURES
Max. 99°F (37°C)	Jan. 34–44°F (1–7°C)
Min. 0°F (−18°C)	July 54–75°F (12–24°C)

Average Rainfall: 38.6 in. (98 cm), evenly distributed throughout the year.

58 clear, 79 partly cloudy, 228 cloudy, and 138 days of precipitation.

This list is provided by Mrs. J. J. Sandifur of Aberdeen, Washington; Knap Harbor Chapter ARS.

RHODODENDRON SPECIES
R. *augustinii* L
R. *davidsonianum* L
R. *yakushimanum* E

RHODODENDRON HYBRIDS—ELEPIDOTE
'Anna Rose Whitney'
'Bow Bells'
'Hallelujah'

'Jean Marie de Montague'
'Lem's Cameo'
'Lem's Monarch'
'Mrs. Furnival'
'Rose Point'
'Virginia Richards'

RHODODENDRON HYBRIDS—LEPIDOTE
'Blue Diamond'

'Bric-a-brac'
'Cream Crest'
'Curlew'
'Pink Snowflakes'
'Ramapo'
'Rose Elf'
'Snow Lady'

DECIDUOUS AZALEA SPECIES
R. albrechtii
R. atlanticum
R. austrinum
R. luteum
R. occidentale
R. prinophyllum (roseum)
R. schlippenbachii
R. vaseyi
R. vaseyi var. *alba*

DECIDUOUS AZALEA HYBRIDS
'Homebush'
'Irene Koster'

'Kathleen'
'Klondyke'
'Narcissaflora'
'Old Gold'
'Strawberry Ice'
'Sylphides'

EVERGREEN AZALEA SPECIES
R. kaempferi
R. kiusianum
R. macrantha

EVERGREEN AZALEA HYBRIDS
'Eikan'
'Everest'
'Hino Crimson'
'Martha Hitchcock'
'Palestrina'
'Rosebud'
'Seneca'
'Sherwood Orchid'
'Sherwood Red'

Australia: Zones 9–11

Weather Data: Melbourne, Zone 9.

TEMPERATURE EXTREMES	AVERAGE TEMPERATURES
Max. 114°F (46°C)	Jan. 57–78°F (14–26°C)
Min. 27°F (−3°C)	July 42–56°F (6–13°C)

Average Rainfall: 26 in. (66 cm), evenly distributed throughout the year.

The Dandenong Ranges at Mt. Dandenong, 20 miles (31 k) east of Melbourne, Victoria, is an ideal growing area for rhododendrons as they can be grown with a minimum of care. This includes azaleas, both deciduous and evergreen, as well as the vireya rhododendrons.

Azaleas, especially the indicas, grow better near Melbourne, Sydney (New South Wales), and Brisbane (Queensland). Some evergreen azaleas grow well into the tropical areas.

The cooler mountain areas around Sydney and Toowoomba (Queensland) and the island state of Tasmania are very suitable for rhododendrons.

Conditions in southern Australia are not favorable for rhododendron culture except in the Mt. Lofty Ranges where the most hardy hybrids will grow.

This list is provided by Lesley Eaton and Mrs. L. Eaton.

RHODODENDRON SPECIES
R. arboreum E
R. yakushimanum E

RHODODENDRON HYBRIDS—ELEPIDOTE
'Alice'
'Antoon Van Welie'
'Blue Peter'

'Britannia'
'Broughtonii'
'Fragrantissimum'
'Mrs. E. C. Sterling'
'Trude Webster'
'White Pearl'

British Isles: Zones 8–9

Weather data is presented for a number of sites:

Belfast, northern Ireland—Zone 9.

TEMPERATURE EXTREMES	AVERAGE TEMPERATURES
Max. 82°F (28°C)	Jan. 34–42°F (1–6°C)
Min. 14°F (−10°C)	July 52–65°F (11–18°C)

Average Rainfall: 38.2 in. (98 cm), the least in February–June.

Birmingham, central England, east of Wales—Zone 8.

TEMPERATURE EXTREMES	AVERAGE TEMPERATURES
Max. 92°F (33°C)	Jan. 35–42°F (2–6°C)
Min. 11°F (−12°C)	July 54–69°F; (12–21°C)

Average Rainfall: 29.7 in. (75.8 cm), evenly distributed through-out the year.

Cardiff, southwestern England—Zone 9.

TEMPERATURE EXTREMES	AVERAGE TEMPERATURES
Max. 91°F (33°C)	Jan. 36–45°F (2–7°C)
Min. 2°F (−17°C)	July 54–69°F (12–21°C)

Average Rainfall: 41.9 in. (106.4 cm), the least in March–June.

Dublin, east central Ireland—Zone 8.

TEMPERATURE EXTREMES	AVERAGE TEMPERATURES
Max. 86°F (30°C)	Jan. 35–47°F (2–8°C)
Min. 8°F (−13°C)	July 51–67°F (11–20°C)

Average Rainfall: 29.7 in. (75.8 cm), evenly distributed through-out the year.

Edinburgh, east central Scotland—Zone 8.

TEMPERATURE EXTREMES	AVERAGE TEMPERATURES
Max. 83°F (28°C)	Jan. 35–43°F (2–6°C)
Min. 15°F (−9°C)	July 52–65°F (11–18°C)

Average Rainfall: 27.6 in. (72.5 cm), evenly distributed through-out the year.

London, southeast England—Zone 8.

TEMPERATURE EXTREMES	AVERAGE TEMPERATURES
Max. 99°F (37°C)	Jan. 35–44°F (2–7°C)
Min. 9°F (−13°C)	July 55–73°F (13–23°C)

Average Rainfall: 22.9 in. (58.2 cm), evenly distributed through-out the year.

Liverpool, west central England—Zone 9.

TEMPERATURE EXTREMES	AVERAGE TEMPERATURES
Max. 87°F (31°C)	Jan. 36–44°F (2–7°C)
Min. 15°F (−9°C)	July 55–66°F (12–19°C)

Average Rainfall: 28.9 in. (73.8 cm), the least in February–April.

Perth, south central Scotland—Zone 8.

TEMPERATURE EXTREMES	AVERAGE TEMPERATURES
Max. 89°F (32°C)	Jan. 32–43°F (0–6°C)
Min. 0°F (−18°C)	July 51–68°F (11–20°C)

Average Rainfall: 30.7 in. (78 cm), the least in March–April.

Plymouth, southeastern England—Zone 9.

TEMPERATURE EXTREMES	AVERAGE TEMPERATURES
Max. 88°F (31°C)	Jan. 40–45°F (5–7°C)
Min. 16°F (−9°C)	July 55–66°F (12–19°C)

Average Rainfall: 37.8 in. (95 cm), the heaviest in the months of November–January.

Wick, northern Scotland—Zone 8.

TEMPERATURE EXTREMES	AVERAGE TEMPERATURES
Max. 80°F (27°C)	Jan. 35–42°F (2–6°C)
Min. 8°F (−13°C)	July 50–59°F (10–15°C)

Average Rainfall: 30 in. (76.2 cm), the least in March–June.

This list is provided by Betty French, Honorable Secretary, The Rhododendron and Camellia Group of the Royal Horticultural Society, England.

RHODODENDRON SPECIES
R. aberconwayi E
R. augustinii var. chasmanthum L
R. campanulatum E
R. fargesii E
R. metternichii E
R. oreodoxa E
R. russatum L
R. smirnowii E
R. wardii E
R. yakushimanum E

RHODODENDRON HYBRIDS—ELEPIDOTE
'Fastuosum Flore Pleno'
'Gladys'
'Goldsworth Orange'
'Lavender Girl'
'Letty Edwards'
'Loder's White'
'Mrs. A. T. de la Mare'
'Mrs. Furnival'
'Mrs. W. C. Slocock'
'Mrs. Tom H. Lowinsky'
'Susan'

RHODODENDRON HYBRIDS—LEPIDOTE
'Alison Johnstone'
'Blue Tit'
'St. Judy'

DECIDUOUS AZALEA SPECIES
R. albrechtii
R. atlanticum
R. bakeri

R. calendulaceum
R. mollis
R. occidentale
R. quinquefolium
R. schlippenbachii
R. vaseyi
R. viscosum

DECIDUOUS AZALEA HYBRIDS
'Coccinea Speciosa'
'Corneille'
'Daviesi'
'Homebush'
'Marion Merriman'
'Persil'
'Prince Henri des Pays-Bas'
'Raphael de Smet'
'Spek's Orange'
'Superba'
'Unique'

EVERGREEN AZALEA SPECIES
R. kaempferi
R. kiusianum
R. mucronatum
R. nakaharae
R. obtusum
R. poukhanense

EVERGREEN AZALEA HYBRIDS
'Addy Wery'
'Hinode Giri'
'Hinomayo'
'Iro-Hayama'

'John Cairns'
'Kirin'
'Leo'

'Naomi'
'Palestrina'

This list is provided by Russel Dyer of Exbury Enterprises Limited, near Southampton, Hampshire County, England.

RHODODENDRON SPECIES
R. *augustinii* L
R. *impeditum* L
R. *johnstoneanum* L
R. *keiskei* L
R. *lutescens* L
R. *ponticum* E
R. *pseudochrysanthum* E
R. *racemosum* L
R. *williamsianum* E
R. *yakushimanum* E

RHODODENDRON HYBRIDS—ELEPIDOTE
'Bud Flanagan'
'Christmas Cheer'
'Hawk Crest' ('Crest')
'Hotei'
'Mrs. G. W. Leak'
'Pink Pearl'
'Vanessa'

RHODODENDRON HYBRIDS—LEPIDOTE
'Blue Bird'
'Blue Diamond'
'Blue Tit'
'Dora Amateis'
'Oudijks Favourite'

'Pink Drift'
'P. J. M.'
'Praecox'
'Princess Anne'

DECIDUOUS AZALEA HYBRIDS
'Annabella'
'Beaulieu Manor' ('Beaulieu')
'Delicatissima'
'Ginger'
'Golden Oriole'
'Narcissiflora'
'Old Gold'
'Royal Command'
'Sunte Nectarine'

EVERGREEN AZALEA HYBRIDS
'Blaauws Pink'
'Blue Danube'
'Hinomayo'
'Iro-Hayama'
'Kirin' ('Coral Bells')
'Mother's Day'
'Palestrina'
'Rose Greeley'
'Rosebud'
'Vuyk's Scarlet'

Scottish Chapter ARS: Zone 8

Weather Data: Manchester, Zone 8

TEMPERATURE EXTREMES	AVERAGE TEMPERATURES
Max. 90°F (32°C)	Winter Low 24°F (−4°C)
Min. 12°F (−11°C)	(during months of Dec.–Feb.)
	Summer High 84°F (29°C)
	(during months of July–Sept.)

Average Rainfall: 50 in. (127 cm), fairly evenly distributed except slightly more during months of March and August.

Total Average Snowfall: 5 in. (15 cm), rarely stays more than 3 days. Occasional snow cover during the months of November–April.

This list is provided by Stephen and Anne Fox.

RHODODENDRON SPECIES
R. *bureavii* L
R. *ciliatum* L
R. *haemotodes* E
R. *orbiculare* E
R. *pseudochrysanthum* E
R. *roxieanum* L
R. *soulei* E
R. *thompsonii* E
R. *wardii* E
R. *wasonii* E
R. *yakushimanum* E

RHODODENDRON HYBRIDS—ELEPIDOTE
'Bow Bells'
'Elizabeth'
'Hawk Crest' ('Crest')
'Jean Marie de Montague'
'May Day'
'Rothenberg'
'Scarlet Wonder'
'Shilsonii'
'Winsome'

RHODODENDRON HYBRIDS—LEPIDOTE
'Blue Diamond'
'Chikor'
'Cilpinense'
'Curlew'
'Dora Amateis'
'Pink Drift'
'Pipit'
'Praecox'
'Sapphire'
'Snow Lady'

DECIDUOUS AZALEA SPECIES
R. *luteum*
R. *occidentale*

EVERGREEN AZALEA SPECIES
R. *amoenum (obtusum)*
R. *kiusianum*
R. *nakaharae* Mariko

EVERGREEN AZALEA HYBRIDS
'Everest'
'Rosebud'
'Vuyk's Rosyred'

Weather Data: Silchester, Zone 8.

TEMPERATURE EXTREMES	AVERAGE TEMPERATURES
Min. 20°F (−7°C)	Winter Low 20°F (−7°C) (during months of Jan.–Feb.) Summer High 80°F (27°C) (during months of July–Aug.)

Average Rainfall: 23 in. (58 cm), evenly distributed throughout the year.

Total Average Snowfall: 1–2 in. (2.5–5.0 cm).

This list is provided by Michael J. Jurgens, The Old House, Silchester, Reading, Berks, England.

RHODODENDRON SPECIES
R. *arboreum* E
R. *argyrophyllum* E
R. *augustinii* L
R. *calophytum* E
R. *ciliatum* L
R. *cinnabarinum* L
R. *dauricum* L
R. *decorum* E
R. *hippophaeoides* L
R. *lutescens* L
R. *morii* E
R. *oreodoxa* E

R. *pseudochrysanthum* E
R. *racemosum* L
R. *rubiginosum* L
R. *uvarifolium* E
R. *yakushimanum* E
R. *yunnanense* L

RHODODENDRON HYBRIDS—ELEPIDOTE
'Carita Inchmery'
'Crest' ('Hawk Crest')
'Cynthia'
'Damaris Logan'
'Elizabeth Hobbie'

'Humming Bird'
'Kate Waterer'
'Loder's White'
'Marcia'
'Pink Pearl'

RHODODENDRON HYBRIDS—LEPIDOTE
'Alison Johnstone'
'Chick'
'Curlew'
'Lady Chamberlain'
'Peace'
'Praecox'
'Seta'
'St. Judy'
'Wongii'
'Yellow Hammer'

DECIDUOUS AZALEA SPECIES
R. albrechtii
R. arborescens
R. atlanticum
R. bakeri
R. luteum
R. occidentale Leonard Frisbe
R. prunifolium
R. schlippenbachii
R. vaseyi
R. viscosum

DECIDUOUS AZALEA HYBRIDS
'Cecile'
'Chicago'
'Coccinea Speciosa'
'Daviesi'
'Homebush'
'Magnifica'
'Narcissiflora'
'Norma'
'Oxydol'
'Tower Dainty'

EVERGREEN AZALEA SPECIES
R. kaempferi Eastern Fire
R. mucronatum
R. nakaharae Mt. 7 Stars

EVERGREEN AZALEA HYBRIDS
'Girard Scarlet'
'H. H. Hume'
'Hino Crimson'
'Hinomayo'
'Mother's Day'
'Palestrina'
'Rosebud'
'Vuyk's Scarlet'

Canada: Zones 1–9

Southwestern British Columbia: the east and west coasts of Vancouver Island, suburban areas around Vancouver, in the delta and lower portions of the Fraser River Valley and surrounding mountain slopes up to 2,500 ft.

Summer drought occurs in Victoria and the lower east coast of Vancouver Island, while the west coast of Vancouver Island has more rain and parts of it are Zone 9a.

Weather Data: Vancouver, Zones 8a–8b.

TEMPERATURE EXTREMES	AVERAGE TEMPERATURES
Max. 92°F (33°C)	Jan. 32–41°F (0–5°C)
Min. 2°F (−17°C)	July 54–74°F (12–24°C)

Average Rainfall: 57 in. (145 cm), the least in May–August.

This list is provided by Clive L. Justice, Vancouver, B.C., Canada.

RHODODENDRON SPECIES
R. augustinii L
R. calophytum E
R. concatenans L
R. dauricum L
R. davidsonianum L
R. fictolacteum E
R. lutescens L
R. morii E
R. williamsianum E
R. yakushimanum E

RHODODENDRON HYBRIDS—ELEPIDOTE
'Albert Close'
'Anna Rose Whitney'
'Beauty of Littleworth'
'Blue Peter'
'Bow Bells'
'Britannia'
'Christmas Cheer'
'Cynthia'
'Elizabeth'
'Jan Dekens'
'Moonstone'
'Mrs. Betty Robinson'
'Mrs. G. W. Leak'
'Olympic Lady'
'Pink Pearl'
'Roseum Elegans'
'Sappho'
'Susan'
'Unique'
'Virginia Richards'

DECIDUOUS AZALEA SPECIES
R. arborescens
R. calendulaceum
R. canadense
R. japonicum
R. occidentale
R. pentaphyllum
R. periclymenoides (nudiflorum)
R. schlippenbachii

R. vaseyi
R. viscosum

DECIDUOUS AZALEA HYBRIDS
'Apple Blossom'
'Bouquet de Flore'
'Coccinea Speciosa'
'Fraserii'
'Gibraltar'
'Irene Koster'
'Koster's Brilliant Red'
'Narcissiflora'
'Oxydol'

EVERGREEN AZALEA SPECIES
R. kaempferi
R. mucronatum
R. poukhanense
R. yedonense

EVERGREEN AZALEA HYBRIDS
'Adonis'
'Aladdin'
'Amy'
'Cameo'
'Christmas Cheer' ('Ima-shojo')
'Corsage'
'Diana'
'Elizabeth Gable'
'Fedora'
'Hino Crimson'
'Hinode Giri'
'Hinomayo'
'James Gable'
'John Cairns'
'Louise Gable'
'Orange Beauty'
'Palestrina'
'Purple Splendour'
'Rosebud'
'Sakata Red'
'Stewartstonian'
'Ward's Ruby'

The climate of Ontario varies considerably (Zones 3a–5b), with the mildest conditions being near the lower Great Lakes (Erie and Ontario). This is the most suitable area for rhododendrons.

Weather Data: Toronto, Zone 5b.

TEMPERATURE EXTREMES	AVERAGE TEMPERATURES
Max. 105°F (41°C)	Jan. 16–30°F (−9– −1°C)
Min. −26°F (−32°C)	July 59–79°F (15–26°C)

Average Rainfall: 32.2 in. (82 cm), evenly distributed throughout the year.

This list is provided by Brian Schram of Fenwick, Ontario.

RHODODENDRON SPECIES
R. *brachycarpum* E
R. *carolinianum* L
R. *catawbiense* E
R. *dauricum* L
R. *dauricum* var. *album* L
R. *ferrugineum* L
R. *hippophaeoides* L
R. *maximum* E
R. *metternechii* E
R. *mucronulatum* L
R. *yakushimanum* E
R. *yakushimanum* E

RHODODENDRON HYBRIDS—ELEPIDOTE
'Blue Peter'
'Calsap'
'Caroline'
'County of York'
'Janet Blair'
'Lodestar'
'Scintillation'
'Sham's Ruby'
'Tony'
'Wyandanch Pink'

RHODODENDRON HYBRIDS—LEPIDOTE
'Fasia'
'Malta'
'Olga Mezitt'
'Pink Carolinianum' × 'Pioneer'
   (Delp)
'P. J. M.'
'Purple Gem'
'Ramapo'
'Wilsonii'
'Windbeam'

DECIDUOUS AZALEA SPECIES
R. *arborescens*
R. *atlanticum*
R. *bakeri*
R. *calendulaceum*
R. *canadense*
R. *japonicum*
R. *luteum*
R. *periclymenoides (nudiflorum)*
R. *prinophyllum (roseum)*
R. *schlippenbachii*
R. *vaseyi*
R. *viscosum*

DECIDUOUS AZALEA HYBRIDS
Exbury Hybrids
Ghent Hybrids
Knap Hill Hybrids

EVERGREEN AZALEA SPECIES
R. *kaempferi*
R. *kiusianum*
R. *poukhanense*

EVERGREEN AZALEA HYBRIDS
'Boudoir'
'Cascade' (Shammarello)
'Corsage'
'Elsie Lee'
'Herbert'
'Karens'
'Kathleen' (Gable)
'Pride's Pink'
'Purple Splendour'
'Rosebud'

FOUR: *Use in the Landscape*

Rhododendrons and azaleas are available in such diversity of flower color, foliage texture, form, season of bloom, and plant size as to fit almost any landscape plan. A landscape plan is necessary to coordinate the planting with the architecture of buildings, to roadways, paths, existing trees, and any other existing features of the landscape, and to determine how many and type of plants needed. As soon as the desired effect is defined and the various elements coordinated, plants can be selected to fit the plan. A landscape plan should be designed for easy maintenance in terms of mowing, pruning, mulching, and so on, providing easy access with as little hand care, such as weeding, pruning, and movement of material, as possible.

The plant collector (a category into which most gardeners fall from time to time) may need to set aside a separate area for collected items which do not fit into the landscape plan yet are so desirable as to deserve space for evaluation or just enjoyment for their own beauty.

Only some basics of landscaping are presented here, together with suggested uses for rhododendrons and azaleas. These are accompanied by illustrations of their application in the landscape. This material is included to assist those new to planning and developing landscape plans and will potentially reduce costly errors of judgment. I would recommend seeking professional help if the development involves a total landscape plan in a new planting area.

In developing the landscape plan a primary decision is whether the garden is to have a formal or informal effect. The trend today is toward informal plantings, edging property in gradual curves and grouping plants. Rhododendrons and azaleas are at their best in such informal settings. Plants grow naturally in rather informal groups with graceful curves; there are no square corners in nature's creations and perhaps the landscape planner is well advised to reflect this design trait. Plantings may be made using gradual, graceful curves around the foundations of buildings, along boundaries, walks, roads, or circling large trees. A very effective method for laying out the boundary of curves and circles is to use a garden hose laid out on the ground to define the shape of the desired bed. The hose can be moved until the desired shape is created. This method permits the gardener to visualize each bed as the landscape plan is being drawn up. Large open areas can be left for lawn and recreational use (see Fig. 65). The landscape design needs to please the user, and no one plan best serves all.

I do not believe the entire garden should be planted solidly to any one type or texture of plant, even though large groups are sometimes very effective. The differing textures and colors of needled evergreens, deciduous trees and shrubs, perennial, and annual flowering plants are needed to provide visual relief in the landscape and will also broaden the highlights when the garden has something in flower.

COLOR GUIDELINES

The integration of flower color is important to the harmony of any landscape design. Observing a few general guidelines can reward the gardener many times over.

1. Remember that bright colors, such as orange and red, are much more difficult to blend into group plantings.

2. It is usually more effective to use a group of at least three plants of a particular kind together rather than have single plants as little spots of many colors.

3. White flowers very effectively separate colors which might otherwise clash, such as the bright orange color of some deciduous azaleas and some of the brilliant reds. Orange seems particularly difficult to blend into plantings so must either be massed or separated from other plants by plants which flower white. Fig. 66 is a good example of using white to balance stronger colors.

4. Colors which are lost or clash with buildings need to be carefully sited. Brick walls are poor backdrops for oranges and light pinks.

5. Light pinks and whites are striking in the woodland or in front of evergreen trees where light intensity is low and could be used for the bulk of plantings of these kinds. (See Fig. 67.)

6. Bright reds can be mixed with pinks and whites in groups of three or five but should not make up over a third of the total planting.

The final planting needs to be fully visualized before any actual ground work is done to minimize surprise color clashes. Planting while plants are in bloom will make it easier to harmonize or blend colors and will also make it easier to consider which plants bloom at the same time. Planting when shrubs are in flower requires that plants receive extra shading and watering in the first growing season. It is fortunate that rhododendrons and azaleas transplant fairly easily, and if a mistake in placement is noticed, plants can easily be moved later.

SPECIFIC USES IN THE LANDSCAPE

The following is a brief outline of specific uses of rhododendrons and azaleas in the landscape. The azaleas, especially the low growing members of the evergreen group, make excellent foundation plants as do many of the dwarf rhododendrons. Some selections of both rhododendrons and azaleas do well as border plants, acting to separate areas in the landscape, while the larger growing forms are supreme in the open landscape and especially in open wooded areas. The very low growing species and cultivars of both rhododendrons and azaleas are very useful in rock gardens and as ground covers. Many of the large growing *Rhododendron* form stunning specimen and accent plants.

Specimen Plants/Accent Plants

Some of the large rhododendrons and azaleas make excellent specimen plants as they can be attractive year-round. When appropriately placed in the landscape such plants are breathtakingly beautiful, especially when viewed against backgrounds of large evergreens or a dark green lawn (Fig. 68). White or light pink, yellow or bright red flower colors contrast well with a dark green background and will add an eye-catching accent, attracting attention to that point in the landscape. Even the small-leaved rhododendron cultivar 'P.J.M.', which matures into a large plant, may be used as a specimen plant. When 'P.J.M.' is in full flower in early spring with drifts of daffodils in front or beside, it offers a sight not soon forgotten.

Plants considered dwarf or slow growing in nature such as *R. yakushimanum* Mist Maiden also form excellent specimen plants for close viewing (Fig. 69). Specimen plants draw attention to themselves and to the area and need to be placed near areas of activity, near paths in the landscape, or in view from the house or road. Specimen plants need to be spaced by themselves and far enough from other plants to allow full development of the natural shape of the individual plant.

Accent plants are also used to heighten interest in a portion of the landscape. They differ from specimen plantings in that accent plants are used with other plants, either in a border planting or a grouping, while specimen plants stand alone in the landscape. When in flower, both rhododendrons and azaleas provide a blast of color quite capable of accenting any point. Care must be taken not to overwork this quality to the point of monotony or to let plantings over power the rest of the landscape. Fig. 70 shows an effective accent planting.

Group Plantings of *Rhododendron*

It is in groups that rhododendrons and azaleas perform at their best, both in relation to the landscape effect and the effect on the well-being of plants and their performance. The group provides shade, interrupts wind, and receives mulch as leaves fall, all of which benefit all the plants in the group.

Shrubs appear more interesting when planted in odd numbers (three, five, seven, etc.) partly because off numbers lend themselves to circles and curves, resulting in more natural-looking beds. Group plantings may be made around building foundations, along walks or roads, around trees, or around the edge of the landscape, as dividers or privacy screens or as a large accent area. Beds or groups may be planted to all the same cultivar or species or to several with care taken to blend or match flower color, plant texture, flowering date, and plant height. A sufficient number of plants of the same flowering date, color, size, and texture will provide a smooth transition rather than giving a shotgun effect. Even small groups require at least three of the same cultivar or species. If bold colors, such as bright reds and oranges, are used, additional plants to provide the light colors of pink and white may be required to blend all colors together. It is often wiser to make solid plantings of bold colors in separate beds.

Spacing of plants within a group depends on the rate of growth and mature size of each plant and the landscape effect desired. If the group is to be solidly planted to rhododendrons and azaleas, with no interplanting of annuals or other plants, a spacing of 3 ft. (0.9 m) results in a completed, more mature effect quickly. When using plants maturing at 6 ft. (1.8 m) in ten years, an initial 6 ft. spacing will not produce a solid planting for ten years. Decisions on plant spacing depend in part on how quickly a solid mass of plants is desired. Closer spacing will require more funds in order to purchase the larger number of plants needed.

Plant height must also be considered in selecting plants for group plantings in order to keep the group in proper scale within itself and with the rest of the landscape. Rhododendrons are sometimes described as tall, which usually means over 6 ft. (1.8 m); medium, 4–6 ft. (1.2–1.8 m); and low growing, 3 ft. (0.9 m) or less. Azaleas have similar descriptions of upright, spreading, low growing, and so forth. Fig. 71 illustrates a large group planting in scale with the landscape.

Where large groups of plants are planted, tall growing forms need to be placed to the center or back, with lower growing plants on the outside or in front. This allows for maximum viewing of all plants and provides the planting with a multi-level effect, especially when in flower (Fig. 72).

Border Plantings, Screens, and Hedges

Borders are used to separate areas in the landscape. They are used to separate property lines, a service area from the rest of the landscape, the parking area from a lawn, the lawn from the garden, or to create secluded areas. Rhododendrons and azaleas, since they are for the most part evergreen plants, make excellent border plants in those locations where the wind is not too severe and some afternoon shade is available (Figs. 73–75).

Natural Screens. The dense evergreen foliage of rhododendrons and some azaleas makes them especially useful in screening undesirable landscape features. For example, a mass planting of evergreen azaleas is used very effectively in Fig. 76 to obscure a large tree stump in my garden. Other situations may require screening activity areas from garbage cans or compost pile, or creating a privacy screen around a swimming pool.

If plants are developed as a low hedge or border, well branched and naturally compact plants are required. Evergreen azaleas and some of the small-leaved rhododendrons are very suitable as small hedges. Rhododendrons are not generally suitable for large formal hedges as their growth habit will not present an attractive appearance if the plants are heavily and regularly pruned as formal hedges require. On the other hand, if there is plenty of room to accommodate natural growth the larger broad-leaved rhododendrons can make a most attractive border. Rhododendrons and azaleas cannot be used as windbreaks as they do not tolerate wind well; other plant species are better suited to this role in the landscape (see Figs. 77 and 78).

Woodland Plantings

It is in the open woodland where rhododendrons and azaleas can truly reign supreme. The informal setting and the backdrop and over-story of trees provide a pleasing landscape effect, yet also provide the benign climate native to many of these species. The high shade and humidity of the forest, its gift of mulch each year, its windbreak qualities, and the vertical emphasis of the tree trunks all serve to enhance the visual effects while proving an environmental benefit to the landscape planting. The larger forms of rhododendrons and azaleas are in better scale for a woodland setting. Smaller species and cultivars are easily lost and when viewed from a distance may appear merely as small dots in the extensive scale of the woodland. Small, low growing plants may be used to best advantage if massed along woodland paths where observers can come in close contact with them.

Plants with fragrant flowers are also more effective when placed near paths where their fragrance can be enjoyed. I think the fragrance of such plants as *R. fortunei* requires that it not be restricted to woodlands, but rather be planted close to foot traffic, upwind of the residence or along activity areas such as patios.

It is best to mass plant in the woodland. In nature one or two plants of a species are seldom noticed growing in one spot, and plants tend to develop large circular or irregular groupings. The naturalized garden indicated by a woodland setting dictates a like manner when plantings are sited.

I recently received an unusual compliment from a carload of sightseers who had stopped to get their shovel out of the trunk in order to lift a rhododendron from my woodland planting along the road. When I confronted them they responded with "We thought they were growing wild!" This is certainly not a valid reason to dig plants, yet I had to feel gratified. The point was that a naturalistic planting had been made which appeared to have evolved by itself. And this is what I consider a successful woodland planting.

As noted earlier, the large woodland tends to overwhelm not only small plants but plantings small in scope as well. To create a satisfactory display, a rather large area containing at least 20–50 plants needs to be included in the original plan. And, if at all feasible, the area should be expanded as soon as possible. Plants may be spaced more widely apart in woodland settings to provide growing room for years of undisturbed growth. Irregular spacing rather than a precise distance between plants also adds to the natural appearance. The large growing hybrids can be spaced 6–9 ft. (2–2.5 m) apart with smaller growing azaleas and dwarf rhododendrons spaced closer. Check the size in ten years, as given in the Good Doer charts, to determine distances for individual cultivars or species. See Fig. 79 for a successful woodland planting of rhododendrons in Hurlock, Maryland.

Fig. 65. Rhododendrons used to border an open area in the garden of Dr. and Mrs. Thomas F. Wheeldon, Richmond, Virginia. Photo by William Bedwell.

Fig. 66. A group planting of *Rhododendron* displaying an excellent use of white to provide color balance. Garden of Jack Ayres, Oakton, Virginia. Photo by Jack Ayers.

Fig. 67. The light pink flowers of 'Cadis' contrast with the dark background of pines in the author's garden, Woodsboro, Maryland. Photo by the author.

Fig. 68. A beautiful specimen plant contrasting well with the dark green lawn border at the Royal Botanical Gardens, Kew, England. Photo by George Ring.

Fig. 69. *R. yakushimanum* Mist Maiden forms a beautiful specimen plant in the author's garden. Photo by the author.

Fig. 70. Azaleas provide an accent point in the garden of Ray and Jane Goodrich, Vienna, Virginia. Photo by Ray Goodrich.

Fig. 71. A large group planting of azaleas and rhododendrons in scale with the landscape in the garden of William Bedwell, Dinwiddie, Virginia. Photo by William Bedwell.

Fig. 72. *Rhododendron* 'Ed's Red' provides needed height and color behind the lower growing 'Yaku King' in the author's garden. Photo by the author.

Fig. 73. Rhododendrons and azaleas successfully used as a transition from the lawn area with the woods in the Hyatt garden, McLean, Virginia. Photo by Don Hyatt.

Fig. 74. Rhododendrons border the driveway in this restful, natural setting in the Goodrich garden, Vienna, Virginia. Photo by Ray Goodrich.

Fig. 75. Rhododendrons used to separate the residential parking area from the lawn in the author's garden. Photo by the author.

Fig. 76. 'Hershey' azaleas used to conceal a tree stump in the author's garden. Photo by the author.

Fig. 77. Azalea 'Rose Greeley' used as a hedge in the garden of Ray and Jane Goodrich of Vienna, Virginia. Photo by Ray Goodrich.

Fig. 78. *Rhododendron* 'P. J. M.' used as a hedge in an unidentified garden. Photo by Harold Greer.

Fig. 79. A woodland planting in the Parsons garden, Hurlock, Maryland. Photo by James Parsons.

Fig. 80. An azalea bonsai in the collection at the National Arboretum, Washington, D.C. Photo by George Ring.

Fig. 81. A foundation planting of azaleas in the garden of Helen and Gilbert Myers, Westminster, Maryland. Photo by Helen Myers.

Container Growing and Bonsai

The smaller rhododendrons and azaleas may easily be grown in containers and, for example, be placed around the patio or in permanent raised planters next to buildings or walkways. Take care to provide a well drained container and planting mix. A mixture of 50% perlite or coarse sand and 50% sphagnum peat moss or other coarse mix works well. Since these materials contain little in the way of plant nutrients or even the minor elements, a complete plant food needs to be used regularly.

Rhododendron roots are much more cold sensitive than is the top growth and can be damaged by temperatures below 20°F, (–6°C). Provide winter protection for the roots of containerized plants wherever temperatures regularly drop below this level. This is best done by insulating the container with bark or other material or by moving the container to a protected winter storage area. While 20°F (–6°C) is a general rule of thumb, there are a few species and cultivars that can withstand lower root temperatures. These are listed in the following table.

ROOT KILLING TEMPERATURES

Variety	°F	°C
R. *prunifolium*	20	–6.7
R. 'Hino Crimson'	19	–7.3
R. Exbury Hybrid	17	–8.3
R. *schlippenbachi*	15	–9.4
R. 'Purple Gem'	15	–9.4
R. 'Gibraltar'	10	–12.2
R. 'Hinode Giri'	10	–12.2
R. *carolinianum*	0	–17.8
R. *catawbiense*	0	–17.8
R. 'P.J.M.'	–9	–23.3

Sources: Harvis, John R. 1976. Root hardiness of woody ornamentals. *HortScience* 11(4):385–386. Steponkus, Peter L., George L. Good, and Steven C. Wiest. 1976. Root hardiness of woody plants. *American Nurseryman* CXLIV(6):16.

Clearly container size will vary by the size of plant. Also, expect that as the plant grows older and larger, it will require transplanting to a larger container.

Plants with small leaves, slow growth, and a crooked or spreading growth habit provide the most suitable forms for bonsai. The small-leaved azaleas and dwarf rhododendrons make ideal plants for miniaturizing. Older plants which have already developed twisted or gnarled stems are superior to immature whips. If only young whips are available, it is still possible to obtain the desired shape by pruning and wiring over a period of years.

I will not attempt to detail the means and objectives of creating a bonsai *Rhododendron*. Instead, I will refer the interested reader to the excellent instruction in *Bonsai: Its Art, Science, History and Philosophy* by Deborah Koreshoff, published by Timber Press in 1984. Fig. 80 illustrates an azalea bonsai.

Not all bonsai plants need to be in containers. Many of the smaller, low growing plant species at home in the rock garden are quite suitable for bonsai development. The azalea *R. nakaharae* and its cultivars are especially well adapted to this form of growing.

Foundation Plantings and Companion Plants

Foundation plantings again seem to require groups of plants. The commonly seen single row of plants lined along a foundation wall is not normally seen as interesting as groups which curve out from and in toward the building and add depth to the area. For maintenance and structural purposes, plants should be placed no closer than 3 ft. (0.9 m) to a building. Also, if plants are sited under a roof overhang they will be more susceptible to drought damage as precipitation will not reach the root area.

The size of the plants to be used in foundation plantings must be coordinated with the size of the building, especially its height. A single-story home requires low growing plants (especially under windows) while the same plants would be out of scale for a multi-story building. The tall growing forms, including the large, broad-leaved rhododendrons, complement taller buildings especially when large landscape trees can unite the planting to the building. The importance of plant selection means it is not a hit-or-miss activity, and a well conceived landscape plan specifies such things as textures and sizes of plants to be used in all situations.

Other plants are often used together with rhododendrons and azaleas in foundation plantings, and can provide an occasion to blend foliage textures and colors. Interestingly, extreme opposites can blend well together. For example, the needlelike foliage of a pine or yew, perhaps used on a windy corner as a windbreak, serves well as a background for the broad-leaved foliage and flowers of rhododendron and azaleas.

Fig. 81 shows rhododendrons and azaleas selected for the foundation planting in Westminster, Maryland.

Trees and Shrubs. Carefully selected trees can add a sense of height to the landscape and provide the light-filtered shade so well suited to many understory plants including rhododendrons. Selection criteria for trees include selecting those with deep root systems that will not seriously compete for water with the more shallow rooted *Rhododendron*. Tree foliage needs to allow adequate light to reach understory plants. Trees and shrubs producing flowers or fruit, as for example dogwoods (*Cornus* spp.), crab apples (*Malus*), viburnum, and hollies (*Ilex*) possess yet another useful quality by extending the season of color and providing food and shelter for birds and other wildlife. Needled evergreens such as fir (*Abies*), pine (*Pinus*), and hemlock (*Tsuga*) with their finer textured foliage and light green color provide a pleasing contrast to rhododendrons and azaleas.

Flowering shrubs which bloom earlier or later than the rhododendrons, like the flowering trees, make good companions by extending the period of color in the landscape not only with flowers but with seeds as well. Shrubs can also provide transitions in size and texture between trees and lower growing azaleas and rhododendrons.

Wild Flowers. Many native flowers are adapted to the same environmental conditions as are rhododendrons and azaleas. Any wild flowers native to the woodland make excellent companions. Specifically this would be such plants as hosta, *Liriope*, lily-of-the-valley (*Convallaria majalis*), bloodroot (*Sanguinaria canadensis*), wood hyacinth (*Endymion non-scriptus*), ferns (various species), lady's slipper (*Paphiopedilum* spp.), and solomon's seal (*Polygonatum* spp.). They could be interplanted between and in front of rhododendrons and azaleas. Purchase such native plants only from businesses selling plants propagated in the nursery. Collected plants should not be purchased as this practice adds to the pressures leading to the destruction of wild plants.

Bulbs. Bulbs may be used to delicately extend the flowering season interest before, during, or following the flowering period of rhododendrons. Early flowering plants such as snowdrops (*Galanthus*), wood hyacinth or grape hyacinth (*Muscari* spp.), lily-of-the-valley, daffodils (*Narcissus*), and tulips (*Tulipa*) add color early in the flowering season and are not highly competitive for nutrients, water, or space. Daffodils planted in front of or beside early flowering rhododendrons such as 'P.J.M.' or azaleas such as 'Springtime' add another dimension to the color scheme. Lilies (*Lilium* spp.) can extend the flowering season into summer. The lighter shades of white, pink, and yellow contrast to great advantage with the dark green foliage of rhododendrons.

Well chosen ground covers between plantings of rhododendrons and azaleas can smoothly unite the planting with a lawn or pathway area. While some root competition may develop, it would not be sufficiently severe to restrict the use of closely grown ground covers when they can add so much to the landscape picture.

Companion plants are used to tie rhododendrons and azaleas into the total landscape, creating a natural-looking, smoothly flowing vision. They can add contrast in height, texture, color, and season of flowering, and fill the spaces between plants to give a look of completion and maturity to the planting.

Some Final Notes on Plant Selection

The flowering times of the plants used in the landscape need careful consideration. Species flowering very early in the season are best placed in view of a window so they can be enjoyed from inside the house. As the weather warms and becomes more suited to outside activity, plants which flower later can be placed in view of the principal areas of outdoor activity.

The genus *Rhododendron* is particularly well suited to a wide range of use in the landscape thanks to the range of shape, size, flower color, and foliage texture. A gardener may consider using rhododendrons and azaleas wherever the site ensures their well-being and wherever they fit into the landscape plan. Where the situation is right, no other plant can give as much beauty for so little effort.

As landscape needs are determined through one's plan, plant selection can be guided by use of the Good Doer lists to identify rhododendron species and cultivars of proper size, flower color, flowering date, and adaptability.

Figs. 82–88 (color photos) show additional examples of landscape uses of rhododendrons and azaleas.

Fig. 82. Foxglove used as a companion plant with rhododendron in the Bedwell garden in Dinwiddle, Virginia. Photo by William Bedwell.

Fig. 83. Companion planting in the Cecil Smith garden in Oregon. Photo by William Bedwell.

Fig. 84. No group of plants add color to the landscape better than rhododendrons. 'Cynthia' in the background, 'Jean Marie de Montague', and 'Pink Pearl' in the foreground at the Crystal Springs Rhododendron Garden, Portland, Oregon. Photo by William Bedwell.

Fig. 85. Dogwood (*Cornus florida*) used as companion plants in the garden of Paul James, Boones Mill, Virginia. Photo by Paul James.

Fig. 86. A formal planting leads up to the entrance in the garden of Ernie Dzurick, Mercer Island, Washington State. Photo by George Ring.

Fig. 87. Spectacular fall color of an Exbury azalea in the Bedwell garden in Dinwiddie, Virginia. Photo by William Bedwell.

Fig. 88. *Rhododendron* 'County of York' provides winter interest in the garden of William Bedwell, Dinwiddie, Virginia. Photo by William Bedwell.

FIVE: *Transplanting to the Landscape*

Planting rhododendrons and azaleas properly is more critical than for some other garden additions since they are somewhat more exacting in their requirements. But if these requirements are met, the results will be at least as successful as with other plant types. This chapter is intended to provide the understanding of those requirements necessary to succeed.

Only plants adequately mature to survive the rigors of the new landscape environment need be purchased. Dwarf species and cultivars can transplant well at a rather small size since age or maturity is best used as the criterion for selection. Such plants may be only a few inches (5 cm) tall, yet will be sufficiently mature with hardened wood to survive the landscape environment. When purchasing larger forms, look for azaleas at least 12–15 in. (30–38 cm) and rhododendrons 18–36 in. (48–91 cm) since they will transplant easier, survive better, and are less costly than larger plants.

Care must be given to the time of planting, particularly in regions or sites less favorable to the growth of rhododendrons and azaleas. In all but the most benign sites, where they can be transplanted in virtually any season, two seasons are best suited for transplanting rhododendrons and azaleas: spring and fall, when plant foliage is not in active growth. *Rhododendron* are sometimes planted as late as the flowering time, but I believe this is usually too late except for the early flowering species. Spring planting can be done as soon as hard freezes have passed and the soil is sufficiently dry to work without forming lumps.

Fall planting is gaining in favor both among nursery people and gardeners since roots have the opportunity to work their way into the prepared soil before the onslaught of winter. Fall planting is most successfully undertaken in those regions in which the soil does not freeze to such a depth that the entire root ball of the transplanted plant is likely to get frozen. In less harsh regions fast root development can occur in early fall since all the plant's resources can be directed to root growth since top growth is no longer active. Lack of tender top growth also reduces moisture demand on the newly transplanted root system. As days shorten and the soil cools, roots continue to grow even well into the fall. This will result in plants better able to support new top growth the following spring and to survive the hot dry conditions the following summer. Fall planting must be completed at least one month before the soil freezes and preferably three to four months before the ground becomes hard and frozen.

PREPARING TO PLANT

It will be assumed that the gardener has familiarized himself or herself with how to select the planting site and modify the soil as outlined in Chapter Two. Questions as to the size of the hole which must be dug and whether raised beds should be used are dependent to a large extent on soil type.

In a heavy, poorly drained soil, plants should *not* be fit into small holes *in* the soil. This is akin to setting them in a container having little or no drainage. On the other hand, smaller holes may be used in well drained soils. In no case should a planting hole be used that is smaller than twice the diameter of the existing root ball. Plantings in heavy soils need to be raised somewhat above the existing soil level or, if internal soil drainage is determined to be very poor, need to be made entirely on top of the existing soil in an amended soil mix.

Many nursery people and horticultural research personnel recommend against adding amendments in heavy soils. Researchers in Georgia have uncovered the fact that the root systems of rhododendrons and azaleas transplanted in an amended backfill were significantly smaller than those transplanted directly into native Georgian clay (*Journal of Environmental Horticulture* 2(2):43–45, 1984). I take issue with this as a general recommendation but have not done extensive research on this matter. In my judgment the problem occurs with method; for example, when a too-small planting hole is dug in heavy clay soil and is then amended only in this area. As water enters the amended medium (that is, the small planting hole) faster than the surrounding native clay soil, it is blocked by the unamended, impervious sides and bottom of the hole. The plant roots can then be damaged by standing water.

The solution would be to dig a larger, wider hole at least 4 ft. (1.2 m) wide and amend all this soil with 50% organic matter. The entire planting bed should then be raised above the existing soil level by adding topsoil to raise the bed 12–18 in. (30–45 cm). The result is an amended rooting medium which drains well and will encourage rhododendron and azalea root extension. This extended area will encompass enough space for several years of normal growth before the unamended soil is encountered. The continued extension of the roots, beyond the amended medium, will be further encouraged by the use of a good mulch extending beyond the interface point.

Organic amendments, in my view, not only will improve soil drainage, except in sandy soils, but will also offer other improvements to the soil environment. One result is to encourage mycorrhizae, the fungi which form a symbiotic association with the roots of ericaceous plants, an association which in turn increases the moisture and nutrients available to the plant.

Incorporate decayed bark as 50–75% of the total organic material for soils that hold too much moisture. The bark will retain less moisture than sphagnum peat moss and greatly improve drainage. A healthy, rapidly growing plant demands less care over the long term, and the extra effort at planting time will prove to be a time-saver with the added dividend of a more attractive plant throughout its lifetime.

These planting instructions apply to planting an individual *Rhododendron* in the landscape. However, rhododendrons and azaleas are generally more attractive in the landscape and seem to perform better when planted in groups of three or five or more. In this case an entire bed can be prepared and amended with organic material as directed for a single planting. Again raise the bed above the soil level in very poorly drained soils or construct a bed on top of the native soil.

Rhododendrons and azaleas are shallow rooted plants, so it is not necessary to dig a very deep hole or bed; 8 in. (20 cm), the usual depth a rototiller works, is deep enough. It is much more effective to prepare the soil area extending around the plant than to prepare the soil area extending much below the plant. This is true even in well drained loam soils. If the subsoil is well drained, the roots will grow downward below the cultivated soil (Fig. 89). If the subsoil is poorly drained, the roots will in no case grow downward. Rhododendron and azalea roots will extend only as deeply as oxygen is available. The only justification for deep soil preparation might be in areas where soils freeze deeply. This would increase aeration at greater depths and allow deeper root penetration. Use of mulch to prevent deep freezing of the soil is an alternative to deep digging in this circumstance.

Caution must be exercised in planting rhododendrons near buildings with concrete foundations as they tolerate lime poorly. Contractors often bury additional concrete, plaster, and other lime-based materials around the building site. These materials greatly affect soil pH, raising it dramatically to alkaline levels. In such cases a

Fig. 89.   A rhododendron with a deep root system grown in a well drained soil. The bed was amended only 8 in. (20 cm) deep, and the root system is now well developed to an 11 in. (28 cm) depth. Photo by the author.

poor-to-intolerable environment for azaleas and rhododendrons results. Furthermore, simple aging of concrete or cement block foundations causes lime to leach into the nearby soil. New concrete foundations can be sealed with asphalt or other waterproofing material to reduce or eliminate the lime problem. Whatever the situation, always plant at least 3 ft. (0.9 m) from any foundation wall or other concrete structure.

If planting areas are prepared at least a week prior to planting, the loosened soil will have time to settle. This reduces the likelihood that either the plant or the soil level will change and altar the desired planting hole depth.

Fertilizer use is mentioned here only to make the point that it is safe to dig organics (including urea formaldehyde as a source of nitrogen) or natural minerals, but not chemical fertilizers, into the soil at planting time. If chemical fertilizers are used they must be dug in at least one week before planting and dissolved through the soil with at least 1 in. (2.5 cm) of water. If the planting area has been prepared as suggested in Chapter Two, no additional fertilizer is needed at planting time.

PLANTING

In digging the planting hole in the bed, attention must be paid to depth, which means the distance from the surface of the planting bed, whether raised above the soil level or not, to the bottom of the planting hole. Rhododendron and azaleas need to be planted about level with the top of the root ball; leaving the top 1 in. (2.5 cm) of the ball above soil level is even better. Under no circumstances should the soil surface be higher than the top of the root ball. The hole therefore needs to be dug to a depth 1 in. (2.5 cm) *less* than the vertical dimension of the root ball. If the root ball is longer than 8 in. (20.3 cm), which was recommended earlier as rototiller depth and adequate to prepare a planting area, dig a small hole, in well drained soil, just large enough to place the root mass. If planting in poorly drained soil, cut off the bottom of the root ball to reduce the dimension. Some readers may be horrified by the latter suggestion, yet it is known that container grown plants benefit from removing the pot-bound roots circling the bottom. Conversely, if the bottom of the planting remains in the loose, prepared soil tamp the bottom surface to forestall settling after planting.

In poorly drained soil the root ball must develop on top of the native soil. This was detailed in Chapter Two. In these situations the planting medium is placed around the ball for a distance of about 2 ft. (0.6 m), resulting in a raised bed as high as the root ball. The native soil beneath the plant requires no digging or amendments and will remain stable, not allowing the root ball to settle below the correct planting depth. Similarly, planting depth is more readily secure if the hole in prepared beds is not dug any deeper than the root ball. The diameter of the planting hole needs to be about twice the width of the root ball. This will allow easy access to pack soil in and around the root ball and to spread the plant roots out into the soil.

Planting considerations are also determined by whether the transplant has been field grown or container grown. Container plants are grown in coarse-textured, soilless media and are often seriously pot-bound. The resulting roots are tightly packed and may circle the inside walls of the container. These two factors present a couple of transplanting hazards. First, rhododendrons and azalea roots prefer the ease of penetrating the coarse, soilless mix to the far less hospitable planting soil and will resist growing into the latter. The gardener must do something to encourage root extension out into the surrounding soil. If the container plant is not pot-bound, the roots may simply be pulled out of the mix and spread in the hole at planting time. A sharp garden weeding tool is helpful in digging away the outer edge of the rooting medium to expose the roots. However, if the roots tightly encircle the pot and cannot be spread out, cut a 1 in. (2.5 cm) deep slit vertically into the root ball at four equally spaced points around the ball with a sharp knife. Also cut 1 in. (2.5 cm) off the bottom of the root ball. This treatment encourages development of new roots which will then grow out into the soil. It is even helpful to the plant if some of the roots are physically spread out in the soil. Do not allow the roots to dry out during treatment.

When filling the hole after the roots have been prepared, hold the plant in position and gradually fill the hole to each succeeding root level. Place roots on top of the fill and firm the soil. Continue this root-covering procedure as the hole is filled. If this procedure is not followed, the exposed roots may be forced back into the original root mass as the hole is filled with growing medium.

Fig. 90.   Cross section of a properly planted *Rhododendron* in well drained soil.

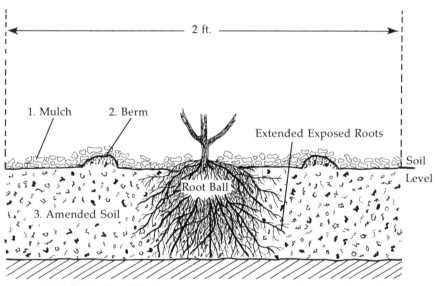

1. Mulch is 1–2 in. (2.5–5 cm) deep and extends past the amended soil area by at least 6 in. (15 cm).
2. Berm area is a 3 in. (7.6 cm) deep circle of soil which rings the plant and helps to hold water from rainfall or irrigation. Note that it is constructed just outside the root ball area.
3. Amended soil extends at least 2 ft. (0.6 m) from each side of the root ball.

Another problem often encountered with container grown plants is the drying out of the root ball. The coarse potting mix dries out more rapidly than the surrounding soil and water cannot move from the finer textured soil back into the root ball. The result is a dry root zone surrounded by a moist soil. Frequent watering of the root ball is necessary to prevent damage to the plant, yet only the root ball should be watered. The surrounding soil is moist, and watering it further can result in a soil too wet to encourage root extension. Additionally, as the root ball dries it will shrink, losing contact with the surrounding soil and making it even more difficult for roots to cross the interface into the surrounding soil. It is in part for this reason that roots are spread when planting. The failure of container grown plants to survive in the landscape can most often be traced to the drying out of the root ball. This results in root death before roots even have a chance to extend into the surrounding soil.

If container grown plants are planted on top of the soil and a totally organic mix is used around them, or they are simply transplanted into larger containers filled with a soilless medium, roots will quickly extend into such media, and it would not be necessary to spread the roots when transplanting.

Field grown plants already growing in a soil similar to the soil at the new planting site can be placed directly into the planting hole after the burlap or other root covering is removed. The soil can simply be packed firmly around the roots to remove any air pockets. If soil texture of the root ball is widely different from that of the planting site (e.g., sand versus clay), the roots need to be exposed and spread as explained previously. This is especially true when the soil in the root ball is of a coarser texture than the new soil environment. Field grown plants are always handled by the root ball and not by the plant stem in order to avoid damaging roots. The soil in the root ball is heavy and roots may be torn loose from the stem area if plants are moved or carried by the stem. A field grown plant will require less frequent watering than a container transplant as the soil in the root ball will not dry out as quickly.

After the plants, whether container or field grown, are planted, the soil needs to be packed firmly around the root ball with the hands, not tamped in with the feet. The planting depth should be rechecked and adjusted. A circle of soil, called a berm, about 3 in. (7.5 cm) high and with a radius about 6 in. (15 cm) outside the root ball will facilitate watering (see Fig. 90).

The entire planting area can then be mulched with about a 2 in. (5 cm) covering and watered to settle the soil around the root ball. Do not place any mulch within 2 in. (5 cm) of the plant stem. An overly deep mulch will severely restrict oxygen supply to the roots and is a major cause of death to rhododendron, azaleas, boxwood, and other plants requiring high oxygen levels around their roots. Do not tamp, pack, or walk on the planting area after watering as this will cause a loss of soil structure and thus a loss of soil aeration due to compaction.

AFTERCARE

Rhododendrons and azaleas require more attention for the first year after planting, and perhaps for the first three to five years, than is required by established plants. *Rhododendron* seem to need this much time to establish a root system adequate to provide the moisture and nutrient requirements of the plant. Older and well established rhododendrons suffer little from periods of drought, whereas newly planted plants are severely affected. New, tender growth on plants of all ages may exhibit some wilting in the heat of the day in full sun. If the foliage recovers a few hours after sundown, this would not be an indication of irreparable water stress.

Misting or fogging with an irrigation system is beneficial even for established plants to control wilting under conditions of extreme or prolonged heat. Provide mist of fog during the hottest part of the day, usually from noon until four or five p.m. Misting with a garden hose is equally helpful if an irrigation system is not available.

Field grown transplants need about 1 in. (2.5 cm) of water, rainfall plus irrigation, per week. If rainfall is inadequate, supplement by irrigating once or twice a week. Container grown plants, since their root balls dry out faster, need more water more often, usually every two days to keep the root ball moist. Obviously more water is needed more often under sunny, hot, low humidity conditions than during periods of cool, cloudy weather.

The watering regime in a woodland area varies much more than for plantings in an open bed. Rhododendrons planted very close to the stump of a tree cut out to thin the area enjoy a generous supply of soil moisture since the area is no longer having moisture pulled for tree growth. Conversely, plants placed within the root zone of a large, actively growing tree have serious competition for water. Given the differing water needs by plant placement in a woodland area, the need for irrigation varies. If all plants receive the same irrigation, some will be overwatered and suffer root damage, while others will not receive enough and suffer from drought stress.

Temporary windbreaks and sunshades are most helpful in the first year and especially through the first winter for newly planted rhododendrons. Such protection reduces the need for moisture and thus improves the likelihood of a successful new planting. Fig. 91 shows burlap used both as a very effective windbreak and as a sunshade for a newly planted rhododendron.

Some protection is advisable for newly transplanted plants even in regions not experiencing extremely cold winters. Protection is most commonly provided to reduce moisture loss and the consequent drying out of the plant which is the most frequent cause of

Fig. 91. Burlap sunshade and windbreak around a newly planted rhododendron. This is particularly helpful for the first year after transplanting, especially during the plant's first winter. Photo by the author.

death in newly transplanted plants. The lack of an extensive root system prevents new transplants from absorbing sufficient moisture to replenish transpiration losses through the leaves. Protection needs to be continued until the root system has extended out into the surrounding soil and the plant is making good top growth annually, perhaps three years or more. There are several measures a gardener can take to encourage moisture loss (transpiration) and intake (root function) into balance.

Sunlight raises foliage temperature and results in a more rapid loss of moisture from the leaves. Shading the plant, therefore, reduces moisture loss. Burlap, snow fencing, or any similar material breaks the sun's rays and reduces heat stress. Do not allow the shade material to touch the foliage as foliage damage will develop.

Air movement across the plant also increases moisture loss through the leaves except when the relative humidity is 100%. Reducing wind velocity will help sustain moisture levels in several ways. Besides the obvious increase from decreasing wind velocity, strong winds also often rock new transplants in the soil. This breaks the fine roots through which the plants absorb most of their moisture. Root extension is delayed, and the period of time the plant is unable to pick up adequate moisture from the soil is extended. Staking and installing a windbreak greatly reduces damage from rocking. As plants grow, their intrinsic bulk serves to slow the effects of wind velocity.

During the winter months plant protection is directed toward the fact that roots cannot absorb moisture as the soil freezes, changing soil moisture to ice. Since the plant is unable to absorb water, it dries out just as surely as it does in constantly high temperatures. Mulching modifies deep soil freezing and when coupled with a windbreak and shading will go far in improving plant survival.

Once plants have established a good root system, extensive protection is no longer necessary.

In transplanting to the landscape, use plants of adequate maturity or size, plant during the best season for the local area, prepare the planting hole properly (keeping good drainage in mind), use only organic fertilizers initially, prepare the root ball to encourage root extension, plant at the proper depth, mulch and water well, and provide shade and wind protection. Never allow the root ball to dry out.

TRANSPLANTING LARGE *RHODODENDRON*

Large rhododendrons or azaleas are usually transplanted for one of several reasons. The most common is to achieve an immediate landscape effect which would otherwise require years of waiting. Another might be to better site a plant which has outgrown its place in the landscape, usually as a result of improper plant selection. Or plants being grown for the landscape may have been left in the garden nursery area too long.

Whatever the reason, large plants with a fully developed root ball are very difficult to move manually. A power-driven tree spade simplifies the task and is the most efficient. But gardeners seldom have access to such a large, specialized piece of equipment and must do the job by hand. The method I use is as follows.

As a general reference, a plant 5 ft. (1.5 m) tall requires a root ball about 3 ft. (0.9 m) in diameter. *American Standards for Nursery Stock*, a publication sponsored by the American Association of Nurserymen, suggests that a grown, broad-leaved, evergreen plant 5–6 ft. (1.5–1.8 m) tall with a well branched root system requires a root ball with a minimum diameter of 20 in. (51 cm). The 3 ft. (0.9 m) ball I recommend is preferable if it can be physically handled as more roots are retained to support the plant in its difficult 2–3 years following transplanting.

Dig the trench 12–18 in. (30–45 cm) deep around the root ball. At this point undercut the root ball which means sever the roots from the underlying soil. In sandy soils that tend to fall apart easily, burlap can be pulled around the ball and wrapped tightly with rope to hold the ball together before the plant is undercut. This is seldom necessary in silt or clay loam soils. Undercutting can be done either by pulling a piece of ¼ in. (0.6 cm) steel cable under the root ball with a tractor or by using a shovel and digging iron around the ball repeatedly until all the roots are severed. With either method the resulting root ball will probably be only 8–12 in. (20–30 cm) deep, which is sufficient.

The next step is to tilt the plant to one side, slide a piece of ½ in. (1.3 cm) plywood under the root ball, and set the plant back down on the plywood. Rope or cable run through two holes previously drilled in the uphill edge of the plywood can be used to pull the plant to its new site. The plywood is pulled directly over and slightly past the prepared new planting site, and the plant is tilted back and the plywood slid from underneath it. Finally soil is placed around the root ball, and care must be given as previously described for all transplants.

SIX: *Care in the Landscape*

The information presented here continues on the assumption that the planting site has been properly selected, the soil well prepared as explained in Chapter Two, and suitable cultivars or species have been planted. Such factors will enable one's *Rhododendron* to be well equipped to survive. As soon as the root system has extended well into the surrounding soil, usually about three years after transplanting, very little aftercare will be needed.

WATERING

Rhododendrons and azaleas are, by virtue of their broad leaves, constantly losing water through transpiration, and an adequate supply of water is the first priority in their maintenance. "Adequate" is indicated by maintaining a uniformly moist soil. In hot, dry areas where moisture loss is high, a steady, dependable source of water is required.

Old, established plants can survive long periods of drought in late summer when they are no longer in soft active growth. Though leaves may wilt for many consecutive days, no damage is indicated as long as the foliage is turgid again by morning. If foliage is still wilted in the morning, a deep, soaking is called for. Sustained daytime wilting over lengthy periods, even though turgor returns overnight, will stress established plants. Consequences of such stress may be the appearance of disease, twig blight, or dieback, as well as symptoms of mineral deficiency in the leaves. A water stressed plant is more susceptible to insect and disease attack as it is not absorbing the soluble nutrients necessary for good health. Water stress induced problems are sometimes reduced by selecting more appropriate plants. Gables' 'Caroline' or any of the *yakushimanum* species or first generation *yakushimanum* hybrids seem seldom to suffer dieback or twig blight under severe stress.

Misting the foliage of established plants during the heat of the day can extend the period between waterings. Mist nozzles controlled by a timer set to the appropriate cycle to prevent serious wilting require relatively small volumes of water.

Newly transplanted plants, on the other hand, require close attention to watering. They cannot be allowed to wilt for any extended period of time. When in active growth, soft, new foliage may wilt on hot afternoons, especially in full sun, but if the foliage recovers an hour or two after sundown, no serious damage will result. Misting new growth during the heat of the afternoon is very beneficial and poses no threat of creating overly wet soil. The root ball and soil around and below newly transplanted plants need to always be kept moist. The amount of water needed to achieve this condition varies with ambient and soil temperatures, evaporation, and other factors, so check the soil beneath the mulch weekly to be sure the soil is moist but not wet.

Watering of newly transplanted container grown plants differs somewhat from that suitable for field grown plants. The soil around the roots of field grown plants dries out more slowly, and thereby plants require less frequent watering. Conversely, the coarse medium surrounding the roots of container grown plants holds little water and will dry out quickly. Container grown plants must therefore be watered every 2–3 days with just enough water to thoroughly wet the root ball. The soil around the root ball needs to be watered only when it starts to dry, not nearly as frequently as the root ball.

The death of newly transplanted plants, and especially container grown plants, can most often be traced to inadequate watering and hence drying out of the root ball. Extra attention to the water needs of newly transplanted plants is necessary for up to three years depending on how quickly the roots extend out into the soil. The intensity of care declines each year, and the frequency and quantity of water can be lessened as the root system develops.

Reduced watering of both old and new plants in late summer and early fall is necessary so that a new growth cycle is not encouraged late in the season. Tender, new growth induced by watering late in the growing season cannot harden off before freezing weather. Vigilance is still in order in the case of new transplants, and in the event that continued heat and sunlight lead to extremely dry soil conditions, water will be needed to maintain plant health and continued root development.

Water quality needs monitoring if extensive irrigation is required. Water with a high pH will cause soil pH to move above the level suitable for best plant growth. Water should not be used that is from sources containing root rot organisms or herbicides. The water quality of flowing streams is usually sufficiently high that no serious problems arise, yet it is best to consult local growers or other knowledgeable persons to be certain.

MULCHING

Mulches which maintain a more consistent soil temperature and moisture level are typically associated with the native habitat of rhododendrons and azaleas. The same benefits can be derived from a mulch when used in the landscape. A loose, coarse mulch extending beyond the root system is of great value in the landscape and helps prevent many problems. By virtue of shading the soil, (thus lowering soil temperature), the mulch greatly reduces moisture loss. The soil moisture level is maintained at a more consistent level, which leads to uninterrupted root development. Since water loss is reduced, the need for irrigation is also reduced.

The soil organisms producing root rot in rhododendrons and azaleas require both high soil temperatures and wet soils to become infectious. The cooling benefits provided by mulch can act as a disease prevention measure. Specific disease control is discussed in Chapter Seven.

Organic mulches also provide plant nutrients as they decompose, helping to maintain soil organic matter levels. Proper mulching is a must throughout the life of the plant and is second only in importance to proper watering, the number one maintenance practice.

Apply new mulch each year late in the fall or early winter after the plants have hardened off and rodents have found other winter homes. Only coarse materials such as wood chips, shredded bark, leaves of most deciduous tree species, or pine needles should be used since they allow better oxygen exchange between the roots and the air. Maple leaves, grass clippings, or peat moss are not good mulching materials as they can pack down too tightly. Very coarse materials such as oak leaves and pine needles can be applied 3 in. (7.6 cm) deep. Finer materials, such as ground pine bark ¼ in. (0.6 cm) in diameter, are applied only 1 in. (2.5 cm) deep since oxygen does not pass through them as readily. Keep mulch a few inches away from the main stem of the plant to avoid an environment conducive to crown rot. Since there are no feeder roots this close to the plant stem, any drying out of the soil in this area is of little consequence. Mulches are often applied too deeply in the landscape, which leads to severe root damage and death for any number of plants including rhododendrons and azaleas.

In *Nurseryman's News,* Dr. Francis R. Gouin, Chairman of the Department of Horticulture, University of Maryland, wrote:

> Not only is over-mulching a waste of mulch, but it is rapidly becoming the number one cause of death to azaleas, rhododendrons, dogwood, andromeda, boxwood, mountain laurel, hollies, cherry trees, ash, linden, spruce, etc. Repeated applications of mulch cause suffocation of the roots of shallow rooted species.

The symptoms of over-mulching are the same as others indicative of root damage, chlorosis, mineral deficiencies, poor growth, dieback, and plant death in extreme cases.

NUTRITIONAL NEEDS

Rhododendrons growing well in the landscape, exhibiting dark green foliage, normal growth rate, and flowering well, require little if any fertilizer. The nutrients released by decaying mulch usually provide sufficient nourishment to maintain healthy, active growth. Soil properly prepared with adequate amounts of organic material encourages the growth and establishment of the symbiotic mycorrhizae in the roots of rhododendrons and azaleas. This mutually beneficial association results in a more efficient transfer of soil nutrients into plant roots so that plant growth is normalized even in soils of low fertility. The need for intensive fertilization is therefore reduced. The fertilizer needs of landscape plantings differ from the needs of plants in a nursery where rapid growth is stimulated to produce a marketable plant as soon as possible.

Plant nutrients are the essential elements needed for plant growth. Plant food elements are divided into two groups: major (or macronutrients) are those consumed in large amounts by plants, and minor (or micronutrients) are those required in very small quantities.

The major elements or macronutrients nitrogen, phosphorus, and potassium are usually the elements in short supply in the soil and the ones that must be added by fertilizing. Calcium, magnesium, and sulfur are used in large quantities by plants and may also be in short supply in some soils.

The minor elements or micronutrients are used by plants in very small quantities and are seldom in short supply in loam or clay soils, though shortages do appear in sandy soils. The minor elements established as essential to plant growth are boron, copper, chlorine, iron, manganese, molybdenum, zinc, and nickel.

The deficiencies most often seen involve the following nutrients.

Major Elements

Nitrogen. Nitrogen is one of the major plant food elements. It promotes rapid growth and dark green leaf color since it is basic to the production of chlorophyll. Nitrogen also produces the most visible growth response in plants. A deficiency of nitrogen results in plant foliage turning uniformly light green or light yellow, and there is a general reduction in growth rate. Leaves may eventually become red in color, and in severe cases older leaves drop after turning yellow.

Since nitrogen is the plant food element most rapidly leached from the soil, it is the element most commonly needed. The amount of leaching varies considerably among different forms of nitrogen fertilizers, and this must be considered when determining which form to use. The nitrate form carries a negative charge as do the soil particles and is leached most rapidly because like charges repel. Furthermore, since ericaceous plants do not handle nitrate nitrogen, this form should not be used. Urea or ammoniacal forms, having a positive charge, do not leach rapidly and are the forms ericaceous plants prefer.

The form of nitrogen recommended for use in the landscape is ammonium sulfate (21% actual nitrogen). It releases nitrogen as ammonium ions that not only do not leach rapidly but are preferred by ericaceous plants. Ammonium sulfate has a further advantage in that it leaves an acidic residue of sulfate ions and continued use will lower soil pH (by removing calcium as calcium sulfate). Since ammonium sulfate is a highly soluble salt, it must be used in small amounts, 0.5–0.75 lb. (0.2–0.3 kg) per 100 sq. ft. (9.3 m²)sprinkled lightly in an area around the outer edge of the plant foliage. Remove any fertilizer accidentally spilled on the leaves as it will burn foliage. Ammonium sulfate is made available slowly over a period of approximately six weeks. Apply it in early spring and if a deficiency appears, as yellow or light green foliage, again in two months. Do not apply nitrogen after June 1 unless a shortage is in evidence.

Organic sources of nitrogen are the safest to use since they release nitrogen slowly which minimizes any likelihood of plant damage. Cottonseed meal (7% nitrogen), soybean meal, or alfalfa meal are good but usually expensive organic fertilizers. Apply at a rate of 3 lbs. (1.35 kg) per 100 sq. ft. (9.3 m²). There are also commercially prepared organic fertilizers that are specially formulated for rhododendrons and azaleas. If these are used, apply according to the manufacturer's directions.

Urea formaldehyde (38% nitrogen) is a synthetic organic fertilizer which releases nitrogen slowly over a period of six months in the form of urea, which in turn breaks down in the soil to ammonium ions. When applied in the fall after the first killing frost or when plants are hardened off for winter, it is a very effective fertilizer. Apply 12 oz. (3.4 kg) per 100 sq. ft. (9.3 m^2). Urea does not change soil pH.

Manures as fertilizer should be used with care. All manures must be composted first and are best dug into the soil prior to planting.

Mulches release nitrogen slowly as soil organisms break the material down at the soil surface. Mulches vary considerably in the amount of nitrogen made available in their decomposition. Materials previously recommended for mulching release very small amounts over a long period of time. The two extremes in the nitrogen content of organic mulches are green, uncomposted sawdust and composted animal manures. Fresh sawdust actively withdraws nitrogen from the soil, and nitrogen fertilizer must be applied to prevent nitrogen deficiency. For this reason sawdust should not be used until it has been well composted. Composted animal manure will add nitrogen to the soil. Cow manure provides the least nitrogen, with horse, hog, sheep, and poultry manure providing progressively more. Composted animal manure used as a summer mulch may result in unwanted succulent growth late in the growing season.

To summarize, nitrogen is the plant food element resulting in the most plant growth response. It is leached from the soil as the ammonium ions are slowly converted to nitrates by soil microorganisms. Nitrogen must be added annually as fertilizer or can be added through the natural breakdown of organic mulch.

Phosphorus. Phosphorus hastens plant maturity and the hardening off process, the reverse of the effect of nitrogen. Phosphorus does not readily leach from the soil, and annual applications are not required. Mycorrhizae associated with the roots of ericaceous plants usually absorb sufficient phosphorus to maintain plant health even in phosphorus deficient soils.

A deficiency of phosphorus serious enough to affect plant growth in the landscape seldom occurs in loam soils or in soil tested and amended according to the soil laboratory recommendations. However, deficiency symptoms can include stunting or lack of new growth, delayed maturity, abnormally dark green leaves, reddish purple spots on the underside of leaves, older leaves turning brown and dropping, and lighter than normal flower color. If phosphorus is deficient, it can best be applied as superphosphate sprinkled lightly on the surface of the mulch at any time of year.

Potassium. Potassium is most commonly known as its compound potash and is the third of the major plant food elements. It is critical to the formation of strong cell walls and thus strong stems. Potassium is not incorporated directly into plant tissue but plays a key role in the synthesis of plant proteins, starch, cellulose, and lignin. It also participates in the opening and closing of leaf stomata and thus gas exchange between the plant and the atmosphere. Adequate potash also improves a plant's ability to fight disease.

Potassium deficiency leads to deficiencies of iron, so symptoms are similar to those for iron deficiency: chlorosis of the leaves between the veins beginning at the leaf edge and tip, rolling up of leaf edges, leaf drop in severe cases, and the appearance of dieback diseases.

Potassium is not as strongly fixed in the soil as phosphorus but does not readily leach except in sandy soils. Most soils contain an adequate supply which is readily available to plants.

Potassium in the form of potash can be applied at any time of year since like phosphorus it does not stimulate vegetative growth. Sulfate of potash (49% potash) is a good form to use with ericaceous plants especially if the acidity of the soil must be lowered. Murate of potash (60% potash) is recommended if soil pH is adequately acidic.

Fertilizers specially formulated for rhododendrons and azaleas and containing all three of the major plant food elements are available and highly recommended for use in the landscape.

Calcium and Magnesium. Calcium and magnesium deficiencies mimic the symptoms of iron deficiency and show as yellowing of the leaf between veins. Calcium deficiency also is displayed by tip burning of leaves. These symptoms are rarely encountered in loam soils of proper soil pH but may occur in sandy soils.

Minor Elements

Minor elements required for adequate plant growth were listed earlier. Although required in very small quantities, they are considered essential to plant health. Availability of minor elements is affected to a large extent by soil pH, which if not properly controlled can result in minor element deficiencies in plants. Soil pH must be maintained between 4.5 and 5.5 to make the minor elements specifically required by rhododendrons and azaleas available in the best proportions. A low pH results in manganese toxicity in some soils, while a high pH leads to iron deficiency. Minor elements are generally available in adequate supply in properly adjusted soil. The minor elements are used by plants in such small quantities and are generally so toxic in excessive amounts that the average gardener cannot accurately apply them to the soil without running the risk of plant damage. Slow release fritted trace element compounds especially formulated for rhododendrons and azaleas have been developed and when carefully used, result in improved plant growth were deficiencies exist.

Iron. Iron deficiency symptoms first appear as a yellowing of leaves between leaf veins while the veins remain dark green. These symptoms usually appear in plants grown in soils with a pH above 6.0. Occasionally iron deficiency results from poorly drained soils, or if soils contain high levels of calcium, phosphorus, and potash, this can lead to iron deficiency at pH levels below 5.5. Maintaining proper soil pH is the best remedy for iron deficiency. Iron is the most important minor element discussed because it is the one most often deficient and symptoms are readily identified. If other minor element deficiencies are suspected, soil tests need to be run to specify the problem. If plant leaves are chlorotic (light green or yellowing between leaf veins while the veins remain green), the probable cause is iron deficiency due to a soil pH above 6.0. The application of soil acidifiers as explained in Chapter Two under site amendment will solve this problem. Iron chelates can be used in either foliar and/or soil applications to correct the deficiency quickly. Chelates should be viewed as only a temporary solution until soil pH can be corrected.

Root Damage

Plant root damage often imitates symptoms associated with minor element deficiencies. Root damage is most often caused by too much mulch or a poorly drained soil, both of which reduce oxygen supply to the roots. Excessive fertilizer use, insect attack, or mechanical injury resulting from hoeing, cultivating, or compacting the soil by walking on it also damage roots. If symptoms appear it is advisable to first check soil aeration before applying fertilizer or other soil amendments.

In summary, to provide good nutrition for rhododendrons and azaleas, plant in a well drained, properly prepared soil of pH 4.5–5.5 amended with nutrient elements as recommended by a soil testing laboratory, and apply a loose organic mulch. These steps, coupled with proper watering to keep the nutrients in solution and available to the plants, can only result in healthy, vigorous growth.

WEEDS

Weeds are present in every landscape. The best weed control is to start with clean soil and never allow any weeds to mature and go to seed. A good mulch can be a very important aspect to control. Since azaleas and rhododendrons should never be cultivated due to their shallow root systems, weeds must be pulled by hand. Weed killers can be used if the weeds are far enough away from garden plants and their roots to allow safe application. Check with your local extension service or horticulture department for the best herbicide to use. The chemical Glyphosate has proved very effective in my garden. It kills only what it is applied to, and the active chemical is inactivated in the soil so root absorption is not a problem. When this herbicide is used with a wick type contact applicator, weeds very close to desirable plants can be controlled.

PRUNING

Rhododendrons and azaleas present their best appearance as informal plants and generally require very little pruning or shaping in the landscape. This is assuming that the plant has the genetic potential to fit the landscape and that the plant has been properly shaped in the nursery. Any necessary pruning can be done with three simple tools—a small hand pruner, a pair of long-handled lopping shears, and a pruning saw.

Plant parts are removed for a number of reasons including deadheading (removal of faded flower trusses), removal of diseased and dead wood, removal of wood to shape or thin the plant, to regenerate an old plant, and root and foliage pruning prior to transplanting a large plant. Pruning needs to be done only for sound reasons, so the objective to be served must be clearly established before any plant parts are removed.

Fig. 92. A well shaped container plant for planting to the landscape. Photo by the author.

While nursery pruning is dealt with later, it can be noted for the benefit of gardeners that growers try to produce a compact plant with many branches. To obtain such a plant growers disbud and summer prune new growth to produce multiple branches resulting in compact plants.

Fig. 93.   A field grown plant nicely branched and compact. Ready for transplanting with no pruning required. Photo by the author.

Pruning in the Landscape

If a newly purchased plant was properly pruned and shaped in the nursery and flower buds are present on most of the terminals, additional pruning is not required at the time of planting. Terminal buds can be pinched out to promote branching if 50% or more of the branches have leaf buds rather than flower buds.

The terminal leaf buds of species or cultivars which naturally branch well seldom require disbudding. If the lateral buds are nearly as large as terminal leaf buds, multiple breaks (branches) will probably develop without pinching. Fig. 94 illustrates a branch with multiple terminal buds of similar size. This plant will probably branch well without pruning the terminal buds. If terminal buds are not pinched out and only single shoots emerge, these must then be pruned or pinched off to produce multiple branching. If the plant receives adequate light, most terminals will set flower buds on the final flush of growth.

Fig. 94. A terminal with buds of similar size. All these buds will probably break, and the plant will develop multiple branches. Photo by the author.

Dead-Heading

Removal of faded flower trusses on large-leaved elepidote rhododendrons is a form of pruning which pays big dividends since it will encourage greater flower bud set. Lepidote rhododendrons and azaleas do not require dead-heading because they flower well every year without it. Elepidote *Rhododendron* need to be dead-headed as soon as the flowers in the truss start to fade. Simply grasp the stem of the flower truss, at the base of the truss just above the terminal leaves, with the thumb and forefinger and twist sideways. If dead-heading is done properly no leaves or buds will be removed along with the truss.

Diseased or Dead Wood

The immediate removal of diseased or dead branches, whatever the cause, is a necessary task. This form of pruning is simply a good sanitary practice because it also helps control disease and insects in the landscape. Dead infected branches must always be pruned below the infected area or area damaged by insects and promptly disposed of by burning or hauling away in the garbage. Pruning tools should be disinfected between each cut with alcohol or a 1:9 mix of Clorox and water.

Shaping Azaleas

Azaleas can be pruned in early spring by simply cutting back long shoots to the point where branching is desired. Azaleas should not be pruned after July 31 in order to allow enough time for the plant to set flower buds for the following year.

At times azaleas send up long, straight stems which dramatically affect plant shape. Depending on how formal the planting is, where the plant is located, or the gardener's desire, this growth habit may or may not be viewed as a problem. If necessary these shoots may simply be cut back to match the height of the rest of the plant; they will branch at this point within a few weeks.

Rhododendrons and azaleas sometimes develop too many branches, which results in smaller flowers and the shading out and death of interior branches. If such a situation begins to develop, remove any weak branches with poor foliage until the desired density is restored.

If cultivars or species have been selected for a particular site and the plants overgrow the space allotted to them, severe pruning is called for and must be repeated periodically. The best time for severe pruning is early spring after the coldest winter weather is past.

Since azaleas have adventitious buds which break easily liberally scattered along the stems, they may be cut back to any point. If the azaleas are vigorous they will branch nicely. Rhododendrons, on the other hand, do not develop as many adventitious buds nor develop new shoots as readily as azaleas. It is very important that rhododendrons be vigorous and in good health before severe pruning. It may be necessary to carefully fertilize and water weaker plants for a year or more before a heavy pruning to improve vigor. Various cultivars or species react more or less favorably to severe pruning. I have pruned a 6 ft. (1.8 m) plant to about 1 ft. (0.3 m) and produced good multiple branching from the crown. On the other hand, some severely pruned plants may require years to regenerate and on occasion die.

The gardener uncertain about a plant's response can use an alternate method of pruning in stages. Remove only a few branches at a time, perhaps ⅓ of the branches each year, over a three-year period. In pruning to reduce height, remove the branches back far enough to allow the plant to grow for at least five years before the next pruning. Plants cannot tolerate severe pruning at close time intervals.

Alternatively, plants may outgrow the width allotted to them, in which case a different type of pruning is required. In this case only the side branches should be removed. Side branches are cut back to the main trunk or to a junction with another branch on the plant. Cuts

Fig. 95.   A large plant re-grown and well branched after being cut back to the soil level. Photo by the author.

should be made about ⅛ in. (0.3 cm) from the other branch or trunk leaving a very short stub. This stub will not only heal over more quickly than a larger cut flush with the trunk, but will also minimize tissue death in the trunk.

Rejuvenating an Old Plant

As plants age they lose vigor and often become open and ungainly due to loss of branches over the years. As a consequence they lose much of their value in the landscape. Only major surgery, either a single massive cutback or spread over 2–3 years, can solve the problem. Although it is surely the more drastic approach (which terrifies many gardeners), I urge cutting the plant back to the desired height, anywhere from 1 ft. (0.3 m) to 3–4 ft. (0.9–1.2 m) above the soil level in a single session. Such a massive reshaping can be done with more confidence if some small shoots have already appeared below the point of pruning. This is often the case if the plant foliage is thin and has allowed light to penetrate to the center. In virtually every case in which I have pruned a plant in this way, I have been rewarded with a vigorous, compact plant in a few years.

The alternate method of cutting back ⅓ of the branches each year over a three-year period is preferable if no new shoots are visible at the base of the plant. The successive thinnings often encourage new shoots to form as light intensity within the plant increases.

In any case, heavy pruning of old plants usually yields much more compact plants within 3–4 years. And if a plant should succumb following such severe pruning, all is not lost because a planting site is opened for one of the newer hybrids which most gardeners are eager to try.

Root Pruning

Root pruning is warranted if larger plants need to be moved. It can best be done in early spring a year before the move and will induce vigorous root branching. It is done by cutting down into the soil to the length of a spade blade in an entire circle around the plant. The circle needs to be about 6 in. (15 cm) smaller than the diameter of a root ball that can easily be handled in transplanting. If it is small enough it will be saturated with old and new roots which will hold the root soil ball together when moving the plant the following year.

Damaged Plants

Large rhododendrons and azaleas can sometimes be badly damaged by strong winds or ice storms felling trees or branches. Damaged *Rhododendron* must be cut back to the nearest undamaged branch or trunk even to soil level. Healthy plants will recover quickly from such damage and the resulting surgery.

Rhododendrons carefully selected for a site seldom need pruning, yet pruning can be used as a regular part of sanitation maintenance. If plants do need pruning, by all means prune and do so with confidence.

Care of plants in the landscape consists of maintaining proper soil moisture, annual mulching, maintaining proper soil pH and nutritional levels, insect and disease control (see Chapter Seven), and annual dead-heading and other forms of pruning as necessary or desired. Proper plant selection and placement greatly reduces the need for most landscape maintenance, allowing time for the gardener to enjoy the fruits of his labor.

SEVEN: *Plant Disorders*

Fortunately rhododendrons and azaleas have few serious insect and disease problems, not enough to limit their use in the landscape. A few are serious enough to require attention based on some knowledge and will be discussed.

Some species/cultivars will exhibit high levels of insect and disease resistance, flourishing with no extra care of any sort, indicating that they are well adapted to the area. Plants weakened either because they are not sufficiently cold hardy or heat tolerant to endure the climate or those not adapted to other cultural conditions are unable to resist insect and disease attack.

The best disease control is prevention. Selecting adapted and disease-resistant plants coupled with maintaining proper soil moisture (moist but not wet) are the best means to control or prevent disease. A well nourished, actively growing plant is much more resistant to both insects and diseases.

Most of the serious rhododendron diseases are caused by fungi, a primitive form of plant life. The first line of defense against fungi is maintaining a high level of garden sanitation. A disease organism can produce an infection or become pathogenic only if it is (1) present in the immediate environment, (2) can make contact with a susceptible host, and (3) environmental conditions favor its growth. Control requires altering only one of these three conditions.

Garden sanitation is part of the first line of defense and needs to be an ongoing practice. Diseased plants, including roots and dying branches, have to be removed and destroyed immediately to destroy pathogenic organisms before they cause further infections. Weeds may act as alternate hosts and must also be controlled, as must other hiding places for insects such as weevils, slugs, and other pests. Clearing brush to provide air movement will encourage drying of foliage surfaces which will discourage the growth of fungi. These are all practices which will discourage plant damage from insects and infectious fungus diseases.

Note of Caution: All chemicals mentioned for control of diseases and insects are listed by the appropriate authorities as materials providing control. I recommend none of them specifically to the reader as I have no way of knowing how well equipped the gardener may be to handle pesticides. If proper safety precautions are taken, there should be no problem. No highly toxic materials are mentioned.

The reader is emphatically advised to always read the label and follow directions exactly.

Some species/cultivars are insect- and disease-resistant and where adapted and suitable for landscape needs are highly recommended.

FUNGUS DISEASES

Fungus diseases are best controlled by sanitation or preventive sprays. Cultural practices and sanitation directed toward altering any one of the three requirements necessary for fungi to become pathogenic should be considered first as prevention will always be the best control. It is quite difficult if not impossible to eliminate or cure a fungus disease once a plant is infected. It is therefore important to carefully monitor and maintain a sanitation program. Remove any known disease organism to prevent or eliminate further contact with plants. In the event sanitation methods fail, chemical control must be initiated as soon as possible after the first sign of infection.

Only the most serious fungal diseases capable of doing extensive damage to rhododendrons and azaleas warrant discussion here. Diseases which produce a few leaf spots but result in little or no lasting damage to the plant are not described.

Root Rot (*Phytophthora cinnamoni*)

Commonly called rhododendron wilt because the entire plant wilts, phytophthora root rot can be one of the most serious diseases of rhododendrons and azaleas. It is not a serious problem in cooler climates where the soil temperature is below 50°F (10°C). Most often it is a disease of small plants recently transplanted, or it can be common to nursery situations. The same disease organism also infects dogwood (*Cornus*), *Pieris, Taxus, Camellia,* laurels (various), *Juniperus, Vaccinium,* and *Pinus,* to list only a few. It can infect large landscape-size plants in poorly drained soils although roots can often regenerate in the well drained upper soil levels.

Root rot symptoms can be noticed in the early morning when plant foliage remains wilted. In contrast are plants that have wilted from heat or low soil moisture which recover by morning in all but the most extreme drought conditions. The foliage of diseased plants will also take on a dull green appearance. *Phytophthora cinnamoni* causes wilting by plugging the conductive tissue in the roots which prevent the movement of moisture into the upper parts of the plant.

There is no known cure. Infected plants should be carefully removed, with great care taken to remove all infected roots and leaves. The plant and all its parts need to be burned or disposed of in the garbage. Do not replant any susceptible species of plant in the same area for several years unless the soil is first sterilized. Freezing will kill the organism in the soil but will not destroy any of the fungus left on plant debris, such as tiny roots left in the soil after the infected plant is removed.

There are now some very effective systemic fungicides for prevention of root rot. However, the best preventive measure is to plant only in well drained soils because the fungus requires free standing water in the soil to become infectious. Poor soil drainage, too much mulch, or any other practice which maintains or encourages high soil moisture and low soil oxygen levels provides favorable conditions for root rot.

Root rot is not necessarily a fatal problem in northerly regions where soils remain cool. Soil temperature must be above 50°F (10°C) for infection to occur. This fungus does not overwinter in soils that freeze as long as a host plant is absent.

The best means of prevention are the following.

1. Purchase disease-free plants from a reputable nursery. Avoid selecting plants lacking normal dark green foliage color or those that remain wilted when the soil around the roots is moist.

2. Plant only in a well drained site; in heavy soils dig in a porous material such as pine bark to improve drainage. Or plant in raised beds in heavy soils.

3. Plant at the same depth or 1 in. (2.5 cm) above the soil level in which the plant was grown in the nursery.

4. Place container plants on a bed of gravel with good drainage, not sitting on plastic.

5. Select disease resistant species/cultivars.

Metalaxyl used as a soil drench reduces the spread of *Phytophthora* into or among plants, but it does not generally kill the fungus in infected plants. Metalaxyl should be used only according to the label instructions for rhododendrons.

To use in the case of small landscape plants, approximately 10 sq.

ft. (0.9 m²) of soil around each plant needs to be drenched. For large rhododendrons and other large shrubs, 20–30 sq. ft. (1.8–2.7 m²) of soil needs to be drenched. Metalaxyl can be applied with a hose applicator or directly through an irrigation system. Metalaxyl, like all chemical pesticides, must be used with extreme care, especially since it is a systemic and can be absorbed through the skin.

In summary, control of root rot depends upon using the following control measures in this order of importance:

1. Do not plant in poorly drained sites except in raised beds.
2. Select disease resistant species/cultivars.
3. Use chemical control as a last resort.

Armillaria Root Rot (*Armillaria mellea*)

Plants suffering from this disease exhibit no specific symptoms, which makes diagnosis difficult. Rather, the plants just appear weak and less thrifty, and the leaves wilt, turn yellow, and drop. Plant death may be sudden or may take years. It is most common to areas in England and the Pacific Northwest.

Control is best achieved by removal and disposal of all infected plant parts.

Other less important root rot diseases such as Crown Rot (*Phytophthora cryptogeal*) are best controlled by providing good soil aeration and maintaining cool soil temperatures with mulches.

Twig Blight (*Botryosphaeria dothideae*)

Twig blight infects larger branches of plants in the landscape. The first symptoms of the disease are wilting of leaves on only one or several branches. The entire plant does not wilt as is the case with root rots. Leaves also take on a dull green appearance. Stems brown, and if the bark is scraped off a reddish brown discoloration is found underneath. Infection can enter through wounds such as pruning cuts, fresh leaf scars, dead branches, and bark cracks. Already stressed plants are more susceptible to the disease.

Twig blight is best controlled by pruning out all infected branches. Branches must be removed below any diseased tissue and the pruning tool sterilized between each cut with rubbing alcohol or a 1:9 solution of Clorox and water. Burn all infected branches after pruning.

Dieback

Phytophthora nicotina var. *parasitica, P. hevaea, P. cactorum, P. cirticola,* and *P. cinnamori* (see Root Rot) have all been isolated from plants exhibiting the symptoms of this disease. Dieback is primarily a disease of nurseries, especially among container grown plants, where it can be devastating.

The disease first appears on young foliage as water-soaked areas on the leaves. This is followed by foliage drying up and dropping off. The disease then moves down the stem and can kill a young liner-size plant in a few days. A film of water and warm weather are needed for infection to occur, which makes prolonged periods of rain in the summer ideal for its spread.

The incidence of dieback may be reduced or controlled by spraying the foliage with a broad spectrum fungicide after flowering and again in two weeks. Additional sprays may be necessary if a second flush of new growth occurs, and again in late summer if dry soil conditions cause plant stress. Some of the new systemic fungicides such as Fosethyl and Metalaxyl look very promising in control of both twig blight and dieback.

Botryosphaeria	*Phytophthora*
1. Mostly in landscape	1. Mostly in container nurseries
2. Entire branch or section of plant wilts quickly (1–2 days) and dies	2. Attacks individual shoots
3. Attacks older wood	3. Attacks succulent leaves and stems
4. Entire leaf rolls downward parallel to midrib	4. Leaf does not roll
5. Entire leaf turns gray-green then brown	5. Dark brown to black discoloration progressing in V-shaped pattern from midrib to leaf margins
6. Leaves remain attached to dead stem	6. Mature leaves drop from stem quickly
7. Brown discoloration in wood on one side of stem	7. Brown discoloration in wood
8. Moves fast in old stems	8. Moves fast in succulent stems
9. Branches die at any time	9. Shoots usually die during growth flush

Fig. 96. Diagnosing *Rhododendron* dieback caused by *Botryosphaeria* and *Phytophthora*. From *Plant Pathology Information* by R. K. Jones and D. M. Benson, Note 232, Dept. of Pathology, North Carolina State University. Rev. 4/84.

Blight (*Phythopthora syringae*)

This dieback disease is a cold or cool weather fungus disease observed in the Pacific Northwest. It causes a leaf spot similar in appearance to leaf scorch. For long term control prune out and destroy infected branches. Metalaxyl used as a drench or foliar spray in mid to late summer gives good chemical control.

Powdery Mildew (*Microsphaera alni*)

Powdery mildew is a serious disease of deciduous azaleas yet seldom appears on rhododendrons and evergreen azaleas. Symptoms are described well by the name; leaves become covered with a white powdery coating, losing some of their photosynthetic effectiveness and presenting a poor appearance in the landscape. Many deciduous azalea cultivars, especially if grown in climates to which they are not adapted, suffer damage starting in late July or August. This may finally result in early defoliation and a gradual weakening of the plant. Poor air circulation contributes to the problem.

Some deciduous azalea cultivars possess high resistance to this disease, and resistant varieties should be selected wherever possible. Chemical sprays, based on wettable sulfur regularly applied from July on, are very effective but should not be used when air temperatures exceed 85°F (29°C).

Petal Blight (*Ovalinia azalea*)

This fungus disease of azalea and rhododendron flowers has become a serious disorder in eastern North America for all mid to late blooming *Rhododendron*. Petal blight can completely destroy flowers in 2–3 days, turning them into a brown, slimy mass if warm, wet weather prevails at flowering time. Infected flowers cling to the plant much longer than normal which further compromises the landscape picture. Flowers not infected fall from the plant with their normal color, but infected flowers turn brown before falling. There are no known resistant varieties to my knowledge, and other control practices such as applying fungicides during wet flowering seasons have limited effectiveness.

Petal blight fungus can overwinter on diseased flower petals which have fallen to the soil surface the previous spring. Primary infection develops the following spring when temperature reaches about 62°F (17°C), although it can be initiated over a range of 49–72°F (9–22°C). Wind and raindrops splash the spores from the soil surface to lower flower petals, and spores are then easily transmitted from blossom to blossom. Picking off and destroying infected flowers will help prevent spread of the disease the following year. Mulch covering fallen flowers prevents spores from initially reaching flower petals, but heavy mulching can cause root damage.

A new fungicide (triadimefon) applied just as the flower buds start to show color offers some but not complete protection. If the disease is severe and the weather remains wet, a second application may be necessary when the flowers open. Early flowing plants such as 'P.J.M.' and 'Mary Fleming' are not affected by this disease as they bloom during cooler temperatures.

Leaf Gall (*Exobasidium vaccinii*)

This disease is not limited to leaves and may appear as thickened swellings on branches, flower parts, or seed pods. Leaf gall affects rhododendrons and some cultivars of evergreen azaleas, but not all. As the galls reach the reproductive stage a white coating appears. All galls need to be removed and destroyed before they can reproduce.

As the fungus can overwinter within the infected plant, control is best achieved by removing and destroying the galls when they first appear. This is not a serious disease, and hand picking is an effective control.

Leaf Rust (*Puccinastrum myrtilli; Melampsoropis peperina;* etc.)

There are a number of rust fungus diseases. Again the common name describes the disease, which appears as a reddish dust on leaves.

Good air circulation and exposure to sun to quickly dry the foliage following rains or irrigation help control rusts. Many cultivars are resistant, and selection of resistant plants is an available preventive measure. Leaf rust is seldom a serious health problem yet does make for an unattractive landscape. The fungicide triadimefon applied on a weekly basis gives control if the problem becomes acute.

Bud Blast (*Pycnostipanus azalea*)

Bud blast is usually first noticed when plants reach their bloom season and flower buds turn brown and fail to open. The actual infection was made through the axils of bud scales during the previous July and August. In the following winter such infected buds are covered with spores that resemble black bristles, and these become the source of infection for next year's buds.

Control is by removing dead buds or spraying with a broad spectrum fungicide which is applied immediately after flowering.

Other fungus diseases such as leaf spots caused by several disease organisms as well as bacterial and viral diseases occasionally attack rhododendrons, yet they are usually of little consequence in the landscape. As noted earlier the best control is prevention. Prevention includes first selecting a site favorable to good plant growth and, second, using resistant species/cultivars. Some nurseries identify resistant plants or are able to give advice as to which plants are the local good doers. Species/cultivars which have grown well in the local area are probably best adapted and most resistant to the principal regional diseases.

INSECTS

Insect pests of rhododendrons and azaleas represent a diverse range of the insect world, including beetles, weevils, true bugs, moths and caterpillars, nematodes, aphids, mites, borers, and scale insects. Only a few of these are of significant economic importance.

Lace Bug (*Stephanitis* **spp.**)

This small, fly-like, sucking insect is one of the worst pests of azaleas and some rhododendron cultivars, particularly in some warm eastern North American regions. Because of natural predators, it is not as serious a pest in Asia where it originated. According to experts the azalea lace bug and the rhododendron lace bug are two different species, alike in appearance but specific to their particular host. They inflict enough damage to weaken and in some cases kill plants that are already weakened by other stress factors.

Damage is usually first observed as a whitening of the upper surface of the plant leaves because the lace bug destroys the chlorophyll in the leaf. By the time this symptom is apparent, the bugs are present in force, as an examination of the underside of the leaf will reveal. It is important to control these insects before extensive leaf damage is done because the chlorophyll removed from the leaf cannot be replaced.

There are as many as four generations of lace bug per year. So it is best to examine the underside of leaves in May, June, July, and August for newly hatched nymphs. If adults are found in the fall it may be assumed that eggs are present and will hatch the following spring. Adults may be present until severe freezing occurs. The lace bug usually overwinters in the egg stage with eggs inserted into the upper leaf surface. Reports from areas in the southern latitudes indicate that adults may also overwinter.

Some rhododendron species, particularly those having a heavy indumentum (the feltlike covering on the leaf underside), are quite resistant to this pest. Hybrids with at least 50% *R. fortunei* in their parentage also are not affected in my plantings.

The most effective control agent is Acephate. This is a systemic insecticide which enters the plant sap, so the spray need not contact the insect to be toxic. All leaves should be wetted for best control. If spray is applied in May after adults have emerged but before eggs are deposited, one application can give control for the whole year. The new, safer insecticidal soap sprays give 85–90% control and are nontoxic. Soap spray must come in direct contact with the insect in order to be effective.

The recent discovery of the lace bug's natural enemy, *Stethoconus japonicus*, in North America has led U.S. Department of Agriculture

researchers at Beltsville, Maryland, to believe this predator will perhaps be as significant in lace bug control in North America as it has
already proved itself to be in Asia.

Whitefly

Whitefly is a pest on a few azaleas and rhododendrons. The small,
white insects are easily seen by shaking a branch to make them fly.
Damage is indicated by a gradual yellowing of leaves, the result of
plant juices being sucked from the underside of the leaf. Whiteflies
also exude a honeydew which results in the growth of a black mold on
the leaf surface. The mold is harmful only in that it reduces the
amount of light to the leaves, thus reducing photosynthesis of plant
food. Whitefly damage is greatest in dry weather and may be especially intense in greenhouses.

The new pyrethrin pesticides are relatively safe to use and result
in good control if applied in the evening since sunlight will destroy
pyrethrin's effectiveness. Whiteflies are attracted to the color yellow
and also can be trapped on yellow sticky strips.

Midge

The midge is a minor pest on rhododendron. A sign that midges
are present is new growth that is stunted and distorted. Leaf tips turn
downward and leaf edges may be spotted red or brown. The small
larvae feed beneath the leaf edges and are hidden under the edges as
the leaves curl.

Midges can be controlled by removing and destroying infected
growth by hand. Two years of surveillance and removal are required
for complete control. Acephate applied just as the new growth is
expanding is also very effective.

Thrips

Thrip damage appears very similar to damage from the lace bug,
with white blotches forming on leaf tops. The underside of the leaf
becomes silvery in color with small black spots of excrement (frass).
Damage is usually worse in hot weather. Eggs are laid in early spring
with a life cycle of about a month when egg laying is repeated. This
brief life cycle results in a rapid population buildup of thrips in a short
time.

Acephate gives control in two applications one week apart during
the height of thrip activity.

Mites

Mites are dry weather pests and almost invisible to the naked eye.
They are not true insects and belong to the same family as spiders,
which also have eight legs. Damage is first noticed as plant foliage
becomes bronze, brown, or pale green in color. A magnifier will be

needed to locate mites, which is most easily done by shaking the leaves over a white piece of paper. Any mites present will fall onto the paper, which can then be examined with the magnifier.

Simply blasting mites from a plant with the full force of a garden hose is usually effective. The new, highly refined spray oils are also very effective, and as they are nontoxic I would recommend their use over toxic chemicals. Apply oil sprays at temperatures below 80°F (27°C).

Leaf Miners

Leaf miners may occasionally be a problem especially on azaleas. Miners tunnel through the leaves contributing to premature leaf drop. The chemical used to control lace bug will also control leaf miners. Repeat the application in ten days.

Scale

A number of different scale insects attack azaleas and rhododendrons, but only occasionally do they become a serious problem on either. Scale insects feed on leaves and stems, and the first symptom is yellow or red spotting on the leaf or on the bark of twigs. Scale insects usually produce a waxy protective coating over their body which makes them difficult to kill with contact sprays. Scale populations appear as small raised bumps on the twig or leaf.

Very effective chemical control can be achieved with the new, highly refined spray oil. The oil penetrates the insects' protective coating and kills them by suffocation. These oils work best if used when the temperature is below 80°F (27°C) to prevent injury to the plant.

Rhododendron Borer (*Synanthedon rhododendri*)

The rhododendron borer, native to eastern North America, is a very destructive pest and one of the most difficult to control. The adult is a blue-black moth with yellow bands on the abdomen, more nearly resembling a wasp than a moth. Adults emerge in May/June. Larvae develop inside the plant stem, and damage is first noted as branches on the plant start to wilt in a manner similar to twig blight.

Close examination of plant stems reveals small holes where the larvae entered the stem or sawdust near tunnel openings. The borer larva consumes the cambium and conducting tissues while working down toward the crown of the plant. Immediate control is directed at infected branches, which must be cut off below the end of the tunnel so as to include the borer; the branch then needs to be burned.

Chemical sprays are used as a control when insects are at the life cycle stage outside of the plant stem. Control is therefore usually directed at the adults and requires 2 or 3 spray applications made in

Fig. 97.   Borer tunnels in rhododendron stem. Photo courtesy of the U.S.D.A. Plant Industry Research Center, Beltsville, Maryland.

May and early June. Sprays can also be applied in mid June to early July, directed against newly hatching larvae. Consult your local horticultural extension agent for insect emergence times and for currently recommended chemicals.

Stem Borer (*Oberea myops*)

The adult stem borer is a small beetle which emerges in mid to late spring. Again the damage is done by the larvae and is very similar to that of the rhododendron borer. However, stem borers enter the plant only through young twigs of the current season's growth. Cut twigs off as soon as wilting is noticed to destroy the borer and prevent further damage. If not controlled the first year, the larvae tunnel downward the second year and may travel to the base of the plant where a pupal chamber is hollowed out. Plants become so weakened at this point that they are easily broken off.

Control is by pruning out infected twigs.

Weevils

Several weevils attack both azaleas and rhododendrons. These include the black vine weevil (*Otiorhynchus sulcatus*), the strawberry root weevil (*Otiorhynchus ovatus*), the two-banded Japanese weevil (*Callirhopalus bifarciatus*), and the woods weevil (*Nemocestes incomptus*). The black vine weevil is native to Europe and most often encountered in the northern half of the U.S. and southern Canada as is the woods weevil. The strawberry root weevil and several other *Otiorhynchus* occur in the Pacific Northwest and in similar climates in Europe and Australia. These insects are widespread and attack many landscape and nursery plants. The damage done and the control measures needed are similar for all weevils.

Damage is first noticed as a pattern of overlapping notches on the leaf edges of rhododendrons and is the result of the nocturnal feeding habit of the weevil.

Although leaf damage is often the first noticeable symptom, it is not nearly as significant as the root damage the larva or grub activity inflicts during the fall and early spring. Plants may be severely weakened or killed due to the loss of feeding roots and the girdling of larger roots. As a consequence the plants wilt or exhibit symptoms associated with a severe drought or root rot. By the time these symptoms are noticed, it is too late for effective control.

Fig. 98. Notched feeding pattern on leaf. Crescent-shaped notches beginning at leaf edges usually indicate the presence of root weevils.

Weevils can be controlled at the adult stage when they emerge in early summer. Chemical spray application needs to start three weeks after the first adults emerge since egg laying begins about a month after emergence. Delayed spraying allows time for most of the adults to emerge and be killed by one or two spray applications. If a daytime hiding place at the base of plants is provided, such as a piece of bark or a board, adults will collect and if the situation is monitored daily will indicate the first adult emergence date. First visible leaf damage is another indicator of adults being present. Acephate is an effective chemical spray yet remains lethal for only two or three days. A second application in two weeks and a third in four weeks is required. Predator nematodes have recently been made available for weevil larvae control. This involves a soil application in the fall or early spring before the larvae pupate or evolve into adults. The *Rhododendron* 'P.J.M.' shows 100% resistance to adult feeding of weevils suggesting no root damage as well.

Other Root Pests

Other types of grubs may occasionally damage azalea or rhododendron roots if plantings are made in areas that were recently in sod. Japanese beetle, June beetle, and others spend their pupal life in the soil eating roots. They are most numerous in sodded areas as they favor grass roots as a food supply.

Milky spore disease, a disease targeted towards Japanese beetle grubs, is very effective but will not control other types of grubs such as June beetle. See your local extension horticulturist for specific control. If sod areas are prepared a year ahead of planting a landscape, the grub problem will be greatly reduced.

Soils may also contain damaging nematodes or other garden pests with potential for damage. Check with your local extension service to see if there are such problems in your area and if so, how to resolve them.

Rhododendron Bud Moth

The bud moth occurs naturally on native azaleas in California and native rhododendrons in Oregon. The small moths lay eggs in July on leaves where the emerging larvae will feed. Bud moths overwinter in the larval stage and in spring eat their way into flower buds and small shoots. Infected flower buds either only partially open or fail to develop entirely.

The bud moth is still a minor pest in landscapes, so handpicking of infested flower trusses and twigs offers the best control.

Other Pests

Other potentially serious rhododendron and azalea pests are various animals. In urban and suburban areas neighborhood dogs can cause the yellowing and eventual death of branches on small plants. Rabbits are fond of azaleas, cutting shoots off at or near ground level, and prefer some cultivars over others. Deer can severely damage azaleas and occasionally rhododendrons. Rodents and moles cause root and stem damage.

Live trapping and relocation can at least temporarily solve any rabbit problem. Deer might be repelled with bars of soap hung among the plants or chemical repellents unless the deer population is under such pressure of numbers that they are eating anything to survive. Although some writers make much of animal problems, damage is usually not so common nor so extensive as to discourage planting azaleas and rhododendrons.

PHYSIOLOGICAL PROBLEMS

The sudden onset of cold weather early in the fall before plants are fully hardened off can cause bark splitting, which severely damages any split stems. To remedy push the bark back tightly against the stem before it has dried out. Then wrap the split portions with grafting tape to hold the bark tightly against the stem. The splits may additionally be coated with grafting wax to prevent drying out or damage from the entry of rainwater.

Any foliage or buds not fully hardened off in fall may also be seriously damaged by the first hard freezes. Symptoms are similar to the foliage drying in summer from excess heat or drought. In both situations death of foliage and buds results.

Winter sun striking only the south side of stems results in widely fluctuating stem temperatures. Severe stem damage may result from heating by sunlight during the day followed by sudden chilling after sundown. This causes the stem bark to first expand and then contract faster than the underlying stem. This condition is known as stem canker. Damage appears as dead areas on the southwest side of the stems as the bark loosens from the stem and is shed. Shading the plant, wrapping the trunk with tree tape, or painting trunks white with diluted latex paint all give protection from stem canker.

Sunscald is often mistaken as a disease because at times secondary fungus infections occur in damaged tissue. It appears as if the fungus caused the problem when the origin is actually sunscald. Primary damage occurs when the sun overheats plant foliage. Symptoms are off-color leaves turning yellow with browning developing on the edges and tips as damage progresses. Badly damaged leaves drop from the plant.

Sunscald is caused by dehydration of the leaves as a result of an increase in temperature. Moisture is lost through transpiration faster than the roots can replenish it. This occurs both in summer and winter as the sun heats plant foliage and is more detrimental to new transplants prior to root establishment.

Shading the foliage to reduce temperature usually remedies the situation. Note that some cultivars are more susceptible to sunscald than others.

A knowledge of disease and insect pests is necessary to both the selection and growing of rhododendrons and azaleas. Proper site and the selection of well-adapted plants, or good doers, go far in preventing problems. Effective methods of control are available when pests are encountered and the potential for serious damage is high.

EIGHT: *Propagation*

The propagation and hybridizing of rhododendrons and azaleas is one of the more rewarding activities a gardener can undertake. Most gardeners are familiar with propagation by seed, a sexual process, and a much smaller group are aware of the almost magical process of asexual propagation. To follow the progress of a stem cutting developing roots, a root cutting developing a new top, parts of two or more individual plants growing together in a graft, or entire plantlets developing in a test tube from a single cell is a wonder to behold. Only plants possess the unique ability to regenerate the entire viable organism from a single cell or plant part.

This unique ability results from the potential of every new plant cell, whether from root tip, stem tip, bud, or cambium, to produce multitudes of undifferentiated cells which in turn develop into leaves, stems, or roots, regardless of origin. Undifferentiated tissue is triggered to develop into the full array of plant parts by hormones and environmental factors.

Propagating does require a commitment of time and energy and a small outlay of capital for the equipment necessary to root cuttings, heal grafts, and so on.

In addition the propagator must have access to plants from which cuttings, scion wood, and other parts can be used. Much of this material can be acquired through the generosity of fellow gardeners, most of whom willingly share propagation material.

Rhododendron species are easily propagated from seed. Such sexual propagation cannot be used for cultivars, however, since they do not come true to form. All cultivars must be propagated by one of the asexual processes which are the subject of this chapter.

Prior to the ready availability of rooting hormones, rhododendron species and cultivars were difficult to propagate from cuttings, though both could be grafted. Deciduous azaleas are as easily rooted yet require special handling to promote shoot development. Tissue culture or micropropagation, the most recently devised asexual method of propagation, is becoming a major method for the rapid reproduction of all rhododendron and azalea species/cultivars and is especially useful for those that are difficult to root from cuttings.

Despite the widespread and growing use of micropropagation, the most common propagation method in North America remains stem cuttings. Grafting remains the propagation mainstay in Europe. Few plants are now propagated by layering since it is a slow process yielding only a limited number of plants. Some deciduous azaleas which are difficult to propagate by stem cuttings continue to be propagated by root cuttings or by tissue culture.

CUTTING BASICS

The availability of clear polyethylene plastic, rooting hormones, rooting media, and fluorescent lights and the knowledge needed to coordinate these elements into a propagation program make it possible for any gardener to successfully root a high percentage of cuttings.

Propagation by cuttings, by virtue of being an asexual method, results in no genetic change in the resulting plants; all are identical to the parent plant as they are clones of the parent. It is one of the most satisfactory methods of propagating many woody plants including Rhododendron.

Some relatively simple criteria must be met to root stem cuttings successfully:

1. Cutting wood must be of proper maturity—before the new season's growth has turned woody yet after the leaves are fully mature.

2. Cuttings must be taken from vigorous, insect and disease free plants.

3. The rooting medium must remain moist yet well aerated.

4. The container must drain well.

5. The medium and container must be free of pathogenic organisms.

6. Cuttings must be treated with a proper rooting hormone.

7. The atmosphere around the cuttings must contain 100% relative humidity.

8. Ample light but not direct sunlight must be provided.

9. Ambient temperatures of 60–75°F (16–24°C) must be maintained to obtain a satisfactory rooting percentage. Providing bottom heat hastens rooting.

Facilities

Stem cuttings can be rooted using one of two facilities: a closed container or a greenhouse with a mist or fog system. The closed container is best suited for the gardener wishing to propagate a small number of plants since it requires neither a significant investment nor skilled management, yet the results can equal those of the more complex systems.

The container used can be of any size or shape as long as it is sterile, at least 4 in. (10 cm) deep to allow space for root development, and has adequate drainage. The container covering must be able to maintain 100% relative humidity and allow maximum light. The gardener wishing to root only a few cuttings can make a satisfactory container out of a Styrofoam soup bowl, a milk jug, or a sterilized flower pot.

Fig. 99.   A homemade rooting facility. Cuttings are placed in a cut-off milk jug which is covered with a polyethylene food bag to maintain 100% relative humidity. Photo by the author.

A person can also use flats converted into small Quonset huts. Three pieces of #9 wire (each about 30 in./76 cm) are bent in a hemisphere with the ends inserted into pre-drilled holes in the flats or inserted in the medium and wired together. After the cuttings are set in and watered, flats are covered with clear polyethylene plastic supported on the wires. Tie string around the bottom to contain moisture levels.

Fig. 100. Quonset hut propagation unit. Notice the flats are placed under fluorescent lights. The moisture collecting on the inside surfaces of the plastic indicate 100% relative humidity. Photo by the author.

If a greenhouse is available, a bench can be covered with plastic in the same way as suggested here for flats.

A Nearing frame is a highly effective rooting structure, requiring very little management. For construction details see Fig. 112 at the end of this chapter.

Mist systems are commonly used in greenhouses to root cuttings. A covering is not required as long as 100% relative humidity is maintained. Cuttings are set directly in the greenhouse bench with a periodic mist spraying over the benches. Cycles are regulated with electric timers, electronic leaves, evaporative pans, or photo cells.

Fogging systems similar to mist systems have recently been developed to maintain a constant 100% relative humidity in the propagation area. The difference between the two systems is that fogging produces smaller water droplets which remain suspended in the air longer. Foggers can easily maintain proper moisture conditions over the entire greenhouse.

Media

There is little consensus as to the absolute best rooting medium, and any formulation that is sterile, holds moisture, and is well aerated will produce satisfactory results. However, rooting media under mist or fog must drain better than those used in a closed container since the medium is constantly being wetted. As a result horticultural perlite is often used as the sole rooting medium under mist propagation systems.

A very effective, widely used container medium consists of 50% coarse sphagnum peat moss, and 50% horticultural perlite or Styrofoam beads by volume. After thoroughly mixing the medium, wet it completely. If dry sphagnum moss is used it will require considerable water. Test for saturation by breaking a piece of the sphagnum moss; if thoroughly wet the color is a uniform brown throughout. After wetting squeeze the propagating mix by hand to force out excess water.

Fill the container level with the top, then firm but do not pack the medium to about 1 in. (2.5 cm) below the top. If using a Nearing frame, fill the rooting bin to within 6 in. (15 cm) of the top to allow space below the sash for cuttings. The top of the medium must be level to assure uniform watering of the cuttings.

Taking Cuttings

Stem cuttings are usually collected from late June to mid August before new stem growth has become woody. Parent plants need to be clearly identified and in good health. Cuttings taken from different plants must be placed in separate bags or containers and labeled to prevent confusion and mislabeling at a later date.

Collect cuttings in the early morning when stems are turgid. During periods of drought, parent plants may need to be thoroughly watered the evening before cuttings are taken to insure turgidity.

Select cuttings from new growth found at the terminal branch ends. Wood of medium diameter and vigor typical of the plant will root better than the thin, weak, wood or large, overly vigorous wood.

Place each cutting in a moistened bag or container maintained at 100% relative humidity. To avoid overheating do not expose cuttings to direct sunlight. Cuttings are best stuck in the rooting medium as soon as possible after collection. However, if cuttings need to be held for a few days (up to a week), they can be stored in a closed container in the refrigerator. There will be little or no loss of viability.

Disease Control

A medium of sphagnum peat and perlite is quite effective in preventing root rot diseases. However, spraying the cuttings and the entire surface of the medium with a broad-spectrum fungicide will prevent mold or algae from growing on the surface. Fungicide sprays are also used to protect the tops of tender softwood cuttings of deciduous azaleas from rot. Caution: follow all label instructions when using fungicides.

Light

Higher rooting percentages result if cuttings are placed in good light but not direct sunlight. One can use fluorescent lights 4 ft. (1.2 m) long each containing two 40-watt tubes placed about 12 in. (30 cm) above the cuttings. These are cycled to be on for sixteen hours continuously each day and provide excellent light for indoor rooting of cuttings. Small containers can be placed in north facing windows or on the north side of a building.

The Nearing frame should be placed in full sun with the front, or open side, oriented exactly true north. True north can be established on a clear night by aligning one side of the frame with the North Star.

Fig. 101.   A Nearing frame properly oriented, showing the shade pattern. Photo by the author.

Keeping the clear covering on all rooting containers clean results in maximum light to cuttings and will result in faster rooting.

If cuttings are rooted in the greenhouse in a closed container, shade must be provided if the interior heats to above 80° F (27°C). If they are rooted under mist or fog in a greenhouse, no shade is necessary unless the entire green house heats up to 80°F (27°C), in which case shade compound or cloth should be used.

Rooting Temperature

Rooting temperature is not critical, as rooting normally occurs over a wide temperature range. Rooting can, however, be speeded up in cool weather by placing heat tapes or cables, and in larger operations hot water tubes, under the rooting medium. Set to maintain a temperature range of 70–75°F (21–24°C).

Watering

Cuttings are watered when first placed in the container to settle the medium around the roots. By virtue of being in an atmosphere of 100% relative humidity, cuttings may not require additional watering until they have rooted. Small containers usually require no additional water until roots develop as long as the medium remains moist and the plastic covering continues to display water droplets. The condensation on the plastic is an indication that 100% humidity is being maintained. Check the medium about every four weeks. Moisture can be lost if condensation is not being totally recycled within the container.

When using the Nearing frame, add water once a week to wash oxygen down through the rooting medium. Air exchange through the bottom of the frame is low.

Cuttings under mist or fog need no water applied after that initially used to settle the medium.

Hardening Off

This is a necessary step to enable cuttings to adapt to the harsher yet normal growing conditions of the landscape. As soon as cuttings have developed a root ball of more than 2 in. (5.0 cm) in diameter, they are ready to begin the hardening off process.

In situations using mist propagation, hardening off is accomplished by gradually reducing the mist cycle until an average watering sequence is reached. Hardening off for cuttings in other situations involves opening the cover on closed containers a bit wider each day. After one week the plants can be fully exposed to the outside environment.

During hardening off the cuttings must be watered and fertilized. For strong growth fertilize every second or third watering with a ½ strength solution of neutral rhododendron fertilizer or the equivalent.

Cuttings rooted under mist will require more fertilizer because the nutrients constantly leach from the leaves, and plants may even require mineral fertilization prior to rooting. If the foliage of plants under mist progressively loses its dark green color, fertilizer at ½ normal rates should be applied to maintain the health of the cuttings.

Fig. 102.   Well rooted cutting being removed for transplanting from the rooting container. Photo by the author.

Aftercare

After the cuttings have rooted and been hardened off, they can be transplanted to flats, beds, or pots for further development. The transplant medium should be either just bark or a combination of bark, sphagnum peat moss, and perlite or Styrofoam.

In a greenhouse situation cuttings are transplanted into flats or benches at a spacing of about 3 in. (7 cm) on center to develop through the winter months. If interior temperatures exceed 40°F (5°C), the cuttings will start to grow and will require adequate light, increased spacing, fertilizer, and water.

Fig. 103.　Flats of transplanted cuttings. Photo by the author.

Rooted cuttings not being grown in the greenhouse must be over-wintered in shade and protected from the wind. In cold climates place them in a shaded, closed cold frame, under Microfoam, a plastic-covered cold house, or in a pit to protect roots against cold and to prevent drying out. Cuttings in flats and pots should never be over-wintered on top of the ground fully exposed to the elements.

While these general principles are common to rooting all stem cuttings, there are some important differences in methodology in rooting stem cuttings of evergreen and deciduous azaleas or rhododendrons. The propagation specifics for each group is discussed separately.

EVERGREEN AZALEAS

These are the easiest of the *Rhododendron* species/cultivars to root from cuttings both in terms of the time required and the success rate. The range in maturity of evergreen azalea cuttings used for rooting is wide, yet wood taken when too soft may rot (or not root at all) while older, harder wood develops roots very slowly (if at all). Cutting wood is best taken from current season's growth that has partially hardened off. Wood needs to be firm enough at the base to break when bent, yet be less firm in the upper part of its length.

The exact date that cuttings are taken is more significant to management concerns than to rooting percentages. Cuttings taken in June will be well rooted by late summer and can be transplanted. If spaced widely enough in the rooting frame (3 in. or 7 cm apart) cuttings may be overwintered in the same container. This spacing will be needed for continued root system development. Cuttings taken later than June may not be well rooted by the time cold weather arrives and will need additional protection. Such cuttings also may not be developed enough to survive in growing beds the following spring. These later cuttings may require overwintering in a heated green house to promote sufficient development for spring planting.

Taking Cuttings

1. Cuttings 3–4 in. (7–10 cm) long are taken from the terminal end of the current season's growth. Immediately place in a moist plastic bag with any excess water removed. Close bag to prevent drying out of the cutting. If a number of different cuttings are made, keep each type separate and carefully labeled. Larger, better branched plants develop more quickly from cuttings with several side shoots. The wood at the base of such cuttings should be current season's growth.

2. The cuttings are prepared for the rooting medium by stripping the leaves from the lower half of the cutting and pinching off the tip of each cutting to prevent flowering and to stimulate branching.

Fig. 104. Evergreen azalea cutting prepared for insertion into the rooting medium. Photo by the author.

3. The cuttings are dipped in a rooting hormone containing approximately 0.1% active rooting hormone or according to the label directions for softwood cuttings. If a liquid rooting material is used, immerse cuttings 1 in. (2.5 cm) deep for five seconds. If a talc dip is used, immerse to 1 in. (2.5 cm) and then tap the cutting to remove excess material. Do not immerse cuttings in the hormone container but transfer the rooting hormone to another container as dipping the cutting will contaminate the material. Excess rooting material should be disposed of as indicated on the label.

4. Place the dipped cuttings in the rooting medium about 2 in. (5.0 cm) apart and 1½ in. (4.0 cm) deep. Carefully label each group as they are inserted to prevent mislabeling. Mist the cuttings during this process to prevent stress until they are placed under cover. As soon as the flat or other container is completely filled with cuttings, water it well to settle the rooting medium. Do not pack the medium tightly around the cuttings.

5. Many growers spray the cuttings and surface of the rooting medium with a fungicide as a preventative measure against root rot.

6. Cover small containers with polyethylene plastic or glass to provide a watertight seal. If using the Quonset hut flat, pull the previously cut plastic over the wire hoops and tuck it under the bottom or secure with string. If placed on/in a greenhouse bench without a mist system, cover with large sheets of polyethylene plastic using wire or other material to hold the plastic up off the cuttings. Shade must be provided on top of this plastic cover if the sun heats up the green house bench during the summer months. If a Nearing frame is used, simply close the north facing sash.

If the propagating containers or facilities are properly sealed and able to maintain 100% relative humidity, evergreen azalea cuttings should root in six to eight weeks. If the inside surface of the plastic or glass covering is consistently covered with small droplets of condensed water throughout the rooting period, the proper humidity level can be assumed. If rooted in a greenhouse, the misting cycle must be of sufficient length and frequency to keep the foliage of the cuttings moist at all times.

After six weeks use a narrow tool to lift a cutting from the medium and check for roots. When cuttings have developed a 2 in. (5.0 cm) root ball, start hardening off preparatory to transplanting or over-wintering the small plants.

DECIDUOUS AZALEAS

Numerous propagation methods are used for deciduous azaleas. A few species of deciduous azaleas are so difficult to propagate that the gardener is well advised to propagate only from seed. Although deciduous azaleas are reluctant to root from stem cuttings, most can be propagated in this way if given proper attention. In this section I will describe stem cuttings, division, and root cuttings and touch briefly on tissue culture. Mound layering is another method used for deciduous azaleas, and both seed propagation and mound layering are discussed later in this chapter.

A few significant differences set the procedure for rooting stem cuttings of deciduous azaleas apart from those used with evergreen azaleas. Cuttings from the evergreen species/cultivars taken over a wide period of time and hardness of cutting wood will root and grow on easily. By contrast the deciduous azalea must be propagated from softwood taken early in the growing season. Cuttings need to be taken as soon as new shoots are 3–4 in. (7.5–10 cm) long. Great care must be taken to keep these cuttings in water from the time of pruning to placement in the rooting container. Deciduous azalea cuttings are taken as softwood cuttings not only because they will root easier but also because early rooting will allow more time during the same growing season for the cuttings to develop new vegetative growth.

Rooted cuttings of deciduous azaleas which do not make some vegetative growth during the season in which they are rooted also seem reluctant to initiate shoot growth at the proper time the following year, even when well rooted. I have found that if left intact in the rooting medium, many reluctant cuttings send out shoots about a month later than cuttings that did make some vegetative growth the previous year.

Taking Cuttings

1. Cuttings about 4 in. (10 cm) in length are taken and the cut ends placed immediately in an inch or two of water in a collecting container. Use a separate container, such as a plastic bag, for each different species/cultivar to reduce the chances for improper labeling.

2. The types of rooting containers and media used to root the cuttings are identical to those used for evergreen azalea cuttings.

3. Dip the cut ends in a broad spectrum fungicide to control fungal diseases. Since the cuttings are soft and easily damaged, prepare holes 1½ in. (3.8 cm) deep into the rooting medium, spaced 3 in. (7 cm) apart, and place a cutting in each hole. The spacing is wider than recommended for evergreen azaleas both to accommodate the larger leaves of deciduous azaleas and to encourage new vegetative growth. If the tips of the cuttings were not pinched prior to collecting they should be pinched when placing them in the rooting medium. Rooting hormone should not be used since it seems to delay vegetative growth later in the summer and is not necessary for rooting to occur.

    The cuttings are watered in to settle the medium around them and then sprayed thoroughly with a fungicide. The rooting container is then closed in the same way as for evergreen azaleas and placed in good strong light but not direct sunlight.

4. Deciduous azalea cuttings must be observed carefully for the first few days to check for unusual wilting. Mist the foliage of any wilted cuttings in closed containers for the first few days.

5. After about six weeks lift and check one of the cuttings for formation of the root ball. If well rooted, apply a soluble fertilizer, especially formulated for azaleas, at ¼ strength to the foliage and medium. Fertilize again with ½ strength fertilizer if no new growth has appeared by early August. This second application usually produces new vegetative growth by autumn and so assures that the cuttings will grow on. Extending day length from sixteen to eighteen hours of light immediately after the cuttings have rooted will also help promote growth.

6. Deciduous azaleas are best overwintered in the rooting container. If overwintering outdoors, cuttings need to be stored under Microfoam, in a cold frame, or a Nearing frame to protect from wind, winter sun, and freezing and thawing if the climate so dictates.

7. Growing-on is carried out in the same way as recommended for evergreen azaleas.

Propagation by Division

Deciduous azaleas are also propagated by division. This method is especially appropriate for the stoloniferous species.

The crown of the plant can be divided at any point where shoots with roots attached can be separated. Also shoots arising from roots at a distance from the parent plant can be dug as separate plants. Division is best done in the fall at the time the leaves start to fall. The separated parts are treated as individual plants and planted in nursery beds for closer attention until a more extensive root system develops.

Recent research has indicated that the severe pruning of transplanted plants often recommended on the theory of balancing top growth with the size of the root system actually reduces growth and survival in many cases. As long as the top remains turgid, it should be left unpruned.

Propagation by Root Cuttings

Deciduous azaleas are also often propagated by root cuttings. Use sections of root from pencil to finger size in diameter, about 4 in. (10 cm) long, and containing some fibrous roots. These cuttings are taken by gently digging around the parent plant or by lifting the parent to expose roots from which the cuttings are taken. Root cuttings are taken in late fall or early spring and immediately placed in the soil or a propagating bed. They are placed horizontally and covered with only 1 in. (2.5 cm) of soil and then mulched to prevent frost heaving. Alternatively they are planted in flats and placed in a greenhouse or under lights to grow on. Shoots emerge from the large end while roots develop at the smaller end in about six to eight weeks.

A mixture of 50% peat and 50% perlite makes a quite satisfactory medium for root cuttings. Treat the cut ends with a wettable sulfur powder before planting to prevent the entrance of root rot organisms.

Tissue Culture

Since some deciduous azalea cuttings are difficult to root from stem cuttings, tissue culture or micropropagation is used extensively in their propagation. This procedure requires a sterile laboratory and is not recommended for the amateur.

RHODODENDRONS

In North America rhododendrons are generally propagated from stem cuttings, while most European growers use grafts as they believe this method produces more uniform, compact plants. Another advantage claimed by European growers is that a widely adaptable rootstock is better suited to sustain grafted plants in a wider range of soils.

Some rhododendron species are propagated from seed, and all can be propagated by layering.

Stem Cuttings

Rhododendron cuttings are taken when the current season's growth is semihard. In the case of the large-leaved forms this is usually July, although cuttings may also be taken again in September. Cutting wood of the small-leaved rhododendrons, especially the early flowering types, is usually sufficiently mature to be taken in June through July and again in September.

Cutting wood needs to be sufficiently mature to break when bent sharply but not completely hardened off. However, 'P. J. M.' and some other Dauricum hybrids root and grow on better if cuttings are taken after the leaves take on their winter color, which indicates the complete hardening off of the wood. Such cuttings must be rooted in a heated building or greenhouse.

Cuttings are made from current season's growth having terminal leaf buds. Medium size stems are best and are usually found on branches with two or more terminal shoots. Large, thick, single shoots often take longer to root and take up more space in the propagating frame even when leaves are trimmed. If stems with flower buds must be used remove the flower buds. It is best not to cut more than 30% of the current season's wood from any parent plant. Only one or two cuttings should be taken from branches bearing 2–4 terminals.

Taking Cuttings

1. Cuttings are removed from the plant at the point where the current season's flush of growth started so no stubs remain on the parent plant. Such cuttings are often too long and can later be shortened to 2½ in. (6.4 cm) in length. Only enough length is necessary to insure that cuttings extend into the medium far enough to stand up and hold the leaves above the medium. Use a sharp knife in preparing cuttings so that the tissue is cut,

not torn. Cuttings must be carefully labeled and kept separate in containers with an atmosphere of 100% relative humidity as explained for azaleas.

2. Shorten the cutting to a length of about 2½ in. (6.4 cm) and remove all lower leaves. The top rosette of four or five leaves on cuttings with average size leaves, such as *R. catawbiense*, can be left. Leave more top foliage on cuttings of plants with small leaves and fewer on larger-leaved types. In order to conserve space in the rooting frame, large leaves are also usually reduced to ½ of their length.

3. Remove a thin sliver of bark and wood starting 1 in. (2.5 cm) from the bottom on two sides of the cutting. This "wounding" results in better root development along the full length of the cut (see Fig. 105).

Fig. 105.   Rhododendron cutting. *Left,* as removed from the parent plant. *Right,* properly prepared for rooting. Note how leaves have been stripped and trimmed and the stem bark removed. Photo by the author.

4. Dip the cutting in a root-inducing hormone, liquid or powder, to a depth of 1 in. (2.5 cm). Since rhododendrons are more difficult to root than azaleas, use a stronger, (0.8% active ingredient) formulation. Alternatively one can soak the cuttings in a rooting hormone for eighteen hours as described by Leach in *Rhododendrons of the World.* I find Leach's soaking system superior to any other method in assuring a higher per-

centage of cuttings which root. Caution: handle all chemicals carefully and according to the label instructions.

5. The types of rooting containers and media used are identical to those described for azaleas.

6. Punch holes about 2½ in. (6.0 cm) apart and 1½ in. (3.8 cm) deep into the medium and insert the cuttings. Spacing may need to be modified to insure that leaves of cuttings do not overlap.

7. Label the cuttings as they are inserted into the container. When the container is full, water to settle the rooting medium around the stems. Apply a fungicide as directed on the label for use on shrubbery.

8. Close the rooting container or place the cuttings under a mist system as explained for azaleas.

Aftercare is much the same as described earlier for azaleas. Most important is that the rooting medium remain moist. Most rhododendron cuttings develop roots in about twelve weeks and need to be checked at this time for root development. Some species/cultivars may require more time, and as long as the foliage remains turgid and green, they will eventually root. After any watering needs are met, close the container or turn the sprinkler system back on. Wait until at least a 2 in. (5 cm) root ball has developed to start the hardening off process as explained earlier for azaleas. Fig. 102 shows a well rooted rhododendron cutting.

Rhododendron cuttings require one additional step in their aftercare. All terminal buds must be pinched out in the fall after cuttings are hardened off. This stimulates lateral bud development and encourages multiple branching to develop earlier the following spring.

Rooted rhododendron cuttings are overwintered in the same manner as described earlier for azaleas.

Grafting

Most European nursery people view grafting as the best means for propagating rhododendrons, and there are indeed some advantages. By using a strong growing, widely adapted rootstock under all species and cultivars, the survival of the resulting plants in a wide variety of conditions is better assured. *Rhododendron* 'Cunninghams White' is widely used as an understock for grafting in Europe because it tolerates higher soil pH and adapts readily to a wide range of soil and climatic conditions. Grafting is also thought to produce more compact plants.

The principal disadvantages of grafting are the tendency of the rootstocks to produce suckers, which frequently engulf the scion, and the fact that graft incompatibility may result in poor growth or separation of the graft union.

Amateur gardeners seeking to augment their collection of species or cultivars or produce duplicates of a rare plant could consider grafting. It is a quite effective way to propagate a limited number of plants and provides another propagation challenge, especially for plants difficult to root by cuttings.

Grafting requires a greenhouse or other indoor growth chamber similar to that used for rooting cuttings, including lights or bright natural light. The most commonly used grafting methods for rhododendrons are the saddle graft, cleft graft, and side graft. (Fig. 106).

Saddle Graft. The saddle graft is a very simple and perhaps the best grafting method for rhododendrons. The rootstock is produced in the same way as described under "Side Graft" below, except that the roots selected are smaller in diameter as they must fairly closely match the diameter of the scion wood.

The scion wood is gathered at the same time and in the same way as for side grafts.

To make a saddle graft:

1. Cut the rootstock off about 2–3 in. (5.0–7.6 cm) above the soil level and below the first rosette of leaves. Less sprouting from the rootstock occurs if the section is taken from below any stem leaves. A straight section of stem at least 1 in. (2.5 cm) long will be needed.

2. Use a sharp knife to make straight, smooth cuts on opposite sides of the stub about ¾ in. (1.9 cm) long to form an inverted V shape.

3. Select a 3 in. (7.6 cm) scion of the current season's growth. Leaves on the scion should have been previously reduced to 3–4, and if the scion is a large-leaved form, cut the leaves in half laterally.

4. Split the scion stem up from the cut end for a distance of about 1 in. (2.5 cm), or cut a V shape in it to match the rootstock.

5. Slide the scion down onto the wedge-shaped rootstock, align the cambium on at least one side, and wrap snugly with a rubber bud tie.

6. Aftercare is as discussed for the side graft.

Cleft Graft. To make a cleft graft:

1. Cut the rootstock off at a right angle 1 in. (2.5 cm) above soil level with a very sharp knife.

2. Split the rootstock stem down the center about 1 in. (2.5 cm).

3. Prepare the scion as in 3. above for the saddle graft.

4. Cut a 1 in. (2.5 cm) slice off opposite sides of the scion to make a smooth wedge shape.

5. Insert the scion in the split stem and align the cambium on at least one side. Push the scion down until no cut wood is exposed, and wrap snugly with rubber grafting tape or a large bud tie. Seal the end of the stem with grafting wax.

6. Aftercare is the same as recommended for the side and saddle graft except in cases where a cleft graft is done on a large plant in the landscape. In this situation clear plastic bags pulled over the grafted branches must be shaded from the sun.

Side Graft. Rootstocks for side grafting are rooted cuttings from a cultivar selected for the vigor of its roots and its adaptability. The rooted cuttings need to attain a size of ¼–⅜ in. (0.6–1.0 cm) in diameter before grafting is undertaken. The rootstock is more easily handled if potted in 4–5 in. (10–12 cm) pots at least a month before grafting. Place pots in a growing environment of about 65–75°F (18–24°C) to encourage active root growth. It is important that the roots be actively growing before a graft is attempted. Grafting is best done in December and January when the scion wood is mature and dormant.

To make a side graft:

1. Cut scions 3–4 in. (7.6–10.2 cm) long from the plant to be propagated. Scions are cut from the previous season's growth. Place immediately in a cool, moist environment to prevent moisture loss. If the scions are not grafted immediately, store in a cool environment of 100% relative humidity until grafted.

2. Remove all leaves from the lower 3 in. (7.6 cm) of the rootstock stem.

3. With a sharp knife, slit the rootstock stem on one side for a distance of 1 in. (2.5 cm) to just above the soil line. Slant the cut slightly toward but not to the exact center of the stem.

Move the knife back and forth slightly while cutting to reduce the downward pressure on the stem. This will avoid tearing the roots off the small plant.

4. Reduce the number of leaves on the scion piece to 3–4. If a large-leaved form is used as the scion, cut away the terminal half of each leaf. Then remove a 1 in. (2.5 cm) long slice on each side of the bottom stem end to make a wedge shape to fit the cut previously made in the rootstock. All cuts must be straight and smooth so contact between the scion and rootstock is continuous along the matching surfaces.

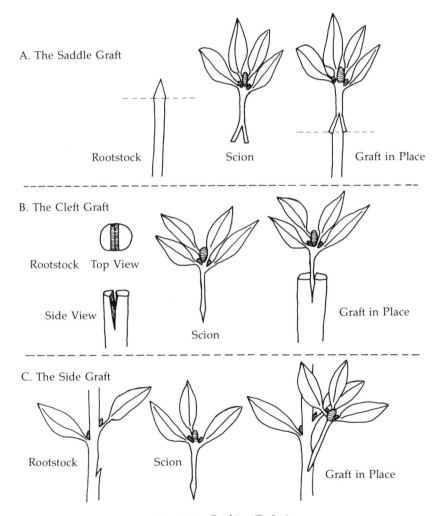

Fig. 106. Grafting Techniques

5. Slide the scion into the slit on the rootstock, being careful to place both cambium layers so as to match on at least one side. The cambium is a very thin layer of cells separating the wood (or xylem) of the stem from the bark (or phloem) and is located just under the bark. The difference between the wood, bark, and cambium layer is easily identified. Precise alignment of the cambium is important since it is the tissue where new cells are formed. This will permit the scion and rootstock to grow together to form new xylem and phloem for the transport of water and nutrients from root to shoot and back.

6. While holding the scion in place, tightly wrap with a rubber bud tie. Begin the wrap by overlapping the bud tie at the bottom of the graft and end by tucking the last wrap under the previous one. The joint needs to be wrapped its entire length with no exposed cut surfaces remaining. Check that the cambium layers of the scion and rootstock have remained aligned during tying.

7. Mist the graft and place it immediately in a grafting case, similar to the containers suggested for cuttings. When using a grafting frame, place a layer of moist, not wet, sphagnum moss in the bottom so the pots are buried in sphagnum deeply enough to cover the grafted area. Or cover individual pots with a polyethylene plastic bag. Before pulling bags over individual pots, place a handful of moist moss around the graft. The case and/or bag must be sealed watertight. Grafts should be placed under plastic immediately after being completed. Never allow the scions to dry out.

8. Maintain a temperature of about 50°F (10°C) and an atmosphere of 100% relative humidity around the grafted plants, and provide sixteen hours of bright light.

9. In about five weeks, remove the peat moss from around the graft union. Prune away any sprouts emerging from the roots or stem of the rootstock, mist the grafts, and reseal the container.

10. About three weeks later, reduce the number of leaves on the rootstock by about 50% and again remove any sprouts from the rootstock. The temperature now needs to be raised to 65°F (18°C). When the grafts are well callused, hardening off can be initiated.

   Open the grafting case or plastic bag slightly and observe

carefully for the first week. Mist and if the grafted scion wilts, close the container. If wilting is not evident, continue to gradually increase the plants' exposure to the outside conditions as outlined in hardening off of cuttings. Plants must be carefully observed during this hardening off period. Any grafts that have not healed completely can be quickly identified as the scions that wilt. If only a few are incompletely healed, move them to a separate container for a few more weeks before attempting to harden them off.

11. Lower the temperature to about 60°F (15°C) when the completely healed plants have been fully hardened off. Remove the rubber bud ties. If the grafts are tightly callused and healed over, prune off the upper portion of the rootstock just above the graft union. If the grafts are not fully healed, give the plants more time. There is no need to rush this pruning, but it should be done before the first flush of growth on the scions is completed. All sprouts from the rootstock are again cut or pinched out. The temperature can now be raised to 70–75°F (21–23°C) to stimulate growth.

Fig. 107.   Side graft in a transplant container. Note graft union. Photo by the author.

OTHER METHODS

Green Grafting

Green grafting is used for propagating both rhododendrons and azaleas and is one of the most successful and easiest methods. It is done in the summer months and uses easier-to-work green wood taken when both rootstock and scion are in active growth. Cleft and saddle grafting are the most successful forms for green grafting. This method is used to increase the number of plants of a particular species/cultivar. In addition, it is used in hybridizing programs. Hybridizers green graft new seedlings to older plants so they can evaluate flower buds more quickly and also to improve the appearance of older plants by what is called "top-working". The latter simply refers to grafting young vigorous scions of new, superior cultivars to the upper stems of older plants.

Green grafting is undertaken after a flush of growth has hardened off to almost the same degree of maturity as would be used for rooting cuttings. In all cases current season's growth is used for both rootstock and the scion.

If plants are grown to provide rootstock for green grafting, one straight stem near the soil level needs to be encouraged. This is easily done by cutting a young plant back in the early spring to just above the first leaves. As shoots arise, remove all but one new shoot to be used as the rootstock.

Layering

Trench or mound layering is seldom used today since large numbers of rhododendron plants are so easily propagated by cuttings or grafting. Layering is a slow process, and only a limited number of plants can be propagated from a single parent plant. Layering is, however, an excellent method for the gardener needing to propagate only one or two additional specimens of a plant to share or to assure survival of a rare form.

The procedure for **trench layering** is as follows:

1. In late summer or early fall, select a propagating branch which is close enough to the soil surface to be bent down and covered with soil. Using a branch on the north side of the plant is best because the soil will be shaded by the parent plant and will retain moisture better.

2. Dig a trench 2–3 in. (5.0–7.6 cm) deep and about 3 in. (7.6 cm)

wide where the current season's growth of the branch can be brought into contact with the ground.

3. Remove all the bark and cambium in a ring 1 in. (2.5 cm) wide or cut ⅔ of the way through the stem at the point where the branch touches the ground. Either of these procedures will restrict the flow of synthesized food from the leaves back to the roots and result in an accumulation of carbohydrates at the girdled area. Remove any leaves that would be buried with the stem. Apply rooting hormone to the wounded area at the same strength as for cuttings.

4. Place the girdled or cut portion in the trench and cover with soil rich in organic matter.

5. Hold the branch in place by placing a brick or stone on top of the soil above the layered branch. Keep the soil in the vicinity of the branch moist but not wet.

6. Rooting usually occurs in the year following layering. If no roots are evident upon cautious examination the following fall, leave the layer in place for another season.

7. When a root system has developed, separate the layer from the parent plant at a point between the parent and the new roots. Transplant the new plant to a nursery area where it can be given careful attention until it is well established.

Mound layering is often used with deciduous azaleas which are difficult to root from cuttings. The procedure is as follows:

1. Prune the parent plant close to soil level in early spring to produce as many new shoots as possible growing near the ground.

2. In the fall build a mound of soil high in organic matter to a depth such that only the tips of the new shoots remain above the mound.

3. Maintain good moisture levels throughout the mound.

4. The following spring clear the mound down to soil level and remove rooted shoots by cutting them from the parent plant just above ground level. The parent plant will produce more shoots in the course of the summer.

5. Transplant the rooted shoots to a nursery bed until well established.

Seed Propagation

Rhododendron and azalea cultivars do not propagate true from seed. Only species plants can reproduce themselves from seed and those only that can grow in a situation well isolated from other plants. Any variation produced would then be within the limits of natural variation typical of sexual reproduction. Hybrid seeds resulting from crosses must always be sown and grown to maturity to identify any worthwhile offspring.

Seeds are available from the ARS Seed Exchange and some commercial sources. If the gardener wishes to collect seed, he or she should do so in early fall before the seed pods open. Store in open, carefully labeled containers in a cool, dry place until the seeds can be prepared for sowing in early winter.

The seed pods of some species/cultivars open easily soon after they dry, but others must be pried open or crushed. The seed can be separated from the pod debris by sifting through a fine sieve. Store seeds in a clearly labeled container in a cool, dry place. Rhododendron and azalea seeds are extremely small and must be handled very carefully.

The conditions required to grow seed are virtually identical to those required to grow rooted cuttings. Germination is highest at temperatures of 70–75°F (21–24°C) in an atmosphere of 100% relative humidity.

The growing medium needs to hold moisture well, be well drained, and be fine enough that a smooth surface can be prepared. If the tiny seeds fall into small holes on the soil surface, they may become too deeply covered. I would recommend a medium composed of 70% sphagnum peat moss and 30% horticultural perlite, but other organic mixes may be equally satisfactory. Many propagators use 100% milled sphagnum peat moss.

The germinating container must be moisture-tight when sealed, must drain well, and must be at least 4 in. (10 cm) deep. The other dimensions depend entirely upon the number of seeds to be sown. Containers must be clean, preferably of plastic, metal, or glass. Plastic food storage boxes with clear tops make excellent seedling growing containers. Bottom holes will allow more careful watering once the seedlings are developed.

The procedure for seeding is as follows:

1. Fill the container with growing medium and firm it to provide a smooth, level surface about 1 in. (2.5 cm) below the top of the container.

2. Water lightly with ¼ strength rhododendron fertilizer since the medium has essentially no available nutrient content.

3. Spray the surface with a broad-spectrum fungicide.

4. Sprinkle the seeds on top of the medium, being careful not to sow too thickly. Do not cover the seed with the medium. Mist the surface with a plant mister so there is moisture available for germination.

5. Cover the container with clear plastic or glass and seal to maintain 100% relative humidity inside.

Fig. 108.   Glass seedling container sown and sealed to encourage germination. Photo by the author.

6. Place the container in a warm (70–75°F or 21–24°C) area for germination. Light is not necessary at this time yet must be provided as soon as the seeds have sprouted. The safest practice may be to place the container under a fluorescent light immediately. Germination occurs in 2—8 weeks in most cases.

    Seeds of some species, such as *R. yakushimanum*, will germinate better if placed in a cool situation, 40°F (5°C) or below, for six weeks immediately after seeding and before placing under lights.

7. As soon as the seedlings have 2–4 true leaves, transplant them to flats or a nursery bed. Fig. 109 shows a group of

seedlings ready for transplanting. Transplanting must be accomplished before seedlings begin crowding each other. Crowding can result in disease problems or the dying out of smaller seedlings.

Fig. 109.   Seedlings in the same glass container with the cover removed. After about six months the seedlings are ready for transplanting. (Note sowing density.) Photo by the author.

The first step in transplanting is hardening off. Do this by gradually exposing the tender seedlings to normal conditions of humidity, as is done with cuttings and grafts, by gradually opening the container over a period of 1–2 weeks. Water needs must be carefully monitored during this time to keep the medium moist but not wet. It is best to water from the bottom as surface watering can wash out or knock over small seedlings.

8. Seedlings can then be transplanted into pots or a larger container containing a medium of 50% coarse sphagnum peat moss and 50% perlite or ground Styrofoam. Alternatively they can be transplanted to nursery beds high in organic matter. Each seedling should be handled by a leaf, not by the stem. If the stem is bruised, the result is death of the plant. Always lift seedlings by prying from underneath the root ball so roots are not torn loose. Fig. 110 shows a seedling lifted from the container ready to transplant.

Spacing in the new container needs to be about 1½–2 in. (3.7–5.0 cm) on center. The seedlings are set at the same depth as they were growing in the germinating container. A

Fig. 110. Seedling with true leaves and a sufficient root mass ready to transplant. Photo by the author.

small hole punched in the medium for each seedling using a dibble board or a finger will facilitate planting. Gently cover the roots; water the seedlings to settle the medium around the roots. Mist the transplanted seedlings several times the first day after transplanting.

9. Place the seedlings under fluorescent lights, 12 in. (30 cm) above the plants.

10. Fertilize by watering with ½ strength, neutral rhododendron food every third watering.

11. Aftercare is similar to that for rooted cuttings except that it will be longer. Seedlings are more tender and cannot be exposed to sun and wind as quickly.

With the knowledge and material available today, a gardener can expect excellent results propagating rhododendrons and azaleas. Not only is it a sound venture economically and in terms of increasing the extent of a collection, but much personal satisfaction can be derived from propagating and growing one's own plants.

Fig. 111.   Seedlings transplanted to wider spacing. Photo by the author.

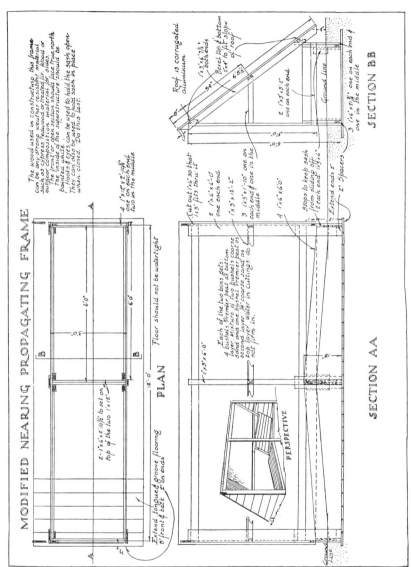

Fig. 112. Building plan for a Nearing frame. From *Rhododendrons of the World*, p. 323. Reprinted with permission.

NINE: *Nursery Growing*

Nearly all rhododendron and azalea growers, large and small, will at some time grow very small, tissue-cultured liners, rooted cuttings, or seedlings to landscape size. Scale of operation makes little difference in the proper method for doing this. The systems discussed here are adequate for both the hobbyist and the nursery person.

Two systems used in the nursery production of plants are, field growing and container growing, with container growing currently gaining popularity. There are some advantages and disadvantages to both systems, as discussed below.

FIELD GROWING

The advantages of field growing include

1. Less water is required and is less frequently applied since plant roots are in a larger water reserve and soils hold more moisture than soilless mixes.

2. Plant roots become acclimated to the soil, resulting in better root extension, and so develop a better root ball.

3. Plants with soil root balls transplant and survive better in the landscape than container grown plants grown in coarse, soilless mixes.

4. Nutrient deficiencies, especially deficiencies of minor elements, do not limit growth if soils are properly prepared. Additionally, overfertilizing is less of a problem since the soil environment acts as a buffer.

5. Roots are not injured from summer heat or winter cold, so they do not require protection from either.

The disadvantages are

1. More labor is required in planting, digging, and potting or balling for market.

2. Root balls are heavier and thus more difficult to handle and transport.

3. It is harder to precisely control growing medium density, aeration, and soil-borne insects and diseases.

4. Plants cannot be dug for market if soils are wet.

5. The root system is reduced during digging.

6. If growing for market, the grower is selling not just a plant but his precious topsoil as well.

Transplanting Liners

One-year-old liners are usually used to begin growth in the nursery field bed. Such plants are purchased by the nursery person as rooted cuttings or tissue culture liners. In some cases one-year-old liners are produced by the nursery using any of the several propagating methods described in the preceding chapter. Liners are then rooted in an organic medium and are given considerable protection throughout the growing period. Under such favorable conditions, plants are relatively tender. Even after hardening off, plants must be given some protection initially, particularly if planted to field beds.

Two major obstacles are encountered in transplanting small plants into the soil: first, encouraging root extension into the soil from the soilless medium in which they were rooted, and second, protecting their foliage.

The problem of getting the roots to venture out into the soil can be solved in one of two ways. One way is to amend the soil with at least 50% organic material. In so doing, I have found no comparable substitute for amending with coarse sphagnum peat moss. Such moss should comprise no less than 50% of the organic amendments used. Pine bark, ¼ in. (0.6 cm) and less in size, may be used to provide the other 50% in heavier soils. Another method to encourage roots is discussed later as part of planting procedures.

The second obstacle is protecting the foliage, especially that of tissue culture plants, which is generally more succulent than foliage of rooted cuttings. Shading, wind protection, and maintaining adequate soil moisture are the most important measures to be taken. This situation is most easily solved by using a modified cold frame. It is not the glass-covered structure commonly used, but rather the cover is made with snow fence, lath, or shade cloth. Walls are high enough to accommodate the top growth of the plants, and it is not heated. Fig. 113 depicts a large cold frame covered with snow fencing and used to grow tissue culture liners and rooted cuttings through the first growing season. The walls are constructed of concrete block, the joints between levels overlapped for stability, though joints are not mortared. The bottom row is set about 4 in. (10 cm) below the soil surface to provide additional stability.

Fig. 113.   A cold frame made from concrete blocks and covered with lath. Photo by the author.

The size of the cold frame depends on the number of plants to be planted. An economical width is 14 ft. (4.3 m) wide as an outside dimension with about a 1 ft. (30 cm) path down the center. This provides space for two beds approximately 6 ft. (1.8 m) wide with enough room for seven rows of liners in each bed spaced 8 in. (20 cm) apart. The plants need to be allowed enough space that the foliage is just touching at the end of the growing season. The center path provides maintenance access for weeding, pruning, and so on. The 14 ft. (4.3 m) width can be spanned with 2 × 4 in. frames which will require no center support if boards can be set on edge. The frames are then covered with snow fence or lath to provide 30–50% shade. Incidentally, a narrower structure may require the same number of blocks for construction but allow less growing space. Both ends of the frame are initially left open to permit passage of a rototiller or other equipment needed to prepare the soil. Plywood ends can be set in place to close the structure after planting. The sash can easily be lifted and stacked by two people when it is necessary to enter the cold frame after planting.

The soil in the cold frame needs to be tested, amended, and in general prepared as for a planting bed. This includes incorporating 1.5 lbs. (0.7 kg) per 100 sq. ft. (9 m²) of urea formaldehyde and at least 50% organic matter. The center path can be about 12 in. (30 cm) wide and 8 in. (20 cm) lower than the planting beds when the path is dug, the soil removed can be placed on each side. Afterwards the two beds are ready to be leveled.

Transplanting liners is done as early in the spring as possible. Planting can begin when the soil and air are still cool and moist yet the soil is sufficiently dry to work without destroying soil structure.

Start rows on one side of the bed using a string to keep them straight. Plant the first row about 8 in. (20 cm) from any walls, spacing plants 8 in. (20 cm) apart in the row. Use a ¾ in. (1.9 cm) plywood board to walk and kneel on while planting to protect the loosely dug soil from compaction. Alternating plants in succeeding rows, spaced midway, will maximize the growing space.

Before setting the liners in the bed, shake or comb off the medium around the roots to expose root ends. If plants are tightly pot-bound, cut off the bottom of the root ball and straighten the roots so they extend from the medium. While preparing the roots takes a little extra time, the result in better growth of plants is warranted. Place the liner in a hole large enough to permit filling in around and below the extended roots and maintain their extended horizontal position. Firm but do not pack the soil tightly around the tender roots; use water later to settle soil around the roots.

Fig. 114.   A liner plant with its extended roots free and ready for the planting bed. Photo by the author.

Each liner needs to be prepared immediately prior to planting so roots do not dry out. Prepared liners should be kept in a flat or other container with the roots covered by moist peat moss or mulch until planted.

Every effort to prevent root damage needs to be made. The fine, tender roots of liners are easily torn, pulled from the plant stem, or bruised. This greatly reduces the effectiveness of the developed root system. When removing liners from pots, squeeze or tap the bottom of the plastic pots or hold the pot upside down and tap to shake the plant out. Lift plants from flats by sliding a putty knife or similar tool under the root ball. Cutting between plants in a flat with a sharp knife: 4–6 weeks prior to transplanting greatly facilitates removal from the flat and will also promote a well branched root system. Never pull the top of the plant to remove it from a container. After careful removal from the container, immediately plant or cover the roots with rooting medium or moist mulch until planting. After planting, mulch the bed from both edges with 1 in. (2.5 cm) of fine pine bark or other suitable material.

When the bed is fully planted and mulched, irrigate to settle the soil around the plant roots and to raise the humidity in the cold frame. If planting is interrupted or when planting a large area which allows time for plant foliage to dry, mist the plants periodically until the entire frame is planted, watered, and mulched.

Immediately after planting and watering, place the lath cover or snow fence over the cold frame (see Fig. 133). During the first week I also add a 50% shade cloth over the lath for additional sun and wind protection.

The single most important requirement after planting is proper watering, this is a practice that cannot be overemphasized, yet the soil should never be overwatered. About 1 in. (2.5 cm) of water per week, as either rain or irrigation or a combination of the two, is a general rule of thumb. Less may be needed in a cold frame covered with shade and a windbreak, so check soil moisture several times a week to determine whether water is needed. The soil should always feel moist but not wet.

To gauge the amount of water the planting bed receives, place a straight-sided container among the plants. Mark a 1 in. (2.5 cm) line on the inside. Check this water gauge regularly to determine when irrigation may be needed.

Newly rooted cuttings or tissue culture plants should not be pruned at planting time as the leaves are necessary to manufacture food for the development of new roots. Wait several weeks until new feeder roots have become established. At this time, pinch or cut back the tips of azaleas to promote early branching.

· To promote low branching, cut the plant back to 2–4 in. (5–10 cm) from the soil surface. New shoots will emerge on the stem to about 2 in. (5 cm) below the cut. Fig. 115 illustrates the pruning needs of an azalea.

Fig. 115.   An azalea liner. A grower holds one of the taller stems where pruning will encourage low branching. Photo by the author.

Later pruning depends upon plant growth. Pruning can be done as necessary to encourage additional branching. Do not prune after August 1, however, since pruning will stimulate tender growth. Fig. 116 shows azaleas after one year of growth. The plant in the center was not pruned; the one to the right was pruned to stimulate low branching.

Fig. 116.   Azalea plants after the first year's growth. The center plant has not been properly pruned and shows gangling growth. Photo by the author.

Spring pinching of azalea flower buds from all tips, as soon as they swell enough to be easily removed, will result in more vigorous, uniform top growth. Obviously this would not be done the year the plants are moved to the landscape or marketed.

Rhododendrons have a growth habit different from that of azaleas and require a different approach to pruning. While azaleas grow by continuous extension of stems, rhododendrons grow in rapid growth flushes. Stem elongation is stopped when a whorl of leaves and a terminal bud with lateral buds in the leaf axils are set. Additional growth does not occur in rhododendrons until soft wood has matured. Young plants usually have two such growth flushes each year.

If terminal buds were removed from rhododendron cuttings the previous fall after rooting, no pruning is required. If terminal buds were not removed, pinch these buds from all cuttings at planting time. During the first flush of growth, additional pinching is necessary only when single shoots are produced. Single shoots can be cut off when they are 1–2 in. (2.5–5 cm) long to promote additional branching. If plants still do not branch well, delay pruning until the first flush of growth has hardened and the root system is developed. Liners with adequate root systems are able to force and support more branches. Fig. 117 shows a well branched liner, the result of pruning back a single shoot after adequate root development had occurred. Tissue culture liners usually develop multiple branches at soil level and readily develop as compact, well branched plants.

Fig. 117. Rhododendron liner. The single shoot was pruned, and six new branches are now originating near the soil surface. Photo by the author.

Pruning of liners is the most important pruning ever done on a plant. No amount of pruning later in the plant's life can correct mistakes made at this stage of development. The goal is to have 3–4 branches starting at or near soil level (see Fig. 118).

Fig. 118. Multiple branching on a rhododendron liner after one year's growth. This specimen illustrates successful pruning of a rhododendron liner. Photo by the author.

Close monitoring is needed to control or prevent damage from insects or diseases in the cold frame. If insects, such as mites, or fungus diseases appear, spray immediately with the proper chemical. See Chapter Seven for control recommendations. ***Handle all chemicals with extreme care.*** However, if the plants were free from insects and diseases when planted in the cold frame and good sanitation is maintained, there probably will be no need to use pesticides.

The number and type of weed seeds in the soil of the cold frame primarily determine the extent of any weed problems. The key to successful weed control is to remove weeds when they are small. Their removal long before maturing and reproducing will go far in controlling any current and future weed populations.

Except for the very vigorous and tall growing weeds, 1 in. (2.5 cm) of mulch prevents most weeds from getting a start. Nearly all types of weeds require light for germination. Mulch blocks light from reaching the soil surface and thereby discourages weed seed germination from the native soil. The few that do emerge can easily be pulled by hand as soon as they are visible. The mulch layer will not be radically disturbed by this process and so will continue to block most attempts at germination.

Chemical weed control is an alternative for use in the cold frame. Contact your local extension horticulturist for recommendations.

In the fall after the first killing frost or when plants are sufficiently hardened off, apply ¾ lb. (0.4 kg) per 100 sq. ft. (9 m²) of urea formaldehyde to the soil surface. This late season organic nitrogen application will promote root development in the fall and will result in evergreen azaleas holding more leaves over winter. Growth the following spring will also be more vigorous as a result of a fall nitrogen application.

The lath cover over the cold frame usually provides adequate winter protection. The plywood ends, if removed during the summer, need to be replaced to protect the plants against rodents and wind. No additional care will be needed until transplanting time the following spring.

Second Year Field Management

After a year spent in the cold frame, the plants are of sufficient size and maturity for transplanting to open field beds for an additional year or two. These beds may be in full sunlight in U.S.D.A. Hardiness Zones 5–6 and possibly Zone 7. It will be necessary to shade plants in sites where sunlight is intense enough to cause foliage damage and subsequent yellowing of leaves.

Raised beds greatly reduce the incidence of root rot and are recommended for field grown plants for all but extremely well drained soils. For best results beds need to be 12 in. (30.5 cm) above the existing soil level and gradually taper down at the edges. Raised beds may require additional irrigation, yet the benefits to plant health usually will outweigh this consideration.

Fig. 119.   Field beds in author's nursery in central Maryland ready for planting. Notice the maintenance path marked in the center area. Each bed is 7 ft. (2.1 m) by 100 ft. (30 m). Beds are raised about 12 in. (30 cm) above the existing soil level. Native soil type is a silt loam. Photo by the author.

In general, prepare the soil in the nursery beds as described in Chapter Five. A few details are different for nursery field bed preparation since it involves more intense plantings. The soil needs to be slightly higher in organic matter. Dig in a 3–4 in. (7–10 cm) layer of organic amendment. Also, it is necessary to pay closer attention to soil test results. Precise amounts of fertilizer elements are required to produce optimum conditions for plant growth. Since nitrogen is generally not part of soil testing, a general recommendation is 1½ lbs. (8 kg) per 100 sq. ft. (9 m²) of urea formaldehyde dug in prior to planting.

The practice of preparing beds in the fall for spring planting can free up valuable time. Most gardeners are fully occupied with numerous other springtime chores, and to have the bed ready for planting seems especially valuable.

Field beds no more than 6 ft. (1.8 m) wide are easier to weed, prune, and otherwise tend and can accommodate 3 rows of plants. If the width is increased by only 1 ft. (to 7 ft. or 2.1 m), 4 rows of azaleas can be planted, but the plants in the center of the beds will be difficult to tend. Do not walk in the beds as that will compact the soil and reduce aeration to the roots.

Plants are spaced 1.5 ft. (0.5 m) apart in the rows for azaleas and 2 ft. (0.6 m) for rhododendrons in rows 1.5 ft. (0.5 m) apart.

Beds can be planted as early in the spring as possible— immediately after the last date on which the soil freezes and after the soil is dry enough to work. Since plants in the cold frame are acclimated to the climate, they are hardened off and will only be frost susceptible at the roots.

Lift each plant from the cold frame bed by cutting around it and prying the root ball loose with a shovel. Handle plants by the root ball, not the top, to avoid tearing roots from the stem. Keep the roots of the newly dug plants covered with mulch or soil until transplanting.

Since the plants were grown in a soil mix similar to the soil being transplanted into, no special preparation of the root ball is necessary.

Dig holes just deep enough so that the top of the root ball is level with the bed. The ball should be resting firmly on the bottom of the hole. Fill soil around but not on top of the roots with the hands. Firm the soil, yet do not tamp tightly. After the bed is planted, mulch with 1–2 in. (3–5 cm) of a loose mulch, such as pine bark, and water well to settle the soil around the roots. If the bed is planted early in the spring, no sun protection is necessary.

The most critical cultural practice from this point on is proper watering. Soil needs to be kept moist but not wet. Some drying of the soil can be encouraged in late summer which will help check active growth and harden plants off for the winter.

Insect and disease control is undertaken only as conditions warrant throughout the growing season. Some growers still apply preventive sprays on a regular schedule, but this procedure is now discouraged. The current view encourages monitoring closely for early pest identification and using spray applications only when damaging pest populations are noticed. During the final growing season, either the second or third year, any damage to foliage will affect plant marketability. It may be necessary to use preventive sprays to prevent such damage since the consumer has every reason to expect an insect and disease free product. Chapter Seven presents control methods for various insects and diseases. It is important to know which of these pests are in the local growing area and how to prepare for control.

When azaleas are planted, only the extra long shoots need to be cut back. In about four weeks, after roots are established, and before new growth starts, additional pruning can be done. How much to prune depends on how well the plant branched during its first year and what level of compactness is desired. If the plant is already well branched, cut back only to the point where additional branching is desired. New shoots originate downward on the stem at a distance of 1–2 in. (2.5–5 cm). Continue cutting back as necessary to promote additional branching.

An alternative method for azaleas is to pinch ½ in. (1 cm) on the soft tips when new shoots reach about 3–4 in. (7.5–8 cm) in length.

No pruning of any kind should be attempted after August 1. Late pruning forces new growth to develop late in the growing season, and this growth may not harden off before freezing weather.

A pruning chemical is available for use as a pruning method for large operations. This chemical works by killing the tender terminal growth. As plant response varies, the chemical should be used only according to label directions.

If rhododendron liners were properly pruned in the cold frame, the plants will have at least 3–4 shoots originating within a few inches of the soil level by the time they are moved into the field beds. If improperly pruned, errors need to be addressed at this time. Fig. 120 shows a rhododendron in need of corrective pruning.

Second year pruning of rhododendrons is largely accomplished by pinching terminal buds before each flush of growth begins. In fall, at the end of the first growing season in field beds, all terminal buds are pinched out, including any flower buds. This may be all the pruning necessary to produce a well branched plant.

Weed control in field beds is partially accomplished through use of a 1.5 in. (3.8 cm) mulch of fine pine bark or other mulching

Fig. 120.   Improperly pruned rhododendron liner ready for field bed move. A grower points to where corrective pruning needs to start. One season's growth has been lost by the initial pruning lapse. Photo by the author.

material. Applied at this depth it is deep enough to shade the soil and thus prevent weed seed germination. If the soil has been managed to provide good weed control several years prior to use as a nursery bed, few weed problems will be encountered.

If weed problems are minimal, hand pulling is a workable control. If the problem is more severe, use herbicides as recommended by the local extension horticulturist.

Wind and sun protection of rhododendrons is important during the winter season in regions where winter winds are strong or temperatures drop below 0°F (−18°C). Snow fencing makes an effective windbreak and also provides shade to plants to the immediate north. Shade is probably most critical the winter before plants are to be sold to help maintain good green foliage color. A windbreak is necessary every winter.

If the organic mulch applied at planting time is decomposed, an additional 1 in. (2.5 cm) can be applied in late fall. Mulching at this time will help prevent deep freezing in the soil, thereby improving moisture availability to plant roots. Apply ¾ lb. (0.3 kg) of urea formaldehyde per 100 sq. ft. (9 m²) prior to mulching.

Assuming a fall application of urea formaldehyde has been applied the first year in the field, no fertilizer applications need to be made until active growth starts the following spring. At this time broadcast ¾ lb. (0.3 kg) of urea formaldehyde per 100 sq. ft. (9 m^2) of bed area. Any fertilizer residue on plant foliage needs to be removed.

Another application of the same fertilizer and rate mentioned needs to be made in the fall of the second year in the field. Fertilize either after the first killing frost or after the plants are hardened off for winter.

Ammonium sulfate can be substituted for urea formaldehyde as a surface application. The rate for ammonium sulfate is 1 lb. (.45 kg) per 100 sq. ft. (9 m^2). Since this material is a salt, it should not be dug into the soil if the area is to be planted immediately following application.

The soil must be kept moist during the active growing season until midsummer when soil can be allowed to dry somewhat to harden plants off for winter. Early hardening off should be encouraged the last year in the nursery and before plants go into the landscape.

If buds (including flower buds) were pinched out the previous fall, there is no need for additional pruning the final year in the field nursery since most terminals are carrying flower buds for next year's display in the landscape.

The year before marketing or landscape placement, both a windbreak and winter shade must be provided. This will protect foliage from sun- and windburn and result in dark green, attractive foliage.

CONTAINER GROWING

Container growing is exactly what the term implies: growing plants in containers rather than in a bed in the ground. The result is an entirely different growing environment. Major differences from field growing include a coarser growing medium, a restricted root zone, wider fluctuations in root temperatures, unique water and fertilizer requirements, and more intensive management of cultural factors.

A large and increasing percentage of nursery plants are grown in containers each year by both commercial and hobbyist gardeners. The advantages of container growing include

1. Greater control of the growing medium since it is mixed in exact proportions of medium and fertilizers. Additionally, commercial mixes are available which are ready for use.

2. Plants can be grown from liner to finished product in the same container. This eliminates the costs and labor of digging and transplanting.

3. Root loss in transplanting to the landscape is likely to be reduced, unless the plants are seriously pot-bound.

4. Plants are easier to transport.

5. Weed control is simplified.

6. A greater number of plants can be grown more intensively in a given area.

7. Plants are available for market regardless of wet soils which prevent digging field grown plants.

The disadvantages include

1. Much more water is required. A gallon pot requires at least 1 pint (400 ml) of water per day because the coarse potting medium drains so rapidly.

2. Plants require daily irrigation during the growing season.

3. Heat from the sun can damage roots growing in the south side of the container.

4. The growing medium is light in weight, so plants can be easily blown or knocked over.

5. Plant roots may become pot-bound.

6. Close management attention must be paid to fertilizer needs since soilless mixes used in containers essentially contain no nutrients.

7. Plant roots can be damaged when temperatures drop below 20°F (−7°C).

8. Plants transplanted to the landscape from containers require more intensive care the first year.

The commercial grower must select a container that is attractive and has a useful life of 1–2 years. Injection molded, polyvinyl pots satisfy both these requirements. The home gardener can use anything with sufficient strength and size to hold the root ball.

Shallow containers do not drain as well as taller ones since gravitational pull is less on short columns of water. A container depth of at least 6 in. (15 cm) is recommended. The diameter of the pot will not affect drainage, but a pot too small for the plant dries out more quickly since a lower volume of medium is available to hold moisture. Gravel or shards placed in the bottom of pots have traditionally been used to improve drainage but in fact do just the opposite. They reduce the depth of the medium and so reduce gravitational pull. Containers with holes extending ½ in. (1.3 cm) up the side drain more efficiently than those with holes only in the bottom.

Questions regarding container size are determined by how long the plant is to remain in the container and how vigorous the plant is. A proper fit can be determined by the size of the root ball. Roots should reach the edge of the container and may circle the walls but should not become solidly matted around the edges or bottom by the end of the growing cycle. Most nurseries use a 2 gallon container to produce 12–15 in. (30–38 cm) plants and a 3 gallon container for 15–18 in. (38–46 cm) plants.

The container medium is made up of three constituents: solids, gases, and liquids. From ⅓ to ½ the total volume is occupied by solid particles. The remaining volume is pore space and is occupied by water or air in varying percentages over time. A growing medium with small pore spaces retains more water and less air than one with large pore spaces. Shallow containers do not drain as well and therefore will require a coarser mix than tall containers.

A good, well draining garden soil will remain saturated longer when placed in a container when compared to its draining capacity in the garden. This is due to the shallowness of the container, which results in a reduced gravitational pull on the column of water through the soil. The outcome of using even good garden soil in a container is a poorly aerated medium; results are poor root development or root death. I hope by this to clarify that a satisfactory container medium must be composed of larger particles than those found in even the best garden loam soil.

Nursery stock can be grown in any medium which is nontoxic, provides anchorage, and provides the plant food elements, water, and oxygen. The selection of materials to be used is usually based on cost and availability as well as quality in terms of providing optimum growing conditions.

Any soil used as part of a container medium needs to be pasteurized before mixing by heating soil to 160°F (72°C) for 30 minutes to kill any resident disease organisms.

Sand is often included to add weight, thus reducing chances for containers to be blown over by wind. The sand too must be pasteurized before it is incorporated. Pasteurization can be achieved in the same manner for soil. Only coarse sand should be used. It should not make up more than 10% of the total volume since sand fills available pore spaces and can seriously reduce drainage and air space in the medium.

Sphagnum peat moss improves moisture retention in a mix, retains plant nutrients well, and lowers the pH of the mixture. If used alone as a container medium, however, it will hold too much moisture.

Conifer bark is probably the most popular container medium in areas where it is readily available. It is quite resistant to decomposition and can be milled and screened to provide a material very uniform in texture or particle size. The best material has 70–80% of the particles in the size range of ¼–⅜ in. (up to 0.9 cm) in diameter and 20–30% of the particles smaller than this. Bark of this particle size can be used alone and requires no additions of sand, sphagnum moss and so on. It will only be necessary to add dolomitic limestone, which adjusts pH, and plant food elements. Pine bark is naturally acidic with a pH range from 4.0 to 5.5.

I have found that a mixture of pine fines with a ¼ inch (0.6 cm) and smaller particle size, mixed with coarse sphagnum peat moss at a ratio of 3:1, provides an excellent medium and does not require watering as often as 100% pine bark. Sphagnum moss improves the moisture and nutrient retention qualities of the mix.

Another container mix widely recommended is

3 parts by volume of bark ¼ in. (0.6 cm) and smaller in diameter
1 part by volume of coarse sphagnum peat moss
0.5 part by volume of sand to add weight

Hardwood bark is not recommended due to its high cellulose content, rapid decomposition, and shrinkage. It also has a high pH (6.5–7.5) after decomposition which is not satisfactory for ericaceous plants.

The gardener growing a small number of plants may be best advised to purchase a commercially prepared container mix formulated for ericaceous plants.

The frequent watering required by plants grown in rapidly draining containers will also result in fertilizer leaching. Since soilless mixes lack virtually all plant food elements, minor elements also need to be included in the fertilizer or added separately in fritted form. Slow release fertilizers mixed into the medium or later sprinkled on the surface will give a consistent level of nutrient input.

Some soluble plant foods generally recommended for ericaceous plants contain too much sulfate for use in container mixes. One result may be the lowering of the pH below levels best suited to *Rhododendron* growth. If a soluble fertilizer is preferred, it is best applied with irrigation water. Soluble plant food formulations used at 50% recommended strength every second or third watering will result in satisfactory plant growth.

The most important considerations in selecting the container growing area are ready accessibility to a water supply, protection from wind, and a gently sloping surface. The reasons for these conditions are quickly apparent. Container plants require virtually daily watering, so a reliable supply of quality water is a must. Because neither small plants nor containers can withstand winds of any magnitude without being injured or tipped, wind protection is required. Likewise, because root rot can be devastating in container growing, the extra drainage provided by a sloping area is a good preventative measure. Fiber mats or gravel on top of black plastic used for weed control also improves drainage.

Fig. 121. Container growing area at Marshy Point Nursery near Baltimore, Maryland. Photo by the author.

Containers are filled with growing medium to within 1 in. (2.5 cm) of the top to provide the largest volume and deepest root zone possible. Liners are planted at the same depth at which they were growing in the flats or small containers. Rhododendrons are planted singly, one liner to each container, yet 2–3 azalea liners are often planted per pot. This double or triple planting of azaleas results in a finished plant in less time (usually in one year) and requires less pruning. Multiple plants result in a composite, many branched plant.

Since liners are planted into an organic mix, little if any problem is encountered with root extension into the soilless mix. However, tightly potbound root balls need to be broken apart to interrupt the circling growth pattern.

Fig. 122. A rhododendron liner that has been properly pruned and displays a good branching pattern. Photo by the author.

Immediately after planting, containers can be watered thoroughly to settle the medium around the roots. Place containers in the growing area as close together as present spread of the foliage allows. Since the sun heats and frosts can cool the growing medium to root-killing temperatures, close spacing will moderate temperature fluctuations. Special attention to watering needs is critical especially during the period immediately after transplanting.

The coarse, rapidly draining potting medium dries out quickly and will require watering once every two days in early spring and daily as summer heat increases. Under conditions of extreme heat (90°F or 32°C and above), water is typically required twice a day to maintain a moist growing medium throughout the container.

Pruning and insect and disease control practices are identical to those for field grown plants.

Weed control for container grown plants is largely a matter of prevention. Since the potting medium is weed-free when made, weed control is a question of preventing weed seeds from blowing into the stored medium or planted containers. Therefore, premixed container medium must be stored inside a windbreak or kept covered. Although some weed seeds can be blown great distances, the area in the immediate vicinity produces the greatest populations. It is imperative to remove all weeds before they go to seed within a radius of 100 ft. (30 m) or more of the medium storage area.

After planting, a weed killer can be spread over the surface of the medium in the containers with a cyclone type spreader. Apply only when plant foliage is dry, and remove any residue from the foliage immediately after application. Check with your extension horticulturist for recommendations. *Handle all chemicals with extreme care.*

The nursery person or gardener growing plants in containers or flats must take extra precautions overwintering plants in cold climates. When plants are grown in the landscape or field, heat continues to rise from the unfrozen soil at deeper levels. So soil temperatures around the roots do not usually go so low as to cause root damage. Because plants in containers are above ground and are unprotected by warmer soil temperatures, plant roots can be killed at temperatures easily endured by soil grown plants. (see Fig. 123). Additionally, when the root balls of container grown plants are solidly frozen, they are unable to absorb needed moisture.

Cultivar or Species	Killing Temperature of	
	Roots	Flower Buds
R. prunifolium	20°F (–7°C)	–15°F (–26°C)
'Hino Crimson', evergreen azalea	17°F (–8°C)	0°F (–18°C)
Exbury Hybrid, deciduous azalea	17°F (–8°C)	–25°F (–32°C)
R. schlippenbachii, "The Royal Azalea"	15°F (–9°C)	–20°F (–29°C)
'Purple Gem'	15°F (–9°C)	–25°F (–32°C)
'Gibraltar', deciduous azalea	10°F (–12°C)	–25°F (–32°C)
'Hinode Giri', evergreen azalea	10°F (–12°C)	0°F (–18°C)
R. carolinianum	0°F (–18°C)	–25°F (–32°C)
R. catawbiense	0°F (–18°C)	–25°F (–32°C)
'P. J. M'	–9°F (–23°C)	–25°F (–32°C)

Fig. 123. Killing temperatures for some container *Rhododendron.* Adapted from the University of Maryland Fact Sheet (H. E. 102-76) by Dr. Francis R. Gouin.

An insulating material such as Microfoam simplifies overwintering container plants where protection of the surface is necessary to help control root temperatures. Plants may be set upright if a frame is used to hold the Microfoam off them, or placed on their sides and closely stacked if the film is to be placed directly on the plants (Fig. 124). All plants should be watered well and sprayed with a fungicide to prevent foliage disease in the moisture-tight enclosure. The Microfoam is placed between two sheets of white (not clear) plastic and spread over the plants with all edges extending to the soil, where they are covered with soil to form a moisture-proof seal (Fig. 125). Plants should be protected only when night temperatures are below 20°F (−7°C) and removed in spring when the danger of such temperatures for longer than a few hours no longer exists.

Fig. 124. Plants laid on side ready for winter covering with Microfoam and white plastic. Photo taken at Marshy Point Nursery, Zone 7. Average winter low is 0°F (−18°C). Photo by the author.

Fig. 125. Same plants as in Fig. 124, now covered with Microfoam and white plastic. Photo taken at the end of December. Photo by the author.

For small numbers of plants, a pit dug 3 ft. (0.9 m) deep also works well to overwinter container plants if a well drained site is available. Cover the pit with any good insulating material, supported so a heavy snow cover does not break it. Remove the cover in early spring.

Container grown plants are often wintered in open poly houses. Fig. 126 shows an example of this system of overwintering. Except in extremely cold areas, no additional heat is needed.

Fig. 126. Poly house at Marshy Point Nursery used for overwintering container grown rhododendrons. Photo by the author.

Where temperatures are not as severe, plant tops can be protected with a snow fence windbreak. Container plant roots can be protected by covering the containers with any mulching material that will adequately insulate and modify temperature extremes in the root zone.

At the end of one or two years, the container grown plant is ready for market or landscape placement. Any plants not sold or moved to the landscape will need to be potted to the next larger size pot to prevent constricting the roots.

In summary, the *Rhododendron* nursery, whether a small hobby venture or of commercial scale, offers many rewards to the grower. The gardener can develop small plants at considerable financial saving, and the nursery person can reap a profit if the business is managed properly. The decision to grow plants in containers or in field beds can be made after careful evaluation of the local advantages and disadvantages. A thoughtful decision can then be reached as to which system is best adapted for the resources available.

Successful growing of small plants to landscape size requires close attention to details, particularly watering and pruning. Yet there is every reason to believe that the average gardener and small nursery person can produce plants of professional quality by following the basics of good culture outlined in these pages.

TEN: *Hybridizing*

INTRODUCTION

Earlier I noted that growing rhododendrons can be contagious and there is no known cure. Hybridizing can be a further symptom of such contagion and a pursuit that injects a kind of mystique and an element of chance. Goals are set, crosses made, seedlings germinated and planted out, and always with the expectation that something new and outstanding is surely in the genes and about to appear—if not this year, maybe next. Or, one hears about the new superior species just discovered which will of course add enormously to the genetic material available. This kind of excitement motivates and keeps thousands of hybridizers around the world at work. The results are seen as the newly listed cultivar registrations each year, some of which will indeed stand the test of time and improve the variety of first-class rhododendron available. Many other crosses, equally as good, are not registered; some may be introduced, yet most will remain unknown.

New and improved cultivars appear only out of the sustained efforts of hybridizers who grow thousands of seedlings. I will never forget the statement I read years ago that all the flowers of all the tomorrows are in the seeds of today. Save for mutants and sports, only seedlings can produce new and exciting plants thanks to the mixing up and rearranging of the genes via the mechanism of sexual reproduction.

A bit of counsel to prospective hybridizers is appropriate here. Only a few hybrids will prove to be superior plants, so there will be many disappointments after thousands of new seedlings have been evaluated. Much patience and a thoroughly disciplined set of judgmental standards are required throughout the long process of evaluation as new crosses are compared to the best available cultivars. Only plants superior to any others in existence at the time should be brought forward for registration and introduction. Complete objectivity is a difficult quality to maintain as one evaluates the seedlings, and advice from others is not only wise but probably necessary. Rhododendron hybridizers are generally friendly, helpful people, ready to assist a new member of the fraternity with hybridizing issues.

The first hybridizers of rhododendrons and azaleas were probably active in Japan over 300 years ago. Evidence of hybrid plants, among the R. *kurume* azaleas in Japanese gardens, dates back at least to the 17th century. Beginning in the 19th century, extensive hybridizing activity developed in Europe as plant explorers brought back an increasing number of new species.

It was not until the early 20th century that hybridizing started in earnest in North America with such greats as Joe Gable, Guy Nearing, C. O. Dexter, Tony Shammarello, and James Barto. I urge the interested gardener to read some of the detailed accounts of the contributions of early hybridizers before starting to work. Since that time many more outstanding hybridizers, too numerous to mention, have been at work.

The genus *Rhododendron* is a hybridizers' paradise. The tremendous diversity of flower color and size, plant size, foliage, cold hardiness, heat tolerance, disease resistance, and other attributes presents such a huge reservoir of genetic variability that it seems possible to make any number of useful combinations. However, some combinations of characteristics have defied the best efforts of numerous hybridizers. For example, there are no yellow flowered, evergreen azaleas; no ironclad, deep yellow rhododendrons; few heat tolerant, deciduous azalea hybrids; no blue Elepidote or red Lepidote rhododendrons; few disease resistant plants; and few ironclad, evergreen azaleas. Yet most of these combinations are within the realm of possibility since the genes are there; it is a matter of cleverly arranging them in the proper order. This is a simple statement, yet for the hybridizer it represents a long, problematic undertaking.

The recent discovery of superior forms of some species offer new potential for the production of superior cultivars. The hybridizer is well advised to search out the best form of each species to use in his or her work. Research at the parent selection stage often makes the difference between achieving hybridizing goals or failing to do so. In any circumstance, parent selection can reduce the time required to meet defined goals.

Probably one of the gravest mistakes a hybridizer can make is to start spreading pollen before thoroughly investigating work already done by others. Another weakness can be in failing to define goals. A third failing quite often lies in parent selection. It is essential to identify the parent plants most likely to achieve the goals that are set.

The first step in any hybridizing program is to become thoroughly familiar with previous work. Since much hybridizing work has been done and the results are on record, it makes no sense to repeat crosses already made, especially those which produced poor results. Such research can also identify parents which consistently pass along certain characteristics to their offspring. Obviously those species/cultivars transmitting traits consistent with the goals of the hybridizing program need to be selected for further evaluation and possible use.

Research can, in addition, often eliminate a step in a hybridizing program by starting with first generation crosses. It is quite possible that two species, identified by the hybridizer as parents, have already been crossed and seedlings selected which carry the genes for the desired characteristic. Since such primary hybrids represent the first step in a successful breeding program, even if the offspring are of mediocre quality, they carry the genetic potential for better things in the next generation where the hybridizers' goal is most likely to be met.

I recommend the following references as the best places for a beginning hybridizer to start his or her research program:

Leach, David G. *Rhododendrons of the World.* New York: Charles Scribner's Sons, 1961.

West, Franklin H., et al. *Hybrids and Hybridizers: Rhododendrons and Azaleas for Eastern North America.* Edited by Philip A. Livingston. Newtown Square, Pennsylvania: Harrowood Books, 1978.

Salley, Homer, and Harold Greer. *Rhododendron Hybrids: Second Edition.* Portland, Oregon: Timber Press, 1992.

The second step is to define goals for the hybridizing program. Since contemporary homes tend to have a low profile, low growing plants are in increasing demand, while the demand for large growing plants is declining as vast estates with wooded grounds are decreasing in number. While many commercial buildings and apartment complexes are of a scale suitable for large growing plants, there is often little interest in rhododendrons and azaleas in these situations because of their special cultural requirements. The beginning hybridizer might be well advised to aim towards the breeding of low growing and dwarf forms as one goal.

The hybridizer is wise to focus on only one or two goals at a time in order to concentrate the focus and to make noticeable progress. Some other goals might include

1. Increased disease resistance, particularly mildew resistance in deciduous azaleas.
2. Increased insect resistance.
3. Increased cold hardiness in evergreen azaleas and yellow rhododendrons.
4. Increased heat tolerance in all rhododendrons and deciduous azaleas.
5. Larger flowers with cleaner colors on rhododendrons.
6. Fragrance in rhododendrons and azaleas.
7. Development of double flowers.
8. Tightly branched plants.
9. Increased amounts of persistent foliage on evergreen azaleas.
10. Improved fall and winter foliage color on evergreen types.
11. A yellow flowered, evergreen azalea.
12. Easier to root deciduous azaleas.
13. A true blue Elepidote rhododendron.
14. A true red Lepidote rhododendron.
15. Indumentum on rhododendron leaves.
16. Stronger root systems.

The careful selection of parents possessing the characteristics being sought in the cultivar is the third major step towards a promising hybridizing program.

Each generation in the hybridizing program requires from three to seven years. Obviously the hybridizer cannot afford to make many mistakes in the selection of parents. Furthermore, if goals are to be met, the parents must be capable of transmitting the characteristics selected by the hybridizer. A thorough knowledge of characteristics most often transmitted by specific parents becomes of utmost importance. This must be researched before the hybridizer can make selections with any degree of accuracy or expectation of success.

AZALEAS

Galle's *Azaleas* (Timber Press, 1987) contains an excellent chapter on hybridizing azaleas written by Dr. August Kehr. It presents detailed information on hybridizing and offers some wise advice on the selection of parents most likely to transmit specific characteristics to their offspring. Kehr writes on p. 346,

An informal poll was taken of several azalea breeders and growers [list omitted] to solicit their choices for parents for some of these specific objectives. As might be expected replies were varied, but significant points of agreement developed. Listed below are some of the plants suggested to realize particular objectives.

EVERGREEN AZALEAS

Most Cold Hardy: 'Corsage', 'Herbert', *R. kiusianum, R. yedoense* var. *poukhanense*
Best Winter Foliage: 'Glacier', 'Hot Shot', 'Polar Bear'
Reddest Color: 'Girard Scarlet', 'Hino Crimson', 'Mother's Day', 'Ward's Ruby'
Yellowest Color: 'Cream Cup', 'Frostburg', 'Mizu no Yuma Buki'
Fragrance: *R. mucronatum*, 'Rose Greeley'
Fully Double Flower: 'Anna Kehr', 'Gardenia', 'Elsie Lee', 'Louise Gable', 'Rosebud'
Fall Flowering: 'Dorsett', 'Indian Summer', 'Opal'
Compact Growth: Beltsville Dwarfs, 'Dragon', 'Girard Border Gem', *R. kiusianum*, 'Myogi'
Lasting Quality of Flowers: 'Ambrosia', 'Chojuho', 'Jeanne', 'Rosebud', 'Scott Gartrell', 'Vuyk's Scarlet'
Best All Around Good-Doer: 'Corsage', 'Herbert', *R. kiusianum*, 'Martha Hitchcock'

DECIDUOUS AZALEAS

Easiest to Root: *R. austrinum, R. atlanticum*, 'Gibraltar', 'Homebush'
Mildew Resistance: 'Coccinea', 'J. Jennings', 'Persil', 'Speciosum'
Compact Growth: 'J. Jennings', 'Klondyke', *R. prunifolium*
Red Flower Color: 'Ilam Red Letter'
Yellow Flower Color: 'Klondyke'
Most Floriferous: 'Gibraltar', 'Knap Hill Red'
Double Flowers: 'Homebush', 'Narcissiflora', 'Norma'
Lasting Quality of Flowers: 'Homebush', 'Norma'
Best All Around Good-Doer: 'Gibraltar'

Azaleas fall into two broad categories, deciduous and evergreen. It is probably sufficient to note that the evergreen species azaleas crossbreed readily, as is also the case among the deciduous species. However, the evergreen species do not readily crossbreed with the deciduous. A handful of hybrids have been produced between an evergreen and a deciduous parent, but they are rare and few of the plants are of much merit.

Most azaleas are self-sterile and cannot pollinate themselves yet will readily crossbreed.

RHODODENDRONS

Rhododendrons also fall into two major groups: the Lepidote or scaly species, which generally also produce small leaves, and the Elepidote or non-scaly, large-leaved species. Lepidotes and elepidotes are cross-sterile. Successful crosses are confined to species or cultivars within each group.

The following plants are suggested as parents with a proven ability to transmit various desirable traits to offspring:

Large Flower Size:
    Elepidote—*R. discolor, R. fortunei,* 'King George'
Cold Hardiness:
    Elepidote—'Catalgla', 'Clark's White', *R. maximum*
    Lepidote—*R. dauricum, R. minus, R. mucronulatum*
Heat/Sun Tolerance:
    Elepidote—*R. catawbiense insularis, R. decorum, R. fortunei,*
        R. hyperythrum, R. maximum, R. metternichii
    Lepidote—*R. chapmanii, R. compactum, R. minus*
Disease Resistance:
    Elepidote—'Caroline', *R. decorum, R. metternichii, R.*
        pseudochrysanthum, R. yakushimanum
    Lepidote—*R. aureum* Wada, *R. keiskei, R. racemosum*
Compact Size:
    Elepidote—*R. metternichii, R. williamsianum, R.*
        yakushimanum
    Lepidote—*R. keiskei* Yaku Fairy
Late Flowering:
    Elepidote—*R. haematodes, R. maximum*
Early Flowering:
    Elepidote—*R. fortunei, R. vernicosum* 18139
    Lepidote—*R. dauricum, R. mucronulatum*
Fragrance:
    Elepidote—*R. fortunei*
Red Flower Color:
    Elepidote—'Essex Scarlet', *R. griersonianum, R. haematodes,*
        R. strigillosum

Yellow Flower Color:
  Elepidote—*R. campylocarpum,* 'Gold Mohur', *R. wardii*
  Lepidote—*R. aureum, R. keiskei*
White Flower Color (usually masked in the first generation and recovered in the second):
  Elepidote—'Clark's White', *R. yakushimanum*
  Lepidote—*R. dauricum* var. *album*
Pink Flower Color: nearly all red × white crosses.

Perhaps one way to further demonstrate the process of selecting suitable parents is to present an example.

Let us say the goal is to develop a compact, large-leaved rhododendron with large, fragrant flowers. The search begins with research to identify parents with a record of transmitting these characteristics to their offspring. The first observation is that typically the less complex or heterogeneous a plant is genetically, the better the prospect of transmitting the desired traits without passing undesirable traits which would require subsequent crosses to eliminate. In other words, a species or primary hybrid possessing the desired characteristics is a better choice than a complex hybrid. A careful search reveals that *R. fortunei* has both large flowers and fragrance plus good foliage and resistance to lace bug. Similar research reveals that the species capable of dwarfing or developing compact offspring among the non-scaly rhododendrons include *R. yakushimanum, R. metternichii,* and *R. williamsianum.*

By carrying crosses of these plants through two or more generations and crossing or backcrossing after each generation (depending on those characteristics needing reinforcing or reducing), the hybridizing goal might possibly be met.

A second example: the goal is to develop a compact plant with a dark red flower. *Rhododendron williamsianum* has a dwarfing effect and also has outstanding foliage. *Rhododendron yakushimanum* also has a dwarfing effect but masks red flower color so completely that the chance of producing a red offspring is very limited. In this case *R. williamsianum* is the better choice for the parent contributing a dwarfing effect. 'Mars' and 'Essex Scarlet' are cultivars which reliably pass red on to their offspring, as does the species *R. haemotodes;* any one of these three is a candidate for obtaining a red flower.

MAKING A CROSS

After the prospective parents have been researched and carefully selected, it is a good idea to start a record book in which the crosses made, subsequent outcomes, further crosses and outcomes, and other data are meticulously recorded. Any cross should be recorded before it is actually made. The female parent or pod parent is always listed first and the pollen parent second. For example, in the cross 'Mars' × 'America', 'Mars' is the female parent. This record book must be carefully maintained so that all significant events and observations are recorded at the time of their occurrence.

The actual process of cross pollinating is very simple if both parent plants are growing in the same garden and flower at the same time. The flowers of both rhododendrons and azaleas are fortunately large enough that the male and female flower parts are easy to identify and work with. See Fig. 127 (A and B) for an illustration of male and female parts.

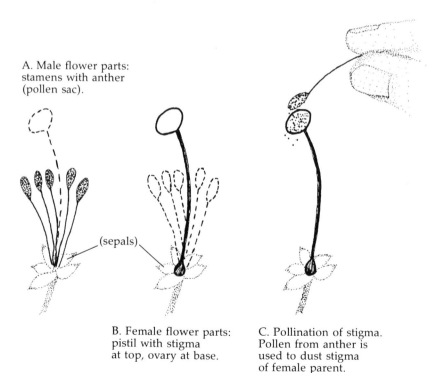

A. Male flower parts:
stamens with anther
(pollen sac).

(sepals)

B. Female flower parts:
pistil with stigma
at top, ovary at base.

C. Pollination of stigma.
Pollen from anther is
used to dust stigma
of female parent.

Fig. 127. Hand pollination: cutaway view of flower parts.

Hand pollination requires the following steps:

1. Identify three or four flower buds on two or more stems. More than one bud will be pollinated to insure against loss through physical damage. Flowers should be just ready to open but not yet accessible to insect pollinators. Next, on the plant to be used as the female parent, reduce the attractiveness of the immediate vicinity to pollinating insects by removing any other flowers within a foot of the selected buds.

2. Carefully remove the flower petals (corolla) of the selected flower buds. Pollen from the anthers or male part of the flower must be prevented from reaching the stigma or female part of the flower. To remove the corolla, separate the flower petals with the fingers and pull or cut them free from their base around the ovary.

3. With a tweezers or small scissors remove the anthers of the selected flowers one at a time and discard.

4. When the top surface of the stigma of the prepared flower exudes a sticky substance, it is receptive and can be pollinated immediately. If it is not sticky, cover the stigma with a small paper bag fastened to the stem to prevent accidental pollination. Check the stigma daily to determine when it is sticky and so receptive to pollen. I will note many hybridizers do not think such stigma protection is necessary as rhododendron pollen is not wind-borne and the emasculated flowers are not attractive to insects.

5. Ideally, when the stigma of the female plant is receptive, remove the corollas to expose anthers on several unopened buds from the male parent plant. Collect the entire flower stem intact and transfer pollen from the anthers to the stigma immediately. If pollen must be held until later, clip the anthers off and place them in a gelatin capsule (#1 or #0). Store the capsule containing the male pollen parts in a refrigerator until the female plant is ready.

6. Apply the pollen from the end of the anther to the sticky surface of the stigma. Since rhododendron pollen is not dusty and does not shake out easily, touch the pollen sac to the surface of the stigma to transfer the pollen. The total surface of the stigma needs to be covered with pollen.

7. Some hybridizers next cover the pollinated flower with a small brown paper bag to protect the fertilized stigma. Others

consider such protection unnecessary for the same reasons mentioned for step 4 above.

8. Label the female parent to show the cross, again listing the name of the female parent first.

9. Check the record book to confirm recording and date the cross.

If the selected parents do not flower at the same time, label and store the pollen as discussed for step 5 above. Pollen may be air dried and stored in the open for up to two weeks at 50°F (10°C). If the male parent flowers after the female flowers, the pollen may be stored in the freezer at 0°F (−18°C) for a year after it is dried or about a week at 50°F (10°C). If stored for an extended period, enclose the capsule in a sealed jar containing calcium chloride or silica gel as a drying agent. Place the drying agent in the bottom of the jar and cover with a layer of cotton on which the capsules are placed. Be certain the capsule is labeled with the parent name.

Warm frozen pollen to ambient temperatures prior to use by setting the jar with the capsules in warm water. When pollinating with stored pollen, insert the receptive stigma into the capsule to transfer the pollen since the pollen frequently sticks to the sides of the capsule. Unused pollen may be refrozen to use later.

Alternatively, off-season flowering of the female parent can be induced. This is most commonly done by transplanting the female parent into a container the previous fall and placing it in a greenhouse or transplanting into a greenhouse bed. By controlling temperature and day length, the time of flowering can be made to coincide with the flowering time of the pollen parent. If a choice can be made, it is easier to store pollen than to alter flowering dates.

If pollination was successful, the ovaries of the female parent will expand rapidly and produce the seed pod containing the new hybrid seed. Seed usually matures about the end of September, at which time the pod can be removed. There is no need to wait until the seed pod turns brown since the seeds are mature and are capable of germinating a month before changes in pod color. Seed pods must be collected no later than the first killing frost as frost accelerates pod splitting and subsequent seed loss.

Place the pods, collected from one plant, in a separate small envelope or cup which has been labeled to identify the cross. Place the seed container in a warm, dry location to dry the pods so they will release the seeds. Crush pods that have failed to open by drying to remove any seeds. Next, separate the pod and other plant material from the seeds. Since the seeds are very small, it is necessary to take great care not to lose them. Seeds may be sown immediately or stored in a cool, dry place for up to a year. Follow the instructions given in Chapter Eight on propagation.

The success or failure of the cross, noted when the seeds are recovered, the disposition of the seed, sowing dates, and other information must all be noted in the record book together with any observations which might prove useful later on. For example, the amount of seed set would indicate the degree of compatibility or success in technique.

The accepted method of ultimately combining in a single cultivar the most desirable characteristics existing separately in the two parent plants is to then cross pollinate two first-generation seedlings which most closely exhibit the desired characteristics. Intended results are most often obtained in the resulting second generation, the grandchildren of the original parents. It is best to grow as many seedlings of this second generation as possible. This will exploit the maximum number of genetic combinations to turn up the one closest to the desired plant.

If the hybridizing goal is to improve only one or two traits of an otherwise outstanding plant, perhaps tightening the truss or increasing disease resistance, backcrossing is undertaken.

The steps in backcrossing are

1. Cross the rhododendron needing improvement with a rhododendron having a proven reputation for transmitting the desired trait.

2. Backcross the F_1 (first generation) seedling which best exhibits the trait desired to the pod parent of step 1 needing improvement.

3. If the desired result is not obtained in the resulting F_2 (second) generation, then proceed to cross two sister seedlings of the F_2 generation.

Backcrossing generally requires fewer seedlings to produce the desired results but is also open to the expression of undesirable qualities.

Any physical characteristic is seldom controlled by a single gene. Rather, a number of genes are involved, some of which may work in opposition to others. This fact is one of the reasons that breeding results are difficult to predict.

Furthermore, some characteristics are linked on a single gene. A good example is color and fragrance in rhododendrons. I know of no fragrant red rhododendron, and to my knowledge fragrance only occurs in white or light colored flowers. These two characteristics are probably located on the same gene, in which case a breeding goal of producing a fragrant red rhododendron may be close to impossible to reach.

Sometimes crosses will not produce seeds. This outcome occurs when the two plants selected as parents are too genetically different. For example, an Elepidote × Lepidote rhododendron cross or a deciduous × evergreen azalea cross usually will not produce seed. In addition, polyploids, that is plants bearing two or three times the normal number of 26 chromosomes, are usually incompatible with plants containing 26 chromosomes. In such cases any seed produced is sterile or weak and yields unthrifty or sterile offspring.

THE SEEDLINGS

The genetic purity and potential of the parents in terms of their ability to transmit the genetic characteristics being sought deter-mines how many seedlings need to be grown. Fewer seedlings are needed with inbred lines, such as species, while more are needed with hybrid parents. The greater the heterogeneity of the parents, the greater the variety of possible results. Accordingly, a greater number of seedlings must be grown to increase the likelihood of arriving at the desired characteristic.

The following are guidelines as to the optimal number of seedlings to be grown for various crosses. As the list progresses from number 1 to number 3, the parents are increasingly more hetero-geneous or variable in genetic makeup, so a greater number of seedlings must be grown.

1. Cross between two different species.

    As few as 20 seedlings are adequate if resulting seedlings are to be used as primary hybrid parents in a second cross. The expectation is reaching the goal in the second generation.

2. Cross between a species and a hybrid.

    A minimum of 50 seedlings are needed if the offspring are to be used as intermediate parents to be crossed again as in number 1. If the expectation is to meet the hybridizing goal in this first generation, several hundred seedlings are a minimum.

3. Cross between two hybrids.

    Since both parents are hybrids and more heterogeneous than

species plants, a minimum of 500 seedlings must be grown on for evaluation.

4. Backcrossing.

The number of seedlings required depends upon the number of characteristics one is attempting to recombine in the progeny. When seeking to recombine two characteristics 100 seedlings are probably adequate.

These estimates are offered as ballpark figures only. In practice, the greater the number of seedlings grown, the better the chance of reaching the goals set.

Recognize that the first generation of seedlings rarely produce the desired results and usually present a group of mediocre plants. The uncertain blending of parental characteristics indicates that efforts must usually be carried on to at least a second generation. Desired characteristics in selected parents (especially if carried on recessive genes) are often absent in the first generation yet will appear in future generations, hopefully in the combination desired.

All plants not meeting the hybridizer's goals must be eliminated as soon as it is clear that any of them fall short of the goals. All such roguing needs to be recorded in the record book. Any seedlings selected for growing on should also be recorded.

All hybridizers could use assistance in the selection process since it is impossible to be objective about one's own work. Some suggested evaluation practices include

1. Evaluating any new hybrid over a period of at least ten years.

2. Comparing by planting the seedlings thought to be better in a test garden beside plants widely agreed to be superior.

3. Share the seedlings with other gardeners in different geographic locations for evaluation under different conditions.

4. Introduce and register only plants that prove superior to existing cultivars after these practices have been completed.

There are far too many new rhododendron and azalea cultivars registered each year simply because many hybridizers fail to reach an objective assessment of their work. This assertion is not meant to criticize the registration system. The registrar is after all only doing the job required by the international code—registering the cultivars submitted. The registrar is not expected to judge the garden worthiness of the cultivars submitted. The issue of selection rests with the hybridizer. This can be a difficult position if a hybridizer lacks knowledge of existing cultivars or understands the plant's performance only under limited conditions. It is for these reasons that objective assistance in determining if a new cultivar is worthy of registration and introduction is warranted. Yet there is some advantage in having too many cultivars registered rather than losing a truly great plant when an amateur hybridizer fails to test it adequately before registration.

Superior selections need to be propagated and shared with other growers, first, to make sure they are not lost to cultivation, and second, to test them as widely as possible. Plant sharing is a critical part of the evaluation process, and if the new cultivar is judged to be superior by a widely diverse number of gardeners, registration may be justified.

Registration forms, available from the American Rhododendron Society (ARS), require the registrant to provide considerable detail so that the cultivar can be well identified. Precise measurements of leaf and flower, precise flower color, truss size, and shape, and parentage are among the details requested. Contact a local hybridizer or the ARS for more information.

Hybridizing is not for everyone. It requires considerable patience, the ability to sustain disappointment, a strong back to transplant thousands of seedlings, and some good, honest gardening friends to help maintain the proper perspective and objectivity for evaluating new hybrids. On the other hand, hybridizing does add an additional level of satisfaction to gardening. Even if the amateur hybridizer never registers or introduces a single plant, the enjoyment of the undertaking can make it all worth the effort.

ELEVEN: *The Flower Show*

Rhododendron flower shows are one of the most rewarding activities any ARS Chapter can undertake. Such a show provides members an opportunity to work together and encourages the formation of rewarding relationships within the membership. In addition it is a multifaceted educational undertaking in which *Rhododendron*, in all its diversity, can be presented to gardeners unacquainted with the plants. It broadens the acquaintance of the genus beyond exhibitors and to all ARS members or visitors. It nurtures, by way of training people to be show judges. It provides an opportunity to reach a more profound understanding of the finer points of the species. And lastly, if a plant sale is made part of the event, it can become not only a source of income for the chapter but a community resource for the acquisition of well-adapted plants.

ORGANIZING

A flower show requires considerable work and planning and therefore a significant time commitment by a large number of members. However, when properly organized and conducted, this potentially daunting task can become a satisfying common undertaking leading to an unparalleled closeness among the club members.

Rhododendron flower shows take many forms yet generally can be described as either competitive or noncompetitive. If the objective of the show is to recruit new members or educate the public by acquainting them with a wide range of *Rhododendron* well suited to the local landscape, a noncompetitive show is the wisest choice. If, on the other hand, the show is intended principally for members, a competitive show may be best since committed growers are generally more greatly stimulated by a competitive show. It is, of course, both possible and often desirable to mount a show which combines features of both.

Advantages of each type of show are enumerated below.

The Noncompetitive Show

1. Since there are no winners or losers, there is little potential for injured feelings.

2. Flowers may be arranged in more attractive and diverse ways than that called for by the formal classes required for judging.

3. The need for judges, ribbons, judging regulations, record keeping, and other formalities is eliminated, which makes the show easier to prepare and conduct.

4. The flowers are labeled for educational objectives and grouped in ways better suited for use in the landscape.

5. The public has more interest in landscape use than in competitive judging and formal plant classification.

The Competitive Show

1. The event provides a forceful incentive to improve plant selection and cultivation.

2. If the reasons winning trusses were selected are posted following judging, the show becomes a powerful educational tool.

3. The required formal grouping of plants leads to a clearer understanding of plant classification.

The choice of show type must be made early in the planning stages because the requirements are very different. For example, competitive shows limited to ARS members can be mounted in quite informal settings.

In order to launch a large public show, a chairperson should form committees, each with a head, to perform the following functions.

1. **Site selection.** This committee would be charged with locating and renting a facility suited to the show objectives.

    When a large public show is conducted, including a plant sale and a display garden to be built on site, the location must have good access, visibility, parking facilities, and a substantial display area. Shopping malls are ideal for such a show, if security is available. Schools with a large cafeteria or gymnasium are also excellent as are some large nurseries with covered display areas. The chances for securing any facility are greatly improved if the show committee guarantees the proprietor that provision will be made to prevent dirt and water damage to the facility and that everything related to show activities will be promptly and thoroughly cleaned following the close of the show. These guarantees must be faithfully met, particularly if the chapter ever expects to use that facility or neighboring facilities again.

After the facility is secured, the space must be allocated to the layouts for display purposes, considering ease of moving plants and equipment in and out and ensuring smooth traffic flow both vehicular and pedestrian. Lighting requirements for displaying the true color of flowers and water to maintain plants and flowers must also be considered.

The owners of most facilities require a renter to provide liability insurance to cover any damage to the facility and to protect the owners against any liability arising from injury to any participant or visitor.

2. **Property.** This committee would be responsible for obtaining the tables, containers, entry cards, and other necessary show props.

3. **Publicity.** The responsibilities of this committee are to advertise the events, targeting groups within the public with most possible interest.

4. **Judging.** This committee is responsible for lining up the judges, clerks, and other staff. It also is responsible for providing the materials such as entry forms and class listings to all prospective exhibitors.

5. **Plant sale.** If a plant sale is included, this committee is charged with establishing the rules and conducting the sale. Several matters need to be resolved. Will chapter members only or local nurseries as well be encouraged to sell? What percentage of sales will be given to the sponsoring chapter? Who will handle the sales, provide advice on how to plant and care for plants purchased, and perform other essential duties?

6. **Education.** Since the principal objective of most shows is educational, considerable time needs to be devoted to providing first-class exhibits. The responsibility of the education committee would be to arrange any such exhibits and/or provide take-home materials.

7. **Display.** This committee is responsible for managing all plants and flowers in the display areas set up for educational and decorative purposes. Fig. 128 illustrates some of the displays and flower arrangements at a recent Mason-Dixon Chapter ARS Show held in Westminster, Maryland. It seems

best to undertake the creation of only as many displays as can be done in a first-class manner. A few outstanding exhibits are more effective than numerous poorly mounted ones.

8. **Clean-up.** The condition in which the facility is left following the show will largely determine whether this facility or similar facilities will be available again.

PREPARING TRUSSES FOR JUDGING

The goals of a competitive, judged show are to teach exhibitors how to grow, select, and prepare flower trusses and sprays, and to broaden their understanding of *Rhododendron* classification.

The following observations are offered to assist exhibitors in cultivating and selecting trusses and sprays which will meet the demands of a well judged show. These recommendations reiterate in brief form the cultural practices required to produce a healthy, attractive plant in the landscape as described earlier.

1. Dead-head plants the previous year to assure good flower bud formation.

2. Water as needed to maintain unstressed growth.

3. Fertilize as necessary to produce healthy, green foliage and vigorous growth.

4. Screen the foliage in the winter to prevent wind- and sunburn. Plants growing in the shade produce better foliage and fewer but larger flower trusses. Plants grown in the sun produce a greater number of trusses on compact plants best suited for display plants.

5. Limit insect and disease damage with an adequate prevention program, especially when leaves are young and tender and easily damaged.

For best appearance, trusses or sprays should be selected either the evening before or the morning of the show date. If need be, they may be stored in a refrigerator up to a week and still remain in good condition. Protect from drying if stored in a frost-free refrigerator.

Guidelines for selection are as follows.

1. Identify the truss or spray on which the greatest number of flowers are fully open. One or two unopened flowers are not

counted against the display when judged. Flower buds just opening usually open fully the following day. Reject any truss or spray on which flowers are starting to fade or have developed brown discoloration around the edges.

2. The stem should preferably be straight. It is especially important that a rhododendron truss sit vertically on top of the stem. Such a truss typically develops on a branch at the top of the plant that can grow straight up; side branches seldom produce winning trusses. The stem needs to be cut sufficiently long that it will fit well down in the display container.

    Trusses which have been grown in the shade are often larger because fewer trusses are produced. This reduces competition for nutrients which in turn results in each truss being larger. In addition the foliage on plants grown in shade is usually a darker green. For these reasons a preponderance of winning trusses come from plants grown in shade.

3. Consider the number of buds. Elepidote (large-leaved, non-scaly) trusses should have a single bud as multiple buds are disqualified in most shows. By contrast, multiple bud trusses and sprays are allowed for Lepidote rhododendrons and azaleas.

4. Select a truss uniformly surrounded by dark green leaves having no insect or disease damage. The leaves need to frame the truss evenly. Remove all dirt and other foreign material from the display. Bud scales and any pips or dead flowers should also be removed. Grooming is a must and can make the difference between a blue ribbon and no ribbon at all. Fig. 133 illustrates a winning truss.

5. Azalea or Lepidote rhododendron sprays must conform to show rules governing overall size, usually a maximum of 12–15 in. (30–38 cm) tall and wide. Sprays are most attractive when balanced with good foliage and flowers at their peak of freshness. Faded flowers with brown edges are not acceptable and can usually be removed without damaging the display. Typically sprays bearing a few unopened flowers are at the best stage for display.

6. Deciduous azaleas are usually entered as a single truss, and the same grooming suggestions apply. The foliage may be removed if it obscures the truss. Sometimes the foliage is used to frame it.

7. Some classes in every show have few entries. It may be a good

idea to enter trusses or sprays in these classes, for not only is it easier to win a blue ribbon, but it helps to enlarge the scope of entries.

Care of the display truss after it is severed from the plant and before it is entered in the show is critical. At no time should the flower be exposed to heat or drying conditions, and the stem must be kept in water at all times. Transporting to the show must be done carefully to prevent bruising or crushing the delicate flowers.

SHOW CLASSES AND RULES FOR ENTRY

The following is an example of the show classes and entry rules used by several ARS chapters and is sufficiently inclusive to be used in conducting regional shows. National shows must necessarily provide more classes since a wider variety of species/cultivars are regularly entered.

SHOW CLASSES

Class 1.0: Rhododendron Species
    Section 1.1   Elepidotes (non-scaly series)
    Section 1.2   Lepidotes (scaly series)
Class 2.0: Rhododendron Hybrids—Elepidote
    Section 2.1   White
    Section 2.2   White with prominent blotch
    Section 2.3   Pink, light
    Section 2.4   Pink, deep
    Section 2.5   Pink with prominent blotch
    Section 2.6   Red, scarlet (orange-red)
    Section 2.7   Red, rose-red, or crimson
    Section 2.8   Red, vermilion, or blackish
    Section 2.9   Red with prominent blotch
    Section 2.10   Blue-purple, lavender-blue
    Section 2.11   Blue-purple, strong purple
    Section 2.12   Blue purple, with prominent blotch
    Section 2.13   Yellow, light shades
    Section 2.14   Yellow, deeper shades
    Section 2.15   Yellow-orange, any shade
Class 3.0: Rhododendron Hybrids—Lepidote
    Section 3.1   White
    Section 3.2   Pink
    Section 3.3   Salmon
    Section 3.4   Lavender shades

Class 4.0: New Rhododendron Introductions*
    Section 4.1   Rhododendron species
    Section 4.2   Elepidote hybrids
    Section 4.3   Lepidote hybrids
Class 5.0: Azalea Species
    Section 5.1   Deciduous
    Section 5.2   Evergreen
Class 6.0: Azalea Hybrids—Deciduous
    Section 6.1   White
    Section 6.2   Yellow
    Section 6.3   Orange
    Section 6.4   Pink
    Section 6.5   Red
    Section 6.6   Bicolored or Tricolored
Class 7.0: Azalea Hybrids—Evergreen
    Section 7.1   White, single
    Section 7.2   White, hose-in-hose or double
    Section 7.3   White with colored blotch, stripe, or border
    Section 7.4   Orange-pink, single
    Section 7.5   Orange-pink, hose-in-hose or double
    Section 7.6   Lavender-pink, single
    Section 7.7   Lavender-pink, hose-in-hose or double
    Section 7.8   Rose-red, single
    Section 7.9   Rose-red, hose-in-hose or double
    Section 7.10   Orange-red, single
    Section 7.11   Orange-red, hose-in-hose or double
    Section 7.12   Lavender-purple, single
    Section 7.13   Lavender-purple, hose-in-hose or double
    Section 7.14   Pink, single
    Section 7.15   Pink, hose-in-hose or double
Class 8.0: New Azalea Introductions*
    Section 8.1   Deciduous
    Section 8.2   Evergreen
Class 9.0: Specimen Plants—Azalea or Rhododendron Plants of Any
           Size
    Section 9.1   Plant in bloom
    Section 9.2   Foliage only (interest and quality; may be budded
              or in bloom)

---

*A special award may be given for the best new rhododendron or azalea not previously exhibited, seed grown from ARS seed-exchange.

ENTRY RULES

1. Only members of the American Rhododendron Society may exhibit. No fee.

2. Only one entry per species/cultivar may be made in each section by an entrant. However, any number of different species/cultivars may be entered in a section.

3. Entries must have been grown and wintered outdoors under ordinary garden conditions.

4. Entries must have been in the possession of the exhibitor for at least six months.

5. Lepidote rhododendrons and azalea entries shall be a single stem spray not longer than 15 in. (38 cm) in height or width above the container. Sprays may not be artificially constrained in any way.

6. Elepidote rhododendron and deciduous azalea entries shall be a single truss from a single bud which need not be fully open.

7. A sweepstakes award shall be made to the exhibitor with the most cumulative points determined as follows:

Best Azalea in Show	8 points
Best Rhododendron in Show	8 points
Best in a Class	5 points
Blue Ribbon in a Section	3 points
Red Ribbon in a Section	2 points
White Ribbon in a Section	1 point
Special Award	5 points

8. All exhibits must be received between 9 and 11:30 a.m. on the day of the show. Late entries will not be judged. Classification and placement will be made by the judging committee.

9. Judging will start at 12:00 p.m. No exhibitors may be present during judging. All judges' decisions are final.

10. Weekend shows will open to the public from 3:00 until 5:00 p.m. on Saturday and from 10:00 a.m. to 3:30 p.m. Sunday. Exhibits and ribbons may be claimed after the awards and business meeting Sunday afternoon. Those exhibits not claimed will be destroyed.

Fig. 128.   Trusses being assembled for a competitive show. Photo by Helen Myers.

Fig. 129.   Trusses displayed for judging, Portland, Oregon, ARS Chapter, 1983. Photo by William Bedwell.

Fig. 130. Prize winning trusses, Portland, Oregon, ARS Chapter Show, 1987. Photo by William Bedwell.

Fig. 131. Display of plants for sale, Mason-Dixon ARS Chapter Show, 1987. Photo by Helen Myers.

Fig. 132. Commercial display garden, Eugene, Oregon. Photo by George Ring.

Fig. 133. A winning truss in a New England show, 1990. Note balance and over-all quality of flower and foliage. Photo by Helen Myers.

Fig. 134. Prospective winning azalea spray. Photo by William Bedwell.

Judging must be as objective as possible, employing rules established before the show. There is no room for personal preferences; only the quality and typical form for the species/cultivar being judged are valid considerations.

A truss or spray must be judged as it is seen on the day of judging. Thus a truss on which half the buds are unopened cannot be evaluated in terms of how it will look in a few days. Conversely, a truss with brown edges on flowers or dropped flowers cannot be judged on how it might have looked yesterday.

Points to consider in judging rhododendron and deciduous azalea trusses include

1. Truss is held upright on a straight stem.
2. Truss is framed by a uniform rosette of leaves.
3. Truss is fresh with no damaged flowers or missing pips. (Most judges prefer tight over loose trusses.)
4. Truss is typical of the size or larger for the species/cultivar.
5. Foliage is a healthy color and free of insect and disease damage.
6. Foliage does not obscure the floral display.
7. Truss is clean and properly groomed.
8. No more than two or three unopened buds are present in the truss.

Points to consider in judging an azalea or Lepidote rhododendron spray include

1. Spray is no larger than 15 in. (38 cm) wide or tall.
2. Shape is pleasing to the eye. Spray may be centered on the stem and balanced or may drift to one side.
3. Foliage is a healthy color and free of insect and disease damage.
4. Spray is clean and properly groomed.
5. Flowers are fresh, clean, and undamaged.

To make judging more objective, it is best to use a point system based on numeric values assigned to each judging consideration listed above.

Members can be encouraged to take a leisurely walk through the exhibits after judging, observing which trusses won ribbons and relating winners to non-winners. Such an exercise is a valuable lesson in what to look for in growing winning trusses. An even better way to learn is by revolving the job of clerk among the members. The clerk's duties are to record show results, providing first-hand experience with winning entries.

Immediately after the show's closing, the chairperson and committee heads need to meet to evaluate the show and determine if show objectives were met. This evaluation should be written up by one of the organizers and reviewed with the entire membership at the earliest possible date.

Feedback from the public as well as members is necessary to accurately assess the need for future changes. One way to obtain public feedback is by distributing survey sheets to all show visitors. Forms could be collected immediately or could be mailed in after completion. The chairperson would be in charge of collecting, reviewing, and sharing these results with members.

All summary evaluations need to be subsequently discussed with the entire membership. This provides a learning experience as well as a foundation for the development of future shows. Such sharing can also encourage member participation in following years.

Show development can be an ongoing process for an ARS chapter. If a positive yet sensitive orientation is maintained, the show will consistently improve and prove more effective each year. This progress will in turn lead to greater community awareness and encourage a larger fraction of the community to improve the appearance of the gardens through familiarity with *Rhododendron*.

APPENDIX A: *Good Doer Tables*

The following tables outline detailed information for all Good Doer rhododendrons/azaleas mentioned in Chapter Three. The tables divide plants into eight groups:

Table 1. Rhododendron Species—Elepidote
Table 2. Rhododendron Species—Lepidote
Table 3. Rhododendron Hybrids—Elepidote
Table 4. Rhododendron Hybrids—Lepidote
Table 5. Evergreen Azalea Species
Table 6. Evergreen Azalea Hybrids
Table 7. Deciduous Azalea Species
Table 8. Deciduous Azalea Hybrids

Information is presented under the following headings.

NAME is the registered name for the particular species/cultivar.

U.S.D.A. HARDINESS ZONES refers to the zone or zones to which the plant is adapted. This is a general guide, and the plant may not be adapted to all specific microclimates within that zone. Both cold and heat limits are provided for azaleas. Hardiness zone data for deciduous azalea hybrids is given by hybrid group. All Knap Hill Hybrids, for example, are cold hardy to Zone 5a and heat tolerant to 8a unless otherwise indicated. The Mollis Hybrids as a group are more heat tolerant than the Knap Hill Hybrids.

Only cold hardiness data is presented for rhododendrons. Also mentioned in this column, for rhododendrons, for those plants for which data is available, is the lowest temperature tolerable to flower buds. Plant foliage is usually more cold hardy than flower buds. Cold and heat tolerance data is not absolute, yet can be valuable as a guide.

HEIGHT IN 10 YEARS is the height the plant, grown under favorable conditions in the landscape, will be after 10 years. In some cases mature height is given instead and is so indicated. Some species, due to natural variation, will diverge somewhat from the measurement given.

QUALITY RATING refers to the numerical rating assigned by judges using the American Rhododendron Society rating system—1 being lowest and 5 highest. The first number is an evaluation of the flower and the second the plant. A plant evaluated 5/3 has an excellent flower on an average plant. In some cases a third number rates plant performance in the landscape. Not all species/cultivars have been evaluated, so quality ratings are not always available.

FLOWER COLOR is given in general color terms such as *pink, red,* or *white* with no reference to a color chart.

FLOWERING SEASON is presented as very early (VE), early (E), midseason (M), late midseason (LM), late season (L), and very late (VL). The designations are relative; no specific dates are given since weather conditions, primarily temperature, vary from place to place and year to year, which in turn advances or delays time of flowering.

COMMENTS include miscellaneous information which may assist in the selection process.

Table 1. Rhododendron Species—Elepidote

NAME	U.S.D.A. HARDINESS ZONES	HEIGHT IN 10 YEARS	QUALITY RATING	FLOWER COLOR	FLOWERING SEASON	COMMENTS
R. aberconwayi	7a 0°F (−18°C)	3 ft. (0.9 m)	4/3/3	white	EM	open, upright growth habit
R. adendopodum	6a −10°F (−23°C)	5 ft. (1.5 m)	3–4/4/3	rose	EM–M	large, long, narrow leaf, fawn-colored indumentum
R. arboreum	7b 5°F (−15°C)	6 ft. (1.8 m)	3/4/3	red	E	name means treelike; white indumentum under leaves
R. argyrophylum	7a 0°F (−18°C)	5 ft (1.5 m)	3/5/3	white	EM	long, narrow leaf, white underside
R. brachycarpum	6a −10°F (−23°C)	3 ft. (0.9 m)	3/4–4/2–3	white	VL	pale indumentum on underside of leaf
R. bureavii	6a −10°F (−23°C)	4 ft. (1.2 m)	3/5/3	white	M	beautiful foliage; needs excellent drainage
R. calophytum	5b −15°F (−26°C)	5 ft. (1.5 m)	4/4/3	pink	E	very beautiful plant and flower
R. campanulatum	6b −5°F (−21°C)	4 ft. (1.2 m)	3/5	lilac to white	EM	superior foliage, cinnamon indumentum on underside of leaf
R. campylocarpum	7a 0°F (−18°C)	4 ft. (1.2 m)	3–4/4/3	pale yellow	EM	round leaf shape
R. catawbiense	4b −25°F (−32°C)	6 ft. (1.8 m)	2/2/4	lilac to pink	ML	widely adapted plant
R. catawbiense alba	4b −25°F (−32°C)	6 ft. (1.8 m)	2/3/4	white	ML	a white form of the species
R. decorum	7a 0°F (−18°C)	5 ft. (1.5 m)	4/3/4	white to pink	EM	compact grower; fragrant flowers
R. degronianum	6b −5°F (−21°C)	3 ft. (0.9 m)	3–4/3–4/3–4	pink	EM	compact grower; reddish indumentum
R. dichroanthum ssp. *scyphocalyx*	6b −5°F (−21°C)	4 ft. (1.2 m)	3/3/3	orange	ML	open, spreading growth habit

Table 1. Rhododendron Species—Elepidote (continued)

NAME	U.S.D.A. HARDINESS ZONES	HEIGHT IN 10 YEARS	QUALITY RATING	FLOWER COLOR	FLOWERING SEASON	COMMENTS
R. fargesii	6a −10°F (−23°C)	5 ft. (1.5 m)	3/3/3	white to pink	E	heavy bloomer; open, upright growth habit
R. fictolacteum	6b −5°F (−21°C)	5 ft. (1.3 m)	3/4/3	white	EM	upright grower; large leaf, brown indumentum on underside of leaf
R. fortunei	5b −15°F (−26°C)	6 ft. (1.8 m)	4/4/4–5	pink to white	EM	treelike growth habit, beautiful, fragrant flowers
R. haematodes	6b −5°F (−21°C)	3 ft. (0.9 m)	3–4/4–5/4	crimson	EM	compact, excellent shrub; brown indumentum
R. houlstonii	6b −5°F (−21°C)	5 ft. (1.5 m)	2–3/3/3	pink	M	upright, open growth habit, to 20 ft. (6 m)
R. hyperythrum (Creech's Narrowleaf Form)	5b −15°F (−26°C)	3 ft. (0.9 m)	3/4/3–4	white	EM	long, narrow leaf
R. makinoi	6a −10°F (−23°C)	3 ft. (0.9 m)	3–4/4/2–3	light pink	ML	excellent foliage; long, narrow leaf; indumentum on underside of leaf
R. maximum	4b −25°F (−32°C)	5 ft. (1.5 m)	2/3/3–4	white	L–VL	large, open, upright growth habit
R. metternichii	5b −15°F (−26°C)	3 ft. (0.9 m)	4/4/3	light pink	EM	compact, rounded growth habit; light indumentum on underside of leaf
R. morii	6a −10°F (−23°C)	4 ft. (1.2 m)	3–4/4/3	white	EM	upright, open growth habit; bell-shaped flowers
R. orbiculare	7b 5°F (−15°C)	3 ft. (0.9 m)	3/4/3	rose	EM	compact, well shaped plant
R. oreodoxa	6b −5°F (−21°C)	5 ft. (1.5m)	2–3/2–3/3	pink	E	open, upright growth habit
R. ovatum	7b 5°F (−15°C)	3 ft. (0.9 m)	3/3/3	white to pink or purple	ML	dense growth habit; new growth red

Table 1. Rhododendron Species—Elepidote (continued)

NAME	U.S.D.A. HARDINESS ZONES	HEIGHT IN 10 YEARS	QUALITY RATING	FLOWER COLOR	FLOWERING SEASON	COMMENTS
R. pachysanthum	6b –5°F (–21°C)	2.5 ft. (0.75 m)	3–4/5/3–4	light pink	EM	beautiful foliage plant; indumentum on underside of leaf
R. ponticum	5b –15°F (–26°C)	4 ft. (1.2 m)	2–4/4/4–5	purple to white	L	open, upright growth habit; excellent foliage
R. pseudochry-santhum (Nelson's Form)	6a –10°F (–23°C)	2 ft. (0.6 m)	3/4–5/4–5	pink	EM	compact grower; several forms available
R. rex ssp. rex	7b 5°F (–15°C)	6 ft. (1.8 m)	3/4/3–4	pink or white	EM	large leaves with brown indumentum on the underside
R. roxieanum	6a –10°F (–23°C)	3 ft. (0.9 m)	3/5/4	white	EM	compact growth habit; heavy, cinnamon indumentum on underside
R. smirnowii	5b –15°F (–26°C)	3 ft. (0.9 m)	3/3–4/2–3	rose-purple	ML	open growth habit; beautiful tomentum and indumentum on leaf
R. smithii	6b –5°F (–21°C)	4 ft. (1.2 m)	4/4/3	red	E	good plant habit; white indumentum on underside of leaf
R. souliei	7b 5°F (–15°C)	5 ft. (1.5 m)	4/3/3	cream or pink	M	compact, upright growth habit
R. sutchuenense	6a –10°F (–23°C)	5 ft. (1.5 m)	4/3/3	lilac to rose	VE	open, upright growth habit
R. thomsonii	7b 5°F (–15°C)	5 ft. (1.5 m)	3/2–4/3–4	blood red	EM	open, upright growth habit
R. uvariifolium	7b 5°F (–15°C)	4 ft. (1.2 m)	3/3–4/3	white	E	treelike growth habit; silvery young growth
R. vernicosum	5b –15°F (–26°C)	5 ft. (1.5 m)	2–3/2–3/3	pink	E–M	upright growth habit; 'Vernicosum 18139' is a good selection
R. wardii	7a 0°F (–18°C)	4 ft. (1.2 m)	4/3–4/3–4	yellow	M	open, growth habit; difficult to grow in some areas

Table 1. Rhododendron Species—Elepidote (continued)

NAME	U.S.D.A. HARDINESS ZONES	HEIGHT IN 10 YEARS	QUALITY RATING	FLOWER COLOR	FLOWERING SEASON	COMMENTS
R. williamsianum	6b −5°F (−21°C)	1.5 ft. (0.45 m)	3/4/4	pink	EM	compact growth habit; very lovely plant
R. yakushimanum	4b −25°F (−32°C)	1–4 ft. (0.3–1.2 m)	5/5/4	pink to white	EM	excellent growth habit; indumentum on underside of leaf
R. yakushimanum Ken Janeck	5a −20°F (−29°C)	2 ft. (0.6 m)	5/4	pink to white	EM	selected, superior clone of R. yakushimanum
R. yakushimanum Pink Parasol	5a −20°F (−29°C)	2 ft. (0.6 m)	5/5	pink to white	EM	selected, superior clone of R. yakushimanum
R. zeylanicum	7b–8a 10°F (−12°C)	5 ft. (1.5 m)	3/3/3	red and pink	EM	open, growth habit; excellent foliage

Table 2. Rhododendron Species—Lepidote

NAME	U.S.D.A. HARDINESS ZONES	HEIGHT IN 10 YEARS	QUALITY RATING	FLOWER COLOR	FLOWERING SEASON	COMMENTS
R. augustinii	5b −15°F (−26°C)	4 ft. (1.2 m)	4/3/3–4	purple or lavender	M	compact growth habit; long, narrow leaf
R. burmanicum	8b 15°F (−9°C)	4 ft. (1.2 m)	4/3/4	yellow	EM	open, upright growth habit; fragrant flowers
R. carolinianum	4b −25°F (−32°C)	4 ft. (1.2 m)	3/3/2–3	rose, pink, or white	M	many-branched plant; sun tolerant
R. chapmanii	6b −5°F (−21°C)	4 ft. (1.2 m)	3/3/2–3	pink	EM	rounded growth habit; heat tolerant
R. ciliatum	7b 5°F (−15°C)	3 ft. (0.9 m)	4/4/3–4	white and pink	EM	cinnamon-colored bark
R. cinnabarium	7b 5°F (−15°C)	5 ft. (1.5 m)	4/4/2–3	pink, red, or yellow	EM–VL	aromatic foliage
R. concatenans	7b 5°F (−15°C)	3 ft. (0.9 m)	3/4–5/2–3	yellow	EM	excellent foliage plant

Table 2. Rhododendron Species—Lepidote (continued)

NAME	U.S.D.A. HARDINESS ZONES	HEIGHT IN 10 YEARS	QUALITY RATING	FLOWER COLOR	FLOWERING SEASON	COMMENTS
R. dauricum	4b −25°F (−32°C)	4 ft. (1.2 m)	4/3/3	rose, purple, or white	VE	upright growth habit; also white form (album)
R. fastigiatum	5b −15°F (−26°C)	1.5 ft. (0.45 m)	4/4/3–4	purple	M	a large number of forms, some of which are excellent
R. ferrugineum	5b −15°F (−26°C)	2 ft. (0.6 m)	3/4/3	rose, pink, or white	M	requires excellent drainage; very attractive foliage
R. glomerulatum	5b −15°F (−26°C)	3 ft. (0.9 m)	4/4/3	lilac	EM	very small leaves and flowers
R. hanceanum	7a 0°F (−18°C)	1 ft. (0.3 m)	3–4/4/4	cream	EM	open, upright growth habit
R. hippophaeoides	4b −25°F (−32°C)	3 ft. (0.9 m)	4/2–3/4	lavender-blue	E	best of the blues; tolerates sun
R. impeditum	5b −15°F (−26°C)	1 ft. (0.3 m)	4/4/3–4	purple	EM	compact growth habit; good ground cover
R. johnstoneanum	8b 15°F (−10°C)	4–12 ft. (1.2–3.7 m)		yellow to white	E–L	varies widely in bloom date
R. keiskei	6a −10°F (−23°C)	1–5 ft. (0.3–1.5 m)	4/3–4/4	yellow	EM	many forms, from the dwarf 'Yaku Fairy' to tall forms
R. keleticum	5b −15°F (−26°C)	1 ft. (0.3 m)	4/4/4	purplish crimson	M	semiprostrate growth habit; good bonsai plant
R. lapponicum	4b −25°F (−32°C)	1.5 ft. (0.45 m)		purple	E–EM	dwarf growth habit
R. leucaspis	7b 5°F (−15°C)	2 ft. (0.6 m)	3–4/3–4/3	white	E	upright, open growth habit; chocolate brown anthers
R. litangense	5b −15°F (−25°C)	.5 ft. (0.2 m)	3/4/3–4	purple	EM	low-growing ground cover; considered the same as R. impeditum
R. lutescens	7b 5°F (−15°C)	6 ft. (1.8 m)	4/3/3–4	yellow	EM	upright, open growth habit; new growth red

Table 2. Rhododendron Species—Lepidote (continued)

NAME	U.S.D.A. HARDINESS ZONES	HEIGHT IN 10 YEARS	QUALITY RATING	FLOWER COLOR	FLOWERING SEASON	COMMENTS
R. micranthum	6b −5°F (−21°C)	4 ft. (1.2 m)	3/2–3/3	white	ML–L	unusual growth habit resembling *Spiraea*
R. minus	5b −15°F (−26°C)	4 ft. (1.2 m)	2–3/2/2–3	white or pink	M–L	varies widely in growth habit
R. moupinense	7a 0°F (−18°C)	2 ft. (0.6 m)	4/3/3	white	VE	open growth habit; new growth is bronze-red
R. mucronulatum	5b −15°F (−26°C)	5 ft. (1.5 m)	3–4/3/3	pink to rose-purple	VE	upright growth habit; deciduous in cold areas
R. mucronulatum Cornell Pink	5b −15°F (−26°C)	5 ft. (1.5 m)	3/3	clear pink	VE	open, upright grower; deciduous
R. oreotrephes	7a 0°F (−18°C)	5 ft. (1.5 m)	3/4/4	pink to lavender	EM	upright, tight grower; variable species
R. racemosum	6b −5°F (−21°C)	2–5 ft. (0.6–1.5 m)	4/3/4–5	rose or white	E–EM	upright, open growth habit; best in sun; variable in size
R. rubiginosum	7a 0°F (−18°C)	6 ft. (1.8 m)	3/2–3/3–4	pink or rose	EM	open, upright growth habit; purplish new growth
R. russatum	5b −15°F (−21°C)	3 ft. (0.9 m)	4/3/4	purple, blue, or pink	EM	open, upright growth habit; variable in form
R. sargentianum Maricee	6b −5°F (−21°C)	2 ft. (0.6 m)	4/3/2	white	M	easier, faster growing selection of *R. sargentianum*
R. veitchianum	8a 20°F (−7°C)	4 ft. (1.2 m)	4/3/3	white	M–L	compact growth habit; fragrant flowers
R. viscosum	5b −15°F (−26°C)	5 ft. (1.5 m)	3/3/3–4	white	VL	upright, spreading growth habit; deciduous
R. yungningense	5b −15°F (−26°C)	2 ft. (0.6 m)	3/3/4	purple	EM	open, upright growth habit; tiny leaf, scaly both sides
R. yunnanense	7a 0°F (−18°C)	6 ft. (1.8 m)	4/2–3/3–4	white to pink	EM–M	open, upright growth habit; extremely variable

Table 3. Rhododendron Hybrids—Elepidote

NAME	U.S.D.A. HARDINESS ZONES	HEIGHT IN 10 YEARS	QUALITY RATING	FLOWER COLOR	FLOWERING SEASON	COMMENTS
'A. Bedford'	6b −5°F (−21°C)	6 ft. (1.8 m)	4/3/5	mauve to lavender	ML	upright growth habit; sun tolerant
'Accomplishment'	6a −10°F (−23°C)	5 ft. (1.5 m)	3–4/3–4	rose	M	good foliage plant; Dexter Hybrid
'Albert Close'	6a −10°F (−23°C)	5 ft. (1.5 m)	3/2/3	rose	L	open growth habit; sun and heat tolerant
'Album Elegans'	5a −20°F (−29°C)	6 ft. (1.8 m)	2/2–3/4	white	L	open growth habit; good foliage
'Alice'	6b −5°F (−21°C)	6 ft. (1.8 m)	4/3–4/4–5	pink	M	upright growth habit; easy to grow; sun tolerant
'America'	5a −20°F (−29°C)	5 ft. (1.5 m)	3/2–3/3–4	red	ML	better plant habit in full sun
'Anah Kruschke'	5b −15°F (−26°C)	6 ft. (1.8 m)	3–4/4/4	lavender	ML–L	compact growth habit; does well in full sun
'Anna H. Hall'	4a −25°F (−32°C)	3 ft. (0.9 m)	3/3/4	white	M	semi-dwarf; good foliage
'Anna Rose Whitney'	6b −5°F (−21°C)	6 ft. (1.8 m)	4/3/5	pink	ML	vigorous, upright grower; well shaped plant
'Antoon van Welie'	6b −5°F (−21°C)	6 ft. (1.8 m)	4/3–4/4	deep pink	ML	vigorous grower; attractive plant
'Apple Blossom'	6a −10°F (−23°C)	5 ft. (1.5 m)	N/A	pink	EM	floriferous; syns. 'Sandwich Apple Blossom', 'Dexter's Pink'
'Atroflo'	6b −5°F (−21°C)	5 ft. (1.5 m)	3/3–4/4	bright rose	M	fawn colored indumentum on underside of leaf
'Autumn Gold'	6b −5°F (−21°C)	5 ft. (1.5 m)	3–4/3–4/4	salmon	ML	tolerates heat
'Baden Baden'	5b −15°F (−26°C)	2 ft. (0.6 m)	3–4/4/3–4	red	M	low growth habit; good foliage
'Bali'	5a −20°F (−29°C)	6 ft. (1.8 m)	4/4	soft pink	ML	excellent growth habit

Table 3. Rhododendron Hybrids—Elepidote (continued)

NAME	U.S.D.A. HARDINESS ZONES	HEIGHT IN 10 YEARS	QUALITY RATING	FLOWER COLOR	FLOWERING SEASON	COMMENTS
'Bass River'	6a −10°F (−23°C)	5 ft. (1.5 m)		pink	LM	glossy foliage; floriferous
'Beaufort'	5a −20°F (−29°C)	5 ft. (1.5 m)	2–3/3–4/3	white	M	compact growth habit
'Beauty of Littleworth'	6b −5°F (−21°C)	6 ft. (1.8 m)	4/3	pink	M	vigorous, upright growth habit; large flowers
'Belle Heller'	6a −10°F (−23°C)	5 ft. (1.5 m)	4/3	white	M	good foliage plant; sun tolerant; sometimes flowers in the fall
'Ben Mosely'	5b −15°F (−26°C)	5 ft. (1.5 m)		purplish pink	ML	*R. fortunei* hybrid
'Besse Howells'	5b −15°F (−26°C)	3 ft. (0.9 m)	3–4/3–4/4	wine red	EM	compact, low growing plant; frilled flowers
'Blue Ensign'	5b −15°F (−26°C)	4 ft. (1.2 m)	4/3/4	lilac-blue	M	well shaped plant; sun tolerant
'Blue Peter'	6a −10°F (−23°C)	5 ft. (1.5 m)	4/2–3/4	lavender-blue	M	spreading growth habit; heat and sun tolerant
'Bonnie Maid'	6a −10°F (−23°C)	5 ft. (1.5 m)		pink	M	saucer-shaped flowers
'Bosley-Dexter 1009'	4a −25°F (−32°C)	7 ft. (2.1 m)	3/3	pink	M	a very hardy Dexter Hybrid selection
'Boule de Neige'	4a −25°F (−32°C)	5 ft. (1.5 m)	4/4/3	white	M	well shaped plant; heat and sun tolerant
'Bow Bells'	6b −5°F (−21°C)	3 ft. (0.9 m)	3/4/3	pink	EM	mound-shaped plant; needs afternoon shade
'Bravo'	5b −15°F (−26°C)	5 ft. (1.5 m)		purplish pink	ML	compact growth habit
'Britannia'	6b −5°F (−21°C)	4 ft. (1.2 m)	4/3–4/3	scarlet	ML	First Class Certificate 1937, Royal Horticultural Society; large pendulous leaf

Table 3. Rhododendron Hybrids—Elepidote (continued)

NAME	U.S.D.A. HARDINESS ZONES	HEIGHT IN 10 YEARS	QUALITY RATING	FLOWER COLOR	FLOWERING SEASON	COMMENTS
'Broughtonii Aureum'	6b −5°F (−21°C)	4 ft. (1.2 m)	3–4/2/4	yellow	ML	yellow azaleadron, sun and heat tolerant
'Brown Eyes'	5b −15°F (−26°C)	6 ft. (1.8 m)		pink	ML	prominent brown blotch in flowers
'Buttermint'	6b −5°F (−21°C)	3 ft. (0.9 m)	3–4/4/4	yellow	M	dense growing; thick leathery leaf; large flowers
'Cadis'	5b −15°F (−26°C)	5 ft. (1.5 m)	3/4/5	pink	ML	Award of Excellence, 1959; fragrant flowers
'Calsap'	4a −25°F (−32°C)	5 ft. (1.5 m)		white	L	dark purple blotch like 'Sappho' but a better plant habit
'Carita'	7a 0°F (−18°C)	5 ft. (1.5 m)	4/4	primrose yellow	M	Award of Merit 1945, Royal Horticultural Society
'Carmen'	6b −5°F (−21°C)	1 ft. (0.3 m)	4/5/4	dark red	EM	very attractive plant
'Caroline'	5b −15°F (−26°C)	6 ft. (1.8 m)	3/4/4	orchid	ML	compact growth habit; easy to grow; fragrant flowers
'Catawbiense Album'	4a −25°F (−32°C)	6 ft. (1.8 m)	3/3/4	white	ML–L	very vigorous and extremely cold hardy
'Catawbiense Boursault'	5a −20°F (−29°C)	6 ft. (1.8 m)	2/3	rose-lilac	ML–L	selection of *R. catawbiense*
'Champayne'	--	--	--	creamy apricot	--	medium to tall grower, wider than tall
'Chesterland'	4a −25°F (−32°C)	6 ft. (1.8 m)		pink	E	
'Chionoides'	6a −10°F (−23°C)	4 ft. (1.2 m)	3/4/4	white	ML	compact growth habit; tolerates sun and cold
'Christmas Cheer'	6a −10°F (−23°C)	4 ft. (1.2 m)	3/4/4	pink	VE–E	well shaped plant; tight growth habit
'County of York'	5b −15°F (−26°C)	6 ft. (1.8 m)	3–4/3/4–5	white	M	vigorous growth habit; large leaves, especially in shade

Table 3. Rhododendron Hybrids—Elepidote (continued)

NAME	U.S.D.A. HARDINESS ZONES	HEIGHT IN 10 YEARS	QUALITY RATING	FLOWER COLOR	FLOWERING SEASON	COMMENTS
'Crest' ('Hawk Crest')	6b −5°F (−21°C)	6 ft. (1.8 m)	4–5/3/3	yellow	M	open growth habit, exposing limbs as the plan gets older
'Cynthia'	5b −15°F (−26°C)	6 ft. (1.8 m)	4/3/4	rose	M	tall growing plan excellent grower; sun and heat tolerant
'Damaris'	7a 0°F (−18°C)	4 ft. (1.2 m)	4/3/3	yellow	M	
'Damozel'	7a 0°F (−18°C)	6 ft. (1.8 m)	4/2/4–5	red	ML	open, spreading growth habit; eas to grow
'David Gable'	5b −15°F (−26°C)	5 ft. (1.5 m)	4/4/3–4	pink	EM–M	large flowers wit strawberry throa good growth hab
'Dexter 974'	5b −15°F (−26°C)	5 ft. (1.5 m)	4/4	deep pink	ML	outstanding plan dependable bloomer
'Dexter's Pink': *see* 'Apple Blossom'						
'Disca'	6a −10°F (−23°C)	6 ft. (1.8 m)	3/3/4	white	ML	compact growth habit; fragrant; best grown in afternoon shade
'Dr. Edward Lufton'	5b −15°F (−26°C)	4 ft. (1.2 m)	--	white	M	excellent foliage; indumentum on underside of lea Pride Hybrid
'Dr. H. C. Dresselhuys'	5b −15°F (−26°C)	6 ft. (1.8 m)	2/3	aniline red	M	upright growth habit; scant foliag
'Edith Pride'	4a −25°F (−32°C)	5 ft. (1.5 m)	2/4	pink	ML	well-branched plant; leaves hol 3 years
'Elizabeth'	5a −20°F (−29°C)	3 ft. (0.9 m)	3–4/4/5	red	EM	outstanding plan Award of Merit, First Class Certificate, ARS
'Elizabeth Hobbie'	6b −5°F (−21°C)	2.5 ft. (0.75 m)	4/4–5/3	scarlet	EM	very compact an heavily foliaged plant
'English Roseum'	4a −25°F (−32°C)	6 ft. (1.8 m)	2–3/3/3–4	rose	ML	compact plant habit; easy to gro under most conditions

able 3. Rhododendron Hybrids—Elepidote (continued)

AME	U.S.D.A. HARDINESS ZONES	HEIGHT IN 10 YEARS	QUALITY RATING	FLOWER COLOR	FLOWERING SEASON	COMMENTS
verestianum'	5b −15°F (−26°C)	6 ft. (1.8 m)	2/3	lilac	ML	vigorous, full plant habit; widely adapted
aggetter's Favorite'	6b −5°F (−21°C)	6 ft. (1.8 m)	5/4/3	white and pink	M	outstanding plant
astuosum Flore Pleno'	5b −15°F (−26°C)	6 ft. (1.8 m)	3/3	lavender blue	ML	semidouble flowers; sun tolerant
rancesca'	6a −10°F (−23°C)	6 ft. (1.8 m)	--	deep red	ML	open growth habit
i Gi'	6b −5°F (−21°C)	5 ft. (1.5 m)	4/3	rose red	ML	compact growth habit; red spotting on flowers
ladys'	7a 0°F (−18°C)	6 ft. (1.8m)	3/3	cream	EM	tall, open plant; syns. 'Gladys Rose', 'Mary Swathling'
lenda Farrell'	6b −5°F (−21°C)	5 ft. (1.5 m)	--	red	EM	compact growth habit; *R. fortunei* hybrid
olden Gala'	5a −20°F (−29°C)	2.5 ft. (0.75 m)	--	ivory	ML	well branched, attractive plant
olden Star'	7a −5°F (−18°C)	5 ft. (1.5 m)	4/3–4/3–4	deep yellow	ML	
oldsworth Orange'	6b −5°F (−21°C)	5 ft. (1.5 m)	3/2	pale orange	L	open, spreading plant; heat tolerant
olfer'	5b −15°F (−26°C)	1 ft. (0.25 m)	--	pink	M	twice as wide as high; good indumentum on underside of leaf
omer Waterer'	5b −15°F (−26°C)	6 ft. (1.8 m)	3/4–5/4–5	white	ML	good foliage plant; sun tolerant
race Seabrook'	6b −5°F (−21°C)	4 ft. (1.2 m)	4–5/4/4	red	E–EM	excellent foliage; good plant habit
reat Eastern'	5b −15°F (−26°C)	5 ft. (1.5 m)	--	pink	ML	free flowering *R. fortunei* hybrid; fragrant
rierosplendour'	6b −5°F (−21°C)	4 ft. (1.2 m)	3/3/4	reddish purple	ML	upright grower when young, spreads as it gets older

Table 3. Rhododendron Hybrids—Elepidote (continued)

NAME	U.S.D.A. HARDINESS ZONES	HEIGHT IN 10 YEARS	QUALITY RATING	FLOWER COLOR	FLOWERING SEASON	COMMENTS
'Halfdan Lem'	6b −5°F (−21°C)	5 ft. (1.5 m)	4–5/4/4–5	red	M	fast grower; good plant habit
'Hallelujah'	5b −15°F (−26°C)	4 ft. (1.2 m)	4–5/5/4–5	rose red	M	excellent foliage; compact growth habit
'Helene Schiffner'	6b −5°F (−21°C)	4 ft. (1.2 m)	4/4/3–4	white	M	plant heavily clothed with narrow leaves and red stems
'Hello Dolly'	6a −10°F (−23°C)	3 ft. (0.9 m)	3–4/3/3–4	yellow and orange	EM	well branched plant; light indumentum on underside of leaf
'Holden'	7a 0°F (−18°C)	4 ft. (1.2 m)	3/3–4/4	rose red	EM–M	compact growth habit; excellent foliage
'Humming Bird'	7a 0°F (−18°C)	2.5 ft. (0.75 m)	3/4/3–4	red	EM	compact growth habit; attractive foliage
'Ice Cube'	5a −20°F (−29°C)	5 ft. (1.5 m)	4/3/4	white	ML	good growth habit; reliable and an easy grower
'Jan Dekens'	6b −5°F (−21°C)	5 ft. (1.5 m)	3–4/3–4/3	bright pink	ML	vigorous grower; frilled flowers
'Janet Blair'	5b −15°F (−26°C)	6 ft. (1.8 m)	4/3/4	light pink	ML	excellent growth habit; easy to grow, widely adapted
'Jean Marie de Montague'	6b −5°F (−21°C)	5 ft. (1.5 m)	4/4/4	bright red	M	good foliage plant; sun tolerant
'Jonathan Shaw'	6a −10°F (−23°C)	3 ft. (0.9m)	4/4	purple	M	hybridized by Jonathan Leonard of Briarwood Nursery
'Joseph Paterno'	3b −35°F (−37°C)	4 ft. (1.2 m)	--	white	LM	compact growth habit; extremely cold hardy
'Kate Waterer'	6a −10°F (−23°C)	5 ft. (1.5 m)	2/3/3	pink	ML	compact upright grower; bright yellow eye in flowers
'Lee's Dark Purple'	5b −15°F (−26°C)	6 ft. (1.8 m)	2–3/3–4/4	purple	ML	outstanding foliage plant; reliable grower

Table 3. Rhododendron Hybrids—Elepidote (continued)

NAME	U.S.D.A. HARDINESS ZONES	HEIGHT IN 10 YEARS	QUALITY RATING	FLOWER COLOR	FLOWERING SEASON	COMMENTS
Lem's Cameo'	7b 5°F (–15°C)	5 ft. (1.5 m)	5/3/3	apricot	M	outstanding foliage; Superior Plant Award 1971
Lem's Monarch'	6b –5°F (–21°C)	6 ft. (1.8m)	4/4/4	pink	M	outstanding flower truss
Loder's White'	7a 0°F (–18°C)	5 ft. (1.5 m)	4/3–4/3–4	white	M	large, upright truss; Award of Merit, Award of Garden Merit, ARS
Lodestar'	5a –20°F (–29°C)	5 ft. (1.5 m)	3/3/4	white	ML	large, vigorous grower; flower buds open pale lilac
Madame Masson'	5b –15°F (–26°C)	5 ft. (1.5 m)	3/3/4	white	M	large growing, well shaped plant; golden eye in flowers
Marcia'	7a 0°F (–18°C)	4 ft. (1.2 m)	4/3/2	yellow	M	slow, upright grower; needs afternoon shade
Markeeta's Flame'	6b –5°F (–21°C)	5 ft. (1.5 m)	4/4/4	rose red	M	vigorous grower, good plant form; red leaf stems
Markeeta's Prize'	6b –5°F (–21°C)	5 ft. (1.5 m)	5/4/4	bright red	M	vigorous grower, good plant form; huge flower truss
Mary Belle'	5b –15°F (–26°C)	5 ft. (1.5 m)	3–4/3–4/4	pink to peach	M	more yellow than most yellow-flowered forms of similar hardiness
Maxecat'	4a –25°F (–32°C)	6 ft. (1.8 m)	--	pink	L	good woodland plant
Maximum Roseum'	4a –25°F (–32°C)	6 ft. (1.8 m)	--	pinkish lilac	L–M	long, narrow leaf
Medusa'	6b –5°F (–21°C)	3 ft. (0.9 m)	3/3/3	orange	M	light indumentum on underside of leaf
Minnie'	6b –5°F (–21°C)	4 ft. (1.2 m)	--	white	L	well formed plant; very floriferous
Moonstone'	6b –5°F (–21°C)	3 ft. (0.9 m)	3–4/4/3	cream	EM	compact growth habit

Table 3. Rhododendron Hybrids—Elepidote (continued)

NAME	U.S.D.A. HARDINESS ZONES	HEIGHT IN 10 YEARS	QUALITY RATING	FLOWER COLOR	FLOWERING SEASON	COMMENTS
'Mrs. A. T. de La Mare'	5b −15°F (−26°C)	5 ft. (1.5 m)	3/3	white	M	large flower truss; tolerates exposure
'Mrs. Betty Robinson'	6b −5°F (−21°C)	4 ft. (1.2 m)	3/3/3	cream	M	compact growth habit; red blotch in flowers
'Mrs. C. S. Sargent'	4a −25°F (−32°C)	6 ft. (1.8 m)	3/3/4	rose pink	ML	easy to grow
'Mrs. E. C. Sterling'	6b −5°F (−21°C)	6 ft. (1.8 m)	4/3/3–4	white	L	upright grower; long, narrow foliage
'Mrs. Furnival'	5b −15°F (−26°C)	4 ft. (1.2 m)	5/3–4/3–4	light pink	M	prominent, deep pink blotch in flowers
'Mrs. G. W. Leak'	7a 0°F (−18°C)	6 ft. (1.8 m)	4/3/4	light pink	EM	tall, vigorous growth habit
'Mrs. Tom H. Lowinsky'	5b −15°F (−26°C)	5 ft. (1.5 m)	4/3/4	white	L	compact plant, vigorous growth; striking orange blotch in flowers
'Mrs. W. C. Slocock'	6b −5°F (−21°C)	--	--	apricot-pink	M	Award of Merit 1929, Royal Horticultural Society
'Newburyport Belle'	5a −20°F (−29°C)	4 ft. (1.2 m)	--	pink	E	
'Nova Zembla'	4a −25°F (−32°C)	5 ft. (1.5 m)	3/3/4	red	M	good growth habit for a red rhododendron; requires good soil drainage
'Odee Wright'	6b −5°F (−21°C)	4 ft. (1.2 m)	4/4/3–4	yellow	M	compact grower; dark green, shiny leaves; large trusses
'Old Port'	5b −15°F (−26°C)	5 ft. (1.5 m)	3/3–4/4	purple	M	vigorous grower
'Olin O. Dobbs'	5b −15°F (−26°C)	4 ft. (1.2 m)	5/3–4/3–4	reddish purple	M	flowers heavy and displayed in large, cone-shaped truss
'Olympic Lady'	6b −5°F (−21°C)	3 ft. (0.9 m)	3–4/4/4	white	EM	compact growth habit; very floriferous

Table 3. Rhododendron Hybrids—Elepidote (continued)

NAME	U.S.D.A. HARDINESS ZONES	HEIGHT IN 10 YEARS	QUALITY RATING	FLOWER COLOR	FLOWERING SEASON	COMMENTS
'Parker's Pink'	5b −15°F (−26°C)	5 ft. (1.5 m)	4/3/3	pink	ML	fragrant flowers, fade to white in center
'Parson's Gloriosum'	4a −25°F (−32°C)	5 ft. (1.5 m)	2/2/3	lavender	ML	hardy, vigorous, compact plant
'Party Pink'	5a −20°F (−29°C)	5 ft. (1.5 m)	5/5/4	pink	ML	one of the very few with a 5/5 rating
'Percy Wiseman'	7b 5°F (−15°C)	3 ft. (0.9 m)	--	peach	M	compact grower; vigorous and floriferous
'Pink Fondant'	5b −15°F (−26°C)	5 ft. (1.5 m)	--	pink	ML	very good foliage plant; flowers of heavy substance
'Pink Pearl'	6b −5°F (−21°C)	6 ft. (1.8 m)	3/3/3	pink	M	one of best pinks; has won many awards
'Pink Walloper'	6b −5°F (−21°C)	6 ft. (1.8 m)	4–5/4–5/4	pink	M	huge trusses; reddish leaf stem; may be same as 'Lem's Monarch'
Platinum Pearl'	6a −10°F (−23°C)	6 ft. (1.8 m)	4/4/4	pink	ML	strong grower with huge trusses; grows in shade
Purple Splendour'	6b −5°F (−21°C)	5 ft. (1.5 m)	4/3/3	purple	ML	good growth habit; excellent foliage; Award of Merit winner
Redder Yet'	4a −25°F (−32°C)	5 ft. (1.5 m)	--	red	ML	introduced about 1988; not widely distributed
Ring of Fire'	7a 0°F (−18°C)	4 ft. (1.2 m)	4/4	yellow ringed in red	M–ML	vigorous, compact plant
Rocket'	5b −15°F (−26°C)	5 ft. (1.5 m)	3/4–5/5	pink	M	full foliaged plant
Rose Point'	7a 0°F (−18°C)	3 ft. (0.9 m)	3–4/4/3–4	pink	EM	round leaves; flowers have some red in them
Roseum Elegans'	4a −25°F (−32°C)	6 ft. (1.8 m)	2/3/4	rosy lilac	ML	dependable in heat or cold
Roseum Pink'	4a −25°F (−32°C)	6 ft. (1.8 m)	2/3/3	pink	ML	dependable in heat or cold

Table 3. Rhododendron Hybrids—Elepidote (continued)

NAME	U.S.D.A. HARDINESS ZONES	HEIGHT IN 10 YEARS	QUALITY RATING	FLOWER COLOR	FLOWERING SEASON	COMMENTS
'Rothenburg'	6a −10°F (−23°C)	4 ft. (1.2 m)	3/4	light yellow	EM	glossy, green foliage
'Ruby Bowman'	6b −5°F (−21°C)	5 ft. (1.5 m)	4/4/4	rose pink	M	formal plant habit
'Ruby Hart'	7a 0°F (−18°C)	2 ft. (0.6 m)	4–5/4–5/5	red	EM	compact, tightly foliaged plant
'Russell Harmon'	4a −25°F (−32°C)	6 ft. (1.8 m)	4/3	pink	L	large, vigorous grower
'Sappho'	5a −20°F (−29°C)	6 ft. (1.8 m)	3/2/4	white	M	open growth habit; prominent purple blotch in flowers
'Scarlet Wonder'	5b −15°F (−26°C)	2 ft. (0.6 m)	4/4–5/4	red	M	low, compact plant; outstanding foliage; prefers sun
'Scintillation'	5b −15°F (−26°C)	5 ft. (1.5 m)	4/4/4–5	pink	M	outstanding foliage plant; beautiful flower
'September Song'	7a 0°F (−18°C)	4 ft. (1.2 m)	4–5/4	orange	M	beautiful flowers for milder climates
'Shamrock'	6b −5°F (−21°C)	1 ft. (0.3 m)	3–4/4/4	chartreuse	EM	very compact, spreads wider than tall
'Sham's Candy'	5a −20°F (−29°C)	5 ft. (1.5 m)	3/3/3	deep pink	ML	tight, conical truss
'Sham's Ruby'	5a −20°F (−29°C)	3 ft. (0.9 m)	3/3/3	red	ML	upright, semi-dwarf
'Shawme Lake'	6b −5°F (−21°C)	6 ft. (1.8 m)	--	rosy lavender	M	open truss, lovely flower; Dexter Hybrid
'Shilsonii'	--	--	--	blood red	--	large grower
'Sir Charles Lemon'	7b 5°F (−15°C)	5 ft. (1.5 m)	4/5/3	white	EM	outstanding foliage; cinnamon brown colored indumentum on underside of leaf
'Spring Parade'	5a −20°F (−29°C)	4 ft. (1.2 m)	3/2/3–4	scarlet	M	recurved, dark green leaf; upright grower

Table 3. Rhododendron Hybrids—Elepidote (continued)

NAME	U.S.D.A. HARDINESS ZONES	HEIGHT IN 10 YEARS	QUALITY RATING	FLOWER COLOR	FLOWERING SEASON	COMMENTS
'Summer Rose'	6a −10°F (−23°C)	5 ft. (1.5 m)	--	rose	VL	
'Susan'	6b −5°F (−21°C)	6 ft. (1.8 m)	4/4–5/4	violet blue	M	excellent plant habit; fast grower
'Taurus'	6b −5°F (−21°C)	6 ft. (1.8 m)	4–5/4/4	red	EM	vigorous, fully clothed plant; leaves hold 3 years
'Terrific'	4a −25°F (−32°C)	--	--	deep pink	M	good foliage; very floriferous and reliable; Pride Hybrid
'Todmorden'	5b −15°F (−26°C)	5 ft. (1.5 m)	3–4/3/3–4	pink	ML	vigorous plant; bicolor flower, pink fading to nearly white in center
'Tom Everett'	6b −5°F (−21°C)	4 ft. (1.2 m)	--	pink	M	large, dark green foliage and a huge, perfect truss
'Tony'	5b −15°F (−26°C)	4 ft. (1.2 m)	3/4/4	red	M	low growing, attractive plant
'Trilby'	5b −15°F (−26°C)	5 ft. (1.5 m)	3/4/4	crimson	ML	red stems add to an already beautiful plant
'Trinity'	5a −25°F (−32°C)	2.5 ft. (0.75 m)	4/4	white	ML	uniform growth habit; leaves hold 3 years
'Trude Webster'	6a −10°F (−23°C)	5 ft. (1.5 m)	5/4/4–5	pink	M	huge trusses and attractive foliage; ARS Superior Plant Award 1971
'Unique'	6b −5°F (−21°C)	4 ft. (1.2 m)	3/4–5/4	cream	E–M	thickly clothed, rounded plant; very floriferous
'Van'	6b −5°F (−21°C)	6 ft. (1.8 m)	3–4/4/4	deep pink	ML	excellent foliage plant; very floriferous
'Vernus'	4a −25°F (−32°C)	5 ft. (1.5 m)	3/3/4	pale pink	VE	one of the earliest large-leaved rhododendrons to flower
'Virginia Richards'	7a 0°F (−18°C)	4 ft. (1.2 m)	4/4/4	pink to yellow	M	compact growth habit

Table 3. Rhododendron Hybrids—Elepidote (continued)

NAME	U.S.D.A. HARDINESS ZONES	HEIGHT IN 10 YEARS	QUALITY RATING	FLOWER COLOR	FLOWERING SEASON	COMMENTS
'Vulcan'	5b −15°F (−26°C)	5 ft. (1.5 m)	4/4/4	red	ML	several forms available
'Vulcan's Flame'	5b −15°F (−26°C)	5 ft. (1.5 m)	4/4/4	bright red	ML	the reverse cross of 'Vulcan' and nearly identical
'Wheatley'	5b −15°F (−26°C)	6 ft. (1.8 m)	3–4/4/4	pink	M	outstanding plant and flower
'White Pearl'	7b 5°F (−15°C)	6 ft. (1.8 m)	3/3–4/4–5	white	M	vigorous, upright growth habit
'Winsome'	7a 0°F (−18°C)	3 ft. (0.9 m)	3–4/4/4	rose	EM	compact plant
'Wyandanch Pink'	5b −15°F (−26°C)	6 ft. (1.8 m)	--	vivid pink	M	excellent foliage; sun tolerant; Dexter Hybrid
'Yaku Duchess'	6a −10°F (−23°C)	3 ft. (0.9 m)	--	pink	ML	semi-dwarf *R. yakushimanum* hybrid; good landscape plant; leaves moderately glossy
'Yaku King'	6a −10°F (−23°C)	3 ft. (0.9 m)	--	deep pink	ML	semi-dwarf *R. yakushimanum* hybrid; good landscape plant
'Yaku Prince'	6a −10°F (−23°C)	3 ft. (0.9 m)	--	pink	ML	semi-dwarf *R. yakushimanum* hybrid; good landscape plant
'Yaku Queen'	6a −10°F (−23°C)	3 ft. (0.9 m)	--	pink	ML	semi-dwarf *R. yakushimanum* hybrid; good landscape plant; pink flowers fade to white; glossy foliage; larger than 'Yaku Duchess', 'Yaku King', or 'Yaku Prince'

Table 4. Rhododendron Hybrids—Lepidote

NAME	U.S.D.A. HARDINESS ZONES	HEIGHT IN 10 YEARS	QUALITY RATING	FLOWER COLOR	FLOWERING SEASON	COMMENTS
'Aglo'	4a −25°F (−32°C)	4 ft. (1.2 m)	--	bright pink	E	good plant habit; sun tolerant
'Alfred Wiacek'	5a −20°F (−29°C)	2.5 ft. (0.75 m)	4/3	lavender pink	EM	rivals 'P. J. M.' in growth habit and flower
'Alice Swift'	5b −15°F (−26°C)	3 ft. (0.9 m)	--	pink	EM	upright plant habit; very floriferous
'Alison Johnstone'	7a 0°F (−18°C)	5 ft. (1.5 m)	4/3/3	golden amber	EM	keep roots cool, Award of Merit, 1945
'April Blush'	4a −25°F (−32°C)	2 ft. (0.6 m)	--	pink	E	frequently deciduous
'April Gem'	5a −20°F (−29°C)	4 ft. (1.2 m)	4/4/4	white	E	double flower; Mehlquist Hybrid
'Arctic Pearl'	4a −25°F (−32°C)	4 ft. (1.2 m)	3–4/3/2	white	E	selected form of *R. dauricum* var. *album*
'Balta'	4a −25°F (−32°C)	3 ft. (0.9 m)	--	pink to white	E	very floriferous
'Barto Alpine'	6a −10°F (−23°C)	3 ft. (0.9 m)	3/4/3	rose	EM	dense, upright growth habit; needs good drainage and moisture
'Blaney's Blue'	6b −5°F (−21°C)	4 ft. (1.2 m)	4/4/4	blue	EM	vigorous grower and very floriferous
'Blue Bird' ('Bluebird')	7a 0°F (−18°C)	3 ft. (0.9 m)	4/3	blue	EM	finely textured; performs best in full sun
'Blue Diamond'	6b −5°F (−21°C)	3 ft. (0.9 m)	4/4/4	blue	EM	well shaped and dense; best in sun
'Blue Ridge'	5b −12°F (−24°C)	2 ft. (0.6 m)	--	violet	M	well branched, rounded plant; fragrant foliage
'Blue Tit'	6b −5°F (−21°C)	--	--	blue	--	
'Bric-a-brac'	7a 0°F (−18°C)	2.5 ft. (0.75 m)	3/3/3	pink and white	VE	fuzzy, attractive leaves

Table 4. Rhododendron Hybrids—Lepidote (continued)

NAME	U.S.D.A. HARDINESS ZONES	HEIGHT IN 10 YEARS	QUALITY RATING	FLOWER COLOR	FLOWERING SEASON	COMMENTS
'Carolina Rose'	6a –10°F (–23°C)	3 ft. (0.9 m)	--	pink	M	a well branched azaleodendron
'Chick'	6b –5°F (–21°C)	3 ft. (0.9 m)	3/—/—	pale yellow	EM	loses most of its leaves in winter
'Chikor'	7a 0°F (–18°C)	1.5 ft. (0.45 m)	4–5/4/3	yellow	EM	requires light and well drained soil
'Cilpinense'	7a 0°F (–18°C)	3 ft. (0.9 m)	4/4/3	pink	E	very attractive; Award of Merit, RHS 1927; First Class Certificate, RHS 1968
'Conewago'	4a –25°F (–32°C)	5 ft. (1.5 m)	3/2/3	rose	E	open growth habit; a reliable grower
Cornell Pink: *see R. mucronulatum* Cornell Pink, 218						
'Crater Lake'	6b –5°F (–21°C)	4 ft. (1.2 m)	4/4/4	violet blue	EM	upright growth habit; new growth yellow
'Cream Crest'	7a 0°F (–18°C)	3 ft. (0.9 m)	3/4/3	cream	EM	compact growth habit; does well in full sun
'Curlew'	6b –5°F (–21°C)	1.5 ft. (0.45 m)	4/5/3	bright yellow	EM	beautiful flowers; fertilize sparingly
'Donna Totten'	6b –5°F (–21°C)	4 ft. (1.2 m)	3/4/3	pink	EM	attractive foliage
'Dora Amateis'	5b –15°F (–26°C)	3 ft. (0.9 m)	4/4/4	white	EM	excellent growth habit, Award of Excellence, ARS; Award of Merit, RHS 1976; First Class Certificate, RHS 1981
'Early Bird'	6a –10°F (–23°C)	5 ft. (1.5 m)	--	lavender	E	spreading growth habit
'Elsie Frye'	8b 15°F (–9°C)	4 ft. (1.2 m)	5/3	white	E	good foliage; fragrant
'Epoch'	6a –10°F (–23°C)	3 ft. (0.9 m)	3/3/2–3	white	M	flowers have strong substance

Table 4. Rhododendron Hybrids—Lepidote (continued)

NAME	U.S.D.A. HARDINESS ZONES	HEIGHT IN 10 YEARS	QUALITY RATING	FLOWER COLOR	FLOWERING SEASON	COMMENTS
'Ethel Mae'	6a –10°F (–23°C)	4 ft. (1.2 m)	--	lavender pink	E	bell-shaped flowers held in large groups
'Fairy Mary'	5b –15°F (–26°C)	2 ft. (0.6 m)	--	white and pink	EM	excellent plant; hardiest of the 'Yaku Fairy' hybrids
'Fasia'	5b –15°F (–26°C)	3 ft. (0.9 m)	--	lavender	E	Delp Hybrid
'Forsterianum'	8b 20°F (–7°C)	5 ft. (1.5 m)	4/4/4	white	EM	upright growth habit; large flowers
'Fragrantissimum'	8b 15°F (–9°C)	3 ft. (0.9 m)	4/2–3/4	white	EM	leggy growth habit; very fragrant flowers
'Ginny Gee'	7a 0°F (–18°C)	2 ft. (0.6 m)	--	pink	EM	very tight compact grower
'Goldstrike'	7a 0°F (–18°C)	4 ft. (1.2 m)	4/4/3	yellow	M	outstanding plant; tubular flowers of heavy substance
'Hudson Bay'	5a –20°F (–29°C)	3 ft. (0.9 m)	--	white	E	well branched, rounded plant
'Jenny' ('Creeping Jenny')	6b –5°F (–21°C)	2 ft. (0.6 m)	3/4	bright red	EM	small leaved plant
'Lady Chamberlain'	7b 10°F (–12°C)	5 ft. (1.5 m)	4/3/2–3	salmon	ML	upright growth habit; flowers of heavy substance
'Lanny's Pride'	5b –15°F (–26°C)	5 ft. (1.5 m)	--	purple	EM	vigorous, upright growth habit; easily pruned
'Laurie'	5a –20°F (–29°C)	2 ft. (0.6 m)	--	pink to white	EM	slow growing; spreading plant
'Lemon Mist'	7b 10°F (–12°C)	3 ft. (0.9 m)	3/4/4	green-yellow	EM	compact growth habit; Award of Excellence, ARS 1969
'Llenroc'	5b –15°F (–26°C)	4 ft. (1.2 m)	--	light pink	E	upright growth habit
'Malta' (Leach)	4a –25°F (–32°C)	4 ft. (1.2 m)	--	light purple	EM	twiggy; red stemmed

Table 4. Rhododendron Hybrids—Lepidote (continued)

NAME	U.S.D.A. HARDINESS ZONES	HEIGHT IN 10 YEARS	QUALITY RATING	FLOWER COLOR	FLOWERING SEASON	COMMENTS
Marisee: *see R. sargentianum* Maricee, 218						
'Mary Fleming'	5b −15°F (−26°C)	3 ft. (0.9 m)	4/3/4	salmon and pink	EM	attractive plant and flower; Award of Excellence, ARS 1973
'Molly Fordham'	5a −18°F (−27°C)	4 ft. (1.2 m)	--	white	E	closest to a white 'P. J. M.'; compact growth habit
'Mother Greer'	6a −10°F (−23°C)	1.5 ft. (0.45 m)	3–4/4/4	blue	M–ML	compact plant with brilliant blue flowers
'Mucram'	5b −15°F (−26°C)	N/A	2/2	rose	E	scarce; Gable Hybrid
'My Lady'	8b 15°F (−9°C)	3 ft. (0.9 m)	4/3/3	white	E	compact growth habit
'Myrtifolium'	5b −15°F (−26°C)	3 ft. (0.9 m)	3/5/4	pink	L	excellent growth habit; tolerates heat and sun
'Olga Mezitt'	5b −15°F (−26°C)	3 ft. (0.9 m)	--	phlox pink	EM	well branched, upright plant
'Olive'	5b −15°F (−26°C)	4 ft. (1.2 m)	3/3/3	orchid pink	VE	vigorous plant; Award of Merit, RHS 1942
'Patty Bee'	6b −5°F (−21°C)	1.5 ft. (0.45 m)	--	clear yellow	EM	small leaves; good growth habit
'Peace'	--	--	--	white	--	Award of Merit, RHS 1946
'Pikeland'	6b −5°F (−21°C)	1 ft. (0.3 m)	--	pink	EM	small leaves and flowers
'Pink Diamond': *see* 'Weston's Pink Diamond'						
'Pink Drift'	6a −10°F (−23°C)	1.5 ft. (0.45 m)	4/4/3	pinkish plum	EM	cinnamon colored foliage; very floriferous
'Pink Snowflakes'	7a 0°F (−18°C)	2 ft. (0.6 m)	4/4/3	pink to white	E	very attractive plant; new foliage bronze-red
'Pioneer'	4a −25°F (−32°C)	4 ft. (1.2 m)	4/3/4	rose-pink	VE	semi-deciduous; upright grower; very floriferous

able 4. Rhododendron Hybrids—Lepidote (continued)

NAME	U.S.D.A. HARDINESS ZONES	HEIGHT IN 10 YEARS	QUALITY RATING	FLOWER COLOR	FLOWERING SEASON	COMMENTS
'ipit'	7a 0°F (−18°C)	1 ft. (0.3 m)	3/3/1	creamy pink	EM	difficult to grow
'P. J. M.'	4a −25°F (−32°C)	4 ft. (1.2 m)	4/4/4	lavender-pink	E	very easy to grow; tolerates sun and cold
'P. J. M. Elite'	--	--	--	--	--	selected form of 'P. J. M
'raecox'	6b −5°F (−21°C)	4 ft. (1.2 m)	3/3/3	lilac	E	upright growth habit; Award of Garden Merit, RHS 1926; First Class Certification, RHS 1978
'rincess Anne'	6a −10°F (−23°C)	2 ft. (0.6 m)	4/4	yellow	EM	compact growth habit; very floriferous
'urple Gem'	4a −25°F (−32°C)	2 ft. (0.6 m)	3/4/3	purple	EM	new foliage blue
'amapo'	5a −20°F (−29°C)	2 ft. (0.6 m)	3/4/4	pinkish violet	EM	good foliage plant; grows more compactly in sun
'ose Elf'	7b 5°F (−15°C)	1.5 ft. (0.45 m)	3/4/3–4	orchid pink	E	well clothed dwarf; extremely floriferous
'ose Marie'	5b −15°F (−15°C)	4 ft. (1.2 m)	--	purple	M	very floriferous
'affron Queen'	8b 20°F (−7°C)	4.5 ft. (1.35 m)	4/3	yellow	EM	upright growth habit
'apphire'	6b −5°F (−21°C)	2.5 ft. (0.75 m)	3/3/3–4	light blue	EM	dwarf; bushy, round shaped plant; small flowers
'enoria Meldon'	7a 0°F (−18°C)	5 ft. (1.5 m)	--	blue	E	upright growth habit; fragrant flowers
'eta'	7a 0°F (−18°C)	5 ft. (1.5 m)	4/3/3	light pink	E	deeper pink stripe on back of flowers; Award of Merit, RHS 1933; First Class Certificate, RHS 1960
'hrimp Pink' ('Shrimp Girl')	7a 0°F (−18°C)	3 ft. (0.9 m)	2/3	rose	M	compact, slow grower

Table 4. Rhododendron Hybrids—Lepidote (continued)

NAME	U.S.D.A. HARDINESS ZONES	HEIGHT IN 10 YEARS	QUALITY RATING	FLOWER COLOR	FLOWERING SEASON	COMMENTS
'Small Gem'	6b −5°F (−21°C)	1.5 ft. (0.45 m)	3/3/4	white	E	very floriferous
'Snow Lady'	7a 0°F (−18°C)	2.5 ft. (0.75 m)	3/4/4	white	E	floriferous even in shade
'Spring Delight'	5a −20°F (−29°C)	2 ft. (0.6 m)	--	purplish pink	EM	well branched plant; broader than tall growth habit
'Spring Song'	6a −10°F (−23°C)	2 ft. (0.6 m)	--	light yellow	E–EM	
'Starry Night'	6b −5°F (−21°C)	--	--	violet blue	--	small leaved; H. Hachmann Hybrid
'St. Judy'	6a −10°F (−23°C)	2 ft. (0.6 m)	4/4	yellow	EM	compact growth habit; very floriferous
'Tiffany'	5b −15°F (−26°C)	2.5 ft. (0.75 m)	3–4/3/4	pink	M	apricot and yellow coloring in flower throat; good foliage
'Tom Koenig'	6a −10°F (−23°C)	2.5 ft. (0.75 m)	3/3	pink	EM	
'Waltham'	5a −18°F (−27°C)	1 ft. (0.3 m)	--	pink	M	low growing, compact plant, wider than tall; grow in shade
'Weston's Pink Diamond'	6a −10°F (−23°C)	5 ft. (1.5 m)	--	light fuschia-purple	E	upright growth habit; double flowers
'Wigeon'	7a 0°F (−18°C)	3 ft. (0.9 m)	--	pink	M	saucer-shaped flowers; Award of Merit, RHS 1982
'Wilsonii'	5b −15°F (−26°C)	3 ft. (0.9 m)	3/3/4	rosy pink	L	spreading growth habit; sun tolerant
'Windbeam'	4a −25°F (−32°C)	4 ft. (1.2 m)	4/3/4	light pink	EM	very hardy; easy to grow
'Wyanoki'	5b −15°F (−26°C)	3 ft. (0.9 m)	3/3–4/4	white	M	very floriferous

Table 4. Rhododendron Hybrids—Lepidote (continued)

NAME	U.S.D.A. HARDINESS ZONES	HEIGHT IN 10 YEARS	QUALITY RATING	FLOWER COLOR	FLOWERING SEASON	COMMENTS
'Yellow Eye'	5a −20°F (−29°C)	3 ft. (0.9 m)	--	white	EM	upright, vigorous growth habit
'Yellow Hammer'	7a 0°F (−18°C)	4 ft. (1.2 m)	4/3/4	deep yellow	EM	upright growth habit; tolerates sun

AZALEA HYBRID GROUPS—A BRIEF DESCRIPTION

Back Acres Hybrids

B. Y. Morrison, of Pass Christian, Mississippi, developed the Back Acres Hybrids after his retirement from the U.S.D.A. Largely an extension of his work with the Glenn Dale Hybrids, his purpose was to develop late blooming, double flowering clones.

Most of the 370 clones selected for testing bloom mid to late midseason, tolerate high temperatures, and are bud hardy in Zone 7b.

Belgian Indian Hybrids

Developed as indoor or greenhouse plants, these hybrids are generally tender. The principle parent is *R. simsii*, usually incorrectly identified as 'Indica'. Hardiness is listed as Zones 9 to 10, and some clones are more cold hardy.

Rutherford Hybrids. These hybrids originated in Rutherford, New Jersey, during the 1920s as an extension of the Belgian Indian Hybrid line. Plants are spreading, compact, medium in height (6–8 ft. or 1.8–2.4 m) and very floriferous, blooming from early to late midseason. Most are hardy to Zone 9 and a few to Zone 7a.

Beltsville Hybrids

Developed and introduced by Guy E. Yerks and Robert L. Pryor of the U.S.D.A., Beltsville, Maryland Station. Parents include *R. kaempferi*, 'Firefly', 'Indica Alba', 'Maxwell', and 'Snow'. The objective was to produce greenhouse azaleas as well as hardy outdoor types. All Beltsville Hybrids are hardy in Zone 7a to 8b.

Brooks Hybrids

Leonard L. Brooks of Modesto, California, developed these hybrids using Belgian and Southern Indian Hybrids crossed on 'Ledifolia Alba' and various Kurume Hybrids. Most flower midseason, are medium in height (4–6 ft. or 1.2–1.8 m), and are cold hardy in Zone 8.

Carla Hybrids

The Carla Hybrids were developed at North Carolina State and Louisiana State universities. Program objectives are cold hardiness, the development of resistance to root rot diseases, floriferousness, and drought resistance. Seventeen clones have been introduced to date, and the program continues at North Carolina State University. Carla Hybrids are hardy in Zones 7b–9a.

Carlson Hybrids

Hybrids of *R. mucronatum*, the Carlson Hybrids were selected for their low spreading habit and are 2–3 ft. or 0.6–0.9 m tall in 10 years.

Plants were selected by Bob and Jan Carlson of South Salem, New York. Plants are hardy in Zone 7a.

Chisolm-Merritt Hybrids

Developed in 1934 by the late Julian J. Chisolm and later introduced by the late Dr. E. I. Merritt. These hybrids were derived using *R. poukhanense* and 'Cleopatra' as seed parents and crossed by numerous pollen parents. Plants bloom early to midseason and are of compact growth habit. All plants are hardy in Zones 7a–9.

Eden Hybrids

The Eden Hybrids were developed by the late W. David Smith at Spring Grove, Pennsylvania. Goals were to produce large flower size, a wide color range, and plants cold hardy in Zone 6. Most are still under observation, and cold hardiness has not been established.

Gable Hybrids

These plants were developed and introduced by the late Joseph B. Gable of Stewartstown, Pennsylvania. His objective was to improve quality and cold hardiness in evergreen azaleas. The species *R. poukhanense* and *R. kaempferi* were used for hardiness, and other parents, including the Kurume Hybrids, were used for other characteristics. The resulting clones are among the hardiest, most widely adapted evergreen azaleas and are widely used in the landscape and as parents in other hybridizing programs. Plants are of medium size and hardy in Zones 6b to 8b.

Girard Hybrids

Starting with Gable hybrids and later using his own seedlings, the late Peter Girard, Sr., of Geneva, Ohio, began a hybridizing program in the late 1940s. His efforts resulted in the development of some of the most cold hardy evergreen azaleas available today. Plants are medium growers, 4–6 ft. (1.2–1.8 m) in height, and are hardy in Zones 6a–9b. See also Girard Hybrids, p. 251.

Glenn Dale Hybrids

Developed by the late B. Y. Morrison, former chief of the Plant Introduction Section and Director of the National Arboretum, U.S.D.A. The Glenn Dale Hybrids represent an extensive and diverse breeding program. Nine principal species and clones were used as parents, and over 70,000 seedlings were grown. From this group 440 clones were selected and introduced.

The plants exhibit wide diversity in flower color, bloom from early to late season, and vary in height from 3–8 ft. (0.9–2.5 m). Breeding objectives were to develop plants with large flowers, cold hardiness, and an extended bloom period. The objectives were met since the Glenn Dale Hybrids bloom from early through late season with large flowers and are hardy in zones 6b–9a. A few clones are hardy to −10°F (−23°C).

Harris Hybrids

Hybridized by James Harris of Lawrenceville, Georgia, most of the Harris Hybrids bloom late midseason and have large flowers. Parents include hybrids of the Kaempferi, Satsuki, and Glenn Dale series. Plants are cold hardy in Zones 7b–9a.

Hershey Hybrids

Hybridized and introduced by the late Ralph Hershey and his son Everett Hershey, these represent an extension of the Kurume Hybrids and have similar characteristics. Hershey Hybrids are hardy in Zones 6b–9b.

Kaempferi Hybrids

The species *R. kaempferi* and the azalea clone 'Malvatica' are the principal parents of this hybrid group originally developed in The Netherlands. *Rhododendron kaempferi* was introduced into the U.S.A. in 1892 by Prof. C. S. Sargent of the Arnold Arboretum, where it was later used in hybridizing.

Plants are medium to tall (4–10 ft. or 1.2–3.0 m) and bloom early to midseason with large flowers. *Rhododendron kaempferi* and its hybrids are often used to transmit cold hardiness. Kaempferi Hybrids are hardy in Zones 5b–9a.

Kehr Hybrids

A retired plant geneticist from the U.S.D.A. now living in Hendersonville, North Carolina, Dr. August Kehr has introduced four outstanding azalea clones. They are medium size plants. Cold hardiness varies from −10–0°F (−23–18°C), Zones 6a–7a.

Kerrigan Hybrids

Developed by Howard Kerrigan of Hayward, California, using Belgian Indian and Kurume Hybrids as parents. Plants are upright, 3–5 ft. (0.9–1.5 m) high, and are hardy in Zones 8b–10.

Kurume Hybrids

Originating near the city of Kurume on the Island of Kyushu, Japan, this is one of the oldest hybrid groups. There is some confusion regarding parentage, but Fred C. Galle states in *Azaleas* "they were probably crosses of *R. sataense* and *R. kiusianum*." The Kurume Hybrids represent one of the largest hybrid groups and are widely used in the landscape. Plants grow slowly yet ultimately reach heights up to 6 ft. (1.8 m). Flowers are single or hose-in-hose. Kurume Hybrids are adapted in Zones 6b–9a.

Linwood Hybrids

Dr. Charles Fisher, Jr., of Linwood, New Jersey, began developing evergreen azaleas for greenhouse forcing in 1950, and in 1953 G. Albert Reid took over the program.

Parentage is very diverse including Kurume and Kaempferi Hybrids as well as Indian greenhouse cultivars. Most plants are hardy in Zones 7 and 8 with a few hardy to −10°F (−23°C), Zone 6a.

Mossholder-Bristow Hybrids

These hybrids were developed by Owen R. Bristow of San Bernardino, California, as greenhouse forcing azaleas. Parents used were Belgian Indian and Rutherford Hybrids. Plants are medium in size, 4–6 ft. (1.2–1.8 m) tall, and are hardy in Zone 8.

North Tisbury Hybrids

Selected by Mrs. Julian (Polly) Hill of Martha's Vineyard, Massachusetts, from seed and cuttings sent by Dr. Tsuneshige of Rokujo, Tokyo, Japan. The North Tisbury Hybrids are generally low growing, ground cover hybrids of *R. nakaharae*. Others are developed from seed of 'Gumpo' collected in a friend's garden in Tokyo, Japan. Most are hardy in Zones 6b–9a.

Pericat Hybrids

Developed by Alphonse Pericat of Collingdale, Pennsylvania, as greenhouse forcing plants. Parentage is unknown.

Plants are of medium height, 3–5 ft. (0.9–1.5 m) tall, and have a dense growth habit. Flowers show much variation, including single, hose-in-hose, semidouble, and petaloid. Pericat Hybrids are hardy in Zones 7a–9b.

Pride Hybrids

Orlando Pride started hybridizing in 1928 using a seedling plant obtained from Joe Gable. Most of his azalea selections came from this seedling which was later named 'Nadine'. Plants are medium to tall, 6–8 ft. (1.8–2.5 m), and hardy in Zones 6a–8b.

Robin Hill Hybrids

Robert Gartrell of Wyckoff, New Jersey, had as his goal to produce hardy, late blooming azaleas with flower size comparable to the Satsuki Hybrids. Most Robin Hill Hybrids bloom mid to late midseason and are 3–5 ft. (0.9–1.5 m) high and hardy in Zones 6b–9b.

Satsuki Hybrids

Highly revered by the Japanese, the Satsuki Hybrids were developed using principally *R. indicum* and *R. tamurae* (*R. eriocarpum*) as parents. They are among the most diverse group of hybrids, presenting a wide range of flower color and growth habit.

The first hybrids occurred naturally in the wild and were used along with other species in development.

The Satsuki Hybrids were widely used as parents in hybridizing the Glenn Dale, Robin Hill, and Harris Hybrids.

Blooming period is late, and flowers are generally single with widely variable color patterns even on the same plant. Satsuki Hybrids are hardy in Zones 7a–9b, and a few are hardy in Zone 6.

H. R. Schroeder Hybrids

Developed by the late Dr. H. R. Schroeder of Evansville, Indiana, in the early 1970s. The goal was to develop compact, evergreen azaleas adapted to the cold, harsh climate of the midwestern states of the U.S.A. Plants flower midseason and are hardy in Zone 5b.

Shammarello Hybrids

Developed and introduced by the late A. M. (Tony) Shammarello. These hybrids, tested in the harsh climate of South Euclid, Ohio, are among the hardiest of evergreen azaleas. *Rhododendron poukhanense* and *R. kaempferi* were widely used as parents. Plants are hardy in Zones 5a–9b.

Southern Indian Hybrids

The Belgian Indian Hybrids were highly prized in the southern U.S.A., and local hybridizing and selection gave birth to the Southern Indian Hybrids. Though not all plants are hybrids, they are all similar to the earlier Belgian Indian Hybrids.

Southern Indian Hybrids can be assigned to two groups based on size and blooming period: an early blooming group which is faster growing, up to 10 ft. (3.0 m) tall; and a later blooming, more compact group ultimately reaching 8 ft. (2.5 m) tall.

The Southern Indian Hybrids are more cold hardy than the Belgian Indian hybrids, being hardy in Zones 8a–10a.

Vuyk Hybrids

Developed in Holland by Aart Vuyk using principally *R. kaempferi* in an effort to produce hardier evergreen azaleas. The Vuyk Hybrids have large flowers, bloom early to midseason, and are adapted in Zones 5b–9a.

Note: Azalea tables which follow do not include a quality rating as this information is not available.

Table 5. Evergreen Azalea Species

NAME	U.S.D.A. HARDINESS ZONES	HEIGHT IN 10 YEARS	FLOWER COLOR	FLOWERING SEASON	COMMENTS
R. *balsaminaeflorum*	7a–10	2–3 ft. (0.6–0.9 m)	medium red	L	selected clone of R. *indicum*; very double flower
R. *indicum* Balsaminiflorum	7a–10a	4 ft. (1.2 m)	pink, red, or white	--	commonly sold as 'Macrantha', 'Balsaminiflora', etc.
R. *kaempferi*	5b–9a	6–8 ft. (1.8–2.5 m)	red to yellowish pink	M–L	many forms available; widely used in hybridizing
R. *kiusianum*	7a–8b	1–2 ft. (0.3–0.6 m)	purple, red, or pink	M	requires good soil drainage; white form also available
R. *macrantha*	7a–10a	1–2 ft. (0.3–0.6 m)	pink and orange	L	several selected clones of R. *indicum*
R. *macrosepalum*	7a–8b	3–4 ft. (0.9–1.2 m)	purple	EM	requires well-drained soil; fragrant flowers
R. *mucronatum*	7a–9b	6–8 ft. (1.8–2.5 m)	white	EM	cultured in Japan for over 300 years; not found in the wild
R. *nakaharae*	6b–9a	1–2 ft. (0.3–0.6 m)	reddish orange	L	excellent ground cover
R. *oldhamii*	8a–9a	6–10 ft. (1.8–3 m)	reddish orange	M–L	recommended for summer flowers in warm climates
R. *serpyllifolium*	6a–8b	3 ft. (0.9 m)	light pink	--	requires well-drained soil; white form also available
R. *simsii*	8a–9a	6 ft. (1.8 m)	pink to red	--	parent of the Belgian Indian Hybrids
R. *yedoense*	6a–9b	4–6 ft. (1.5–1.8 m)	light purple	--	deciduous in colder climates; fragrant flowers; double flowering forms also available
R. *yedoense* var. *poukhanense*	6a–9b	5–6 ft. (1.5–1.8 m)	purple	E	excellent for cold climates; pink form also available.

Table 6. Evergreen Azalea Hybrids

NAME	U.S.D.A. HARDINESS ZONES	HEIGHT IN 10 YEARS	FLOWER COLOR	FLOWERING SEASON	COMMENTS
'Addy Wery'	6a–8a	4 ft. (1.2 m)	--	EM	upright habit; Kurume Hybrid
'Adelaine Pope'	7a–8a 5°F –15°C)	4–5 ft. (1.2–1.5 m)	purplish red	--	dense, upright grower; Carla Hybrid
'Adonis'	--	--	white	E	hose-in-hose, frilled; Kurume Hybrid
'Aladdin'	--	--	vivid red	E	Kurume Hybrid
'Alexander'	6a–8a –10°F (–23°C)	3 ft. (0.9 m)	reddish orange	VL	ground cover plant; North Tisbury Hybrid
'Amoenum'	6b–9a 0°F (–18°C)	6–8 ft. (1.8–2.5 m)	purplish red	EM	spreads up to 15 ft. (4.5 m); *R. obtusum* clone
'Amy'	--	--	pink	--	compact grower; glossy foliage; flower double; Kurume Hybrid
'Anna Kehr'	6b–8a 0°F (–18°C)	2 ft. (0.6 m)	pink	M	easy to grow, compact plant; double flowers; Kehr Hybrid
'Atlanta'	--	2–3 ft. (0.6–0.9 m)	reddish purple	--	Kaempferi Hybrid
'Beni Kirishima'	6b–8a –5°F (–21°C)	4 ft. 1.2 m)	orange-red	--	excellent azalea; flower double; Glenn Dale Hybrid
'Ben Morrison'	7a–9a 5°F (–15°C)	5 ft. (1.5 m)	scarlet and white	EM	beautiful bicolor scarlet; Glenn Dale Hybrid
'Big Joe'	6b–8b	4 ft. (1.2 m)	purplish pink	EM	spreading habit; Gable Hybrid
'Blaauw's Pink'	6a–8a	5 ft. (1.5 m)	yellowish pink	E	hose-in-hose flower; Kurume Hybrid
'Blue Danube'	6b–8a	4 ft. (1.2 m)	violet	M	easy growing plant; excellent foliage; Vuyk Hybrid
'Boudoir'	6b–8a	--	purplish red	--	introduced by Old Kent Nursery; Gable Hybrid
'Buccaneer'	6b–9a	5 ft. (1.5 m)	orange-red	E	erect growing; best in afternoon shade; Glenn Dale Hybrid
'Cameo'	--	--	light pink	L	hose-in-hose; Gable Hybrid
'Caroline Gable'	6b–8a	4 ft. (1.2 m)	vivid red	LM	hose-in-hose; Gable Hybrid
'Cascade' (Glenn Dale)	--	4 ft. (1.2 m)	white	E	upright grower; hose-in-hose; Glenn Dale Hybrid

Table 6. Evergreen Azalea Hybrids (continued)

NAME	U.S.D.A. HARDINESS ZONES	HEIGHT IN 10 YEARS	FLOWER COLOR	FLOWERING SEASON	COMMENTS
'Cascade' (Shammarello)	6a–8b –10°F (–23°C)	2 ft. (0.6 m)	white	M	*R. poukhanense* hybrid; Shammarello Hybrid
'Cavalier'	6b–9a	6 ft. (1.8 m)	yellowish pink	E	dense, bushy plant; Glenn Dale Hybrid
'Christmas Cheer'	--	5 ft. (1.5 m)	rose red	E	hose-in-hose; Kurume Hybrid
'Cloud Nine'	8b	4 ft. (1.2 m)	white	--	flowers double; Kerrigan Hybrid
'Conversation Piece'	6b–8a 0°F (–18°C)	2 ft. (0.6 m)	light pink	M	flowers vary in color, Robin Hill Hybrid
'Coral Bells'	6b–8a –5°F (–21°C)	2 ft. (0.6 m)	rose pink	E	syn. of 'Kirin'; hose-in-hose; Kurume Hybrid
'Corsage'	5b–8a –15°F (–26°C)	5 ft. (1.5 m)	purple	E	fragrant, very floriferous; Gable Hybrid
'Dayspring'	6b–9a –5°F (–21°C)	6 ft. (1.8 m)	white center, purple edge	M	striking floral display; Glenn Dale Hybrid
'Debonnaire'	6a–8a	3 ft. (0.9 m)	vivid pink	LM	flower petal edge deeper pink; Back Acres Hybrid
'Delaware Valley White'	6b–8b –5°F (–21°C)	3 ft. (0.9 m)	white	EM	hardier form of *R. indica alba*
'Desiree'	6a–8b –10°F (–23°C)	5 ft. (1.5 m)	white	EM	flowers frilled; Shammarello Hybrid
'Diana'	6b–8a	5 ft. (1.5 m)	yellowish pink	EM	hose-in-hose; Kurume Hybrid
'Dorothy Clark'	7a–7b 0°F (–18°C)	3 ft. (0.9 m)	light pink	--	light red border on flowers; Harris Hybrid
'Dream'	7a–9a 0°F (–18°C)	6 ft. (1.8 m)	purplish pink	E	spreading habit; frilled flowers; Glenn Dale Hybrid
'Easter Parade'	8a–8b	4 ft. (1.2 m)	light pink	M	semidouble hose-in-hose flower; Mossholder-Bristow Hybrid
'Eikan'	7a–9b	3 ft. (0.9 m)	white with pink stripe	ML	vigorous, spreading habit; Satsuki Hybrid
'Eliza Hyatt'	5b–8a –15°F (–26°C)	2 ft. (0.6 m)	light pink	M	flowers double; H. R. Schroeder Hybrid

Table 6. Evergreen Azalea Hybrids (continued)

NAME	U.S.D.A. HARDINESS ZONES	HEIGHT IN 10 YEARS	FLOWER COLOR	FLOWERING SEASON	COMMENTS
'Elizabeth Gable'	6b–8b –5°F (–21°C)	4 ft. (1.2 m)	red	L	flowers frilled; Gable Hybrid
'Elsie Lee'	5b–8a –15°F (–26°C)	3 ft. (0.9 m)	orchid	LM	flowers semidouble; Shammarello Hybrid
'Eureka'	7a–8b 0°F (–18°C)	3 ft. (0.9 m)	light purplish pink	--	hose-in-hose; spreading habit Beltsville Hybrid
'Everest'	7a–9a	4 ft. (1.2 m)	white	M	broad, spreading habit; Glenn Dale Hybrid
'Fascination'	7a–9a	5 ft. (1.5 m)	light pink	EM	Chisolm-Merritt Hybrid
'Fashion'	7a–9a	5 ft. (1.5 m)	pink	E	purple blotch in flower, hose-in-hose; Glenn Dale Hybrid
'Fedora'	6b–9a	5 ft. (1.5 m)	purplish pink	M	Kaempferi Hybrid
'Festive'	6b–9a	5 ft. (1.5 m)	white	E	flowers striped purplish red; Glenn Dale Hybrid
'Flamingo'	N/A	5 ft. (1.5 m)	deep pink	LM	hose-in-hose; Brooks Hybrid
'Forest Fire'	6b–8b	4 ft. (1.2 m)	deep pink	--	hose-in-hose; Gable Hybrid
'Gaiety'	7a–9a	4 ft. (1.2 m)	purplish pink	EM	flowers single with darker blotch; Glenn Dale Hybrid
'Gay'	8b–10	3 ft. (0.9 m)	white	--	dark red edge on flower petals, Kerrigan Hybrid
'Girard Border Gem'	6a–9a –10°F (–23°C)	2 ft. (0.6 m)	deep pink	E	dwarf; dense growth habit; Girard Hybrid
'Girard Chiara'	5b–9a –15°F (–26°C)	3 ft. (0.9 m)	purplish pink	EM	hose-in-hose, flowers ruffled; Girard Hybrid
'Girard Fuschia'	6a–9a –10°F (–21°C)	3 ft. (0.9 m)	deep reddish purple	EM	wavy lobes on flowers; Girard Hybrid
'Girard Hot Shot'	6b–9a –5°F (–21°C)	2 ft. (0.6 m)	reddish orange	EM	wavy lobes on flowers; Girard Hybrid
'Girard Rose'	6a–9a 0°F (–18°C)	2 ft. (0.6 m)	deep pink	EM	wavy lobes on flowers; Girard Hybrid
'Girard Scarlet'	5b–9 –15°F (–26°C)	2 ft. (0.6 m)	strong red	EM	deep red blotch on flower; Girard Hybrid

Table 6. Evergreen Azalea Hybrids (continued)

NAME	U.S.D.A. HARDINESS ZONES	HEIGHT IN 10 YEARS	FLOWER COLOR	FLOWERING SEASON	COMMENTS
'Glacier'	6b–9a	5 ft. (1.5 m)	white	E	dark green foliage; Glenn Dale Hybrid
'Glamour'	6b–9a	5 ft. (1.5 m)	rose red	E	beautiful, dark green leaves; Glenn Dale Hybrid
'Gumpo'	6b–9b	1 ft. (0.3 m)	pink, red, or white	L	various color selections; Satsuki Hybrid
'Guy Yerkes'	7a–8b	5 ft. (1.5 m)	pink	--	hose-in-hose; Beltsville Hybrid
'Hampton Beauty'	7a–9b	5 ft. (1.5 m)	deep pink	EM	partially petaloid sepals; Pericat Hybrid
'Hardy Gardenia'	7a–9b	5 ft. (1.5 m)	white	ML	double, gardenia-like flowers; Linwood Hybrid
'Helen Curtis'	5b–9 –15°F (–26°C)	3 ft. (0.9m)	white	ML	semidouble flowers; Shammarello Hybrid
'Helena'	--	4 ft. (1.2 m)	yellowish pink	--	vivid red blotch; Eden Hybrid
'Herbert'	6a–8b –10°F (–23°C)	4 ft. (1.2 m)	reddish purple	EM	hose-in-hose, frilled fowers; Gable Hybrid
'Hershey's Red'	6b–9b –5°F (–21°C)	2 ft. (0.6 m)	red	EM	outstanding grower; Hershey Hybrid, Kurume type
'H. H. Hume'	7a–8b	--	white	--	hose-in-hose, 2 in. (5.0 cm) flowers; Beltsville Hybrid
'Hino Crimson'	6b–8a –5°F (–21°C)	3 ft. (0.9 m)	crimson	E	easy to grow; Kurume Hybrid
'Hino Pink'	6a–8b –10°F (–23°C)	3 ft. (0.9 m)	purplish pink	EM	Shammarello Hybrid
'Hino Red'	5b–8b –15°F (–26°C)	1.5 ft. (0.45 m)	moderate red	EM	very hardy; Shammarello Hybrid
'Hinode Giri'	6b–8a –5°F (–21°C)	3 ft. (0.9 m)	rose-crimson	E	easy to grow; Kurume Hybrid
'Hinomayo'	6b–8a	5 ft. (1.5 m)	purplish pink	EM	Kurume Hybrid
'Iro-Hayama'	6b–8a	2 ft. (0.6 m)	white	--	Kurume Hybrid
'Iveryana'	8a–10a	2 ft. (0.6 m)	white	L	deep red flecks in flower petals; Southern Indian Hybrid

Table 6. Evergreen Azalea Hybrids (continued)

NAME	U.S.D.A. HARDINESS ZONES	HEIGHT IN 10 YEARS	FLOWER COLOR	FLOWERING SEASON	COMMENTS
'James Gable'	6a–8b –10°F (–23°C)	2 ft. (0.6 m)	strong red	EM	hose-in-hose, darker blotch; Gable Hybrid
'John Cairns'	5b–9a	4 ft. (1.2 m)	vivid red	EM	hybridized at Exbury; Kaempferi Hybrid
'John Haerens'	--	--	white	M	syn. 'Jean Haerens'; purplish red edge on flower petals; Belgian Indian Hybrid
'Karens'	4b–8a –25°F (–32°C)	4 ft. (1.2 m)	reddish purple	E	wavy, fragrant flowers; tolerates pH 7; Kurume Hybrid
'Kathleen' (Gable)	--	--	light pink	--	Gable Hybrid
'Kathleen' (Glenn Dale)	6b–9a –5°F (–21°C)	4 ft. (1.2 m)	yellowish pink	L	spreading habit; Glenn Dale Hybrid
'Kirin'	6b–8a	2 ft. (0.6 m)	strong pink	E	syn. 'Coral Bells'; Kurume Hybrid
'Leo'	6b–8a	2 ft. (0.6 m)	vivid orange	LM	Exbury Hybrid
'Lorna'	6b–8a –5°F (–21°C)	3 ft. (0.9 m)	pink	L–M	beautiful, double flowers; reliable; Gable Hybrid
'Louise Gable'	6a–8a –5°F (–21°C)	5 ft. (1.5 m)	salmon	M	very dependable; large, semidouble flowers; Gable Hybrid
'Margaret Douglas'	7a–8a	4 ft. (1.2 m)	light pink	M–L	deep, yellowish pink edge on flower petals; Back Acres Hybrid
'Marjorie'	6a–8a –10°F (–23°C)	4 ft. (1.2 m)	reddish purple	M	Pride Hybrid
'Martha Hitchcock'	6b–9a –5°F (–21°C)	4 ft. (1.2 m)	white	EM	reddish purple edge on flower petals; Glenn Dale Hybrid
'Mary Dalton'	6b–8b –5°F (–21°C)	6 ft. (1.8 m)	reddish orange	EM	hose-in-hose; Gable Hybrid
'Maybelle'	6a–8b –10°F (–23°C)	1.5 ft. (0.45 m)	deep pink	LM	semidouble flowers; Shammarello Hybrid
'Mildred Mae'	6b–8b –5°F (–21°C)	4 ft. (1.2 m)	reddish purple	EM	spreading, large grower; Gable Hybrid
'Modesty'	6b–9a	5 ft. (1.5 m)	purplish red	E	flowers flushed purplish pink from center; Glenn Dale Hybrid

Table 6. Evergreen Azalea Hybrids (continued)

NAME	U.S.D.A. HARDINESS ZONES	HEIGHT IN 10 YEARS	FLOWER COLOR	FLOWERING SEASON	COMMENTS
'Moonbeam'	6b–9a	5 ft. (1.5 m)	white	M	frilled flower margins; Glenn Dale Hybrid
'Mother's Day'	6b–8a	2.5 ft. (0.75 m)	vivid red	EM	hose-in-hose to semidouble flowers; Kurume Hybrid
'Mrs. G. G. Gerbing'	8a–10a	5 ft. (1.5 m)	white	M	large flowers; Southern Indian Hybrid
'Mrs. Henry Schroeder'	6b–7a	2 ft. (0.6 m)	purplish pink	ML	very double flowers; H. R. Schroeder Hybrid
'Mrs. Nancy Dipple'	5b–7a	2 ft. (0.6 m)	pale pink	ML	double flowers; H. R. Schroeder Hybrid
'Nadine'	6a–8b	6 ft. (1.8 m)	light pink	--	not widely distributed; Pride Hybrid
'Nancy of Robin Hill'	6b–9b	2 ft. (0.6 m)	light pink	ML	semidouble flowers; Robin Hill Hybrid
'Naomi'	6b–8a	5 ft. (1.5 m)	strong pink	LM	Exbury/Kaempferi Hybrid
'Orange Beauty'	5b–9a	4 ft. (1.2 m)	light orange	EM	Kaempferi Hybrid; Kurume Hybrid by the same name
'Palestrina'	6a–9a –10°F (–23°C)	5 ft. (1.5 m)	white	E	syn. 'Wilhelmina Vuyk'; Vuyk Hybrid
'Parfait'	6a–9a –10°F (–23°C)	--	pink	--	hose-in-hose, ruffled flowers; Kaempferi Hybrid
'Pink Pearce'	--	--	purple	M	origin unknown
'Pink Pearl'	6b–8a	--	strong pink	E	hose-in-hose; Kurume Hybrid
'Pink Ruffles'	9a–10a	6 ft. (1.8 m)	deep pink	M	semidouble, hose-in-hose; Rutherford Hybrid
'Polaris'	6b–8a	2.5 ft. (0.75 m)	white	LM	hose-in-hose; Gable Hybrid
'Pride's Pink'	6a–8a	--	pink	L	introduced shortly before 1990, not widely distributed; Pride Hybrid
'Purple Splendour'	6a–8a	3 ft. (0.9 m)	reddish purple	EM	similar to 'Herbert'; Gable Hybrid
'Red Red'	5b–8b	3 ft. (0.9 m)	strong, deep red	EM	Shammarello Hybrid
'Red Ruffles'	9a–10a	6 ft. (1.8 m)	strong red	M	semidouble, hose-in-hose; Rutherford Hybrid
'Refrain'	6b–9a	6 ft. (1.8 m)	white and purplish pink	E	hose-in-hose; Glenn Dale Hybrid
'Roehr's Peggy Ann'	6b–9a	--	white	L	purplish pink petal edge; Kaempferi Hybrid

Table 6. Evergreen Azalea Hybrids (continued)

NAME	U.S.D.A. HARDINESS ZONES	HEIGHT IN 10 YEARS	FLOWER COLOR	FLOWERING SEASON	COMMENTS
'Rose Greeley'	6a–8a	3 ft. (0.9 m)	white	E	hose-in-hose, fragrant; Gable Hybrid
'Rosebud'	6a–8a	2 ft. (0.6 m)	pink	M–L	double, hose-in-hose; Gable Hybrid
'Sakata Red'	6b–9a	2.5 ft. (0.75 m)	vivid red	E	Kurume Hybrid
'Seneca'	6b–9a	5 ft. (1.5 m)	strong purple	E	ascending branches; Glenn Dale Hybrid
'Sherwood Orchid'	6b–8a	4 ft. (1.2 m)	reddish purple	EM	darker blotch in flower; Kurume Hybrid
'Sherwood Red'	6b–8a	2 ft. (0.6 m)	vivid red	E	heavy bloomer; Kurume Hybrid
'Snow'	6b–8a	2 ft. (0.6 m)	white	E	hose-in-hose; Kurume Hybrid
'Springtime'	6a–8a	4 ft. (1.2 m)	purplish red (pink)	EM	one of the best pinks; Gable Hybrid
'Starlight' (Kerrigan)	8b–10a	4 ft. (1.2 m)	yellowish pink	--	semidouble; Kerrigan Hybrid
'Starlight' (Carlson)	4a–8a	2–3 ft. (0.6–0.9 m)	yellowish pink	M	Carlson Hybrid
'Stewartstonian'	5b–8a	5 ft. (1.5 m)	vivid red	EM	reddish winter foliage; Gable Hybrid
'Sunglow'	7b–9b	4 ft. (1.2 m)	purplish red	--	rounded, upright grower; Carla Hybrid
'Surprise'	6b–9a	3 ft. (0.9 m)	medium red	--	flower margins irregular white; Glenn Dale Hybrid
'Twenty Grand'	7a–9b	5 ft. (1.5 m)	purplish red	EM	David Leach Hybrid
'Vespers'	6b–9a	5 ft. (1.5 m)	white	M	purplish red stripes in flowers; Glenn Dale Hybrid
'Vuyk's Rosyred'	6b–8a	3 ft. (0.9 m)	deep pink	EM	2.5–3 in. (7.5–7.6 cm) flowers; Vuyk Hybrid
'Vuyk's Scarlet'	5a–8a	4 ft. (1.2 m)	deep red	EM	2.5–3 in. (7.5–7.6 cm) flowers; Vuyk Hybrid
'Wakaebisu'	7a–8a	1.5 ft. (0.45 m)	medium red	--	very pale throat, dark blotch in flower; Kurume Hybrid
'Ward's Ruby'	7a–8a	--	strong red	E	one of the best reds; Kurume Hybrid
'White Rosebud'	6a–8b	4 ft. (1.2 m)	white	M	double flower, fragrant; Kehr Hybrid
'Yankee Doodle'	5b–9a	--	pink	M	introduced by Abbott; Kaempferi Hybrid

DECIDUOUS AZALEA HYBRIDS

Beasley Hybrids
Developed and introduced by George, Mary, and Jeffrey Beasley of Lavonia, Georgia. The Beasley Hybrids are derived from the following North American species: *R. arborescens, R. atlanticum, R. bakeri, R. calendulaceum, R. periclymenoides,* and *R. viscosum.* Most plants are hardy to −15°F− −10°F (−26− −23°C), Zone 5b.

Carlson Hybrids
Clones of the North American species were selected by Bob and Jan Carlson in an effort to extend the blooming season into summer. All plants are hardy to −25°F (−32°C), Zone 4b.

Ghent Hybrids
These hybrids were developed in Ghent, Belgium, using *R. calendulaceum, R. japonicum, R. luteum, R. molle, R. periclymenoides,* and *R. viscosum.*
Flower color is white, pale yellow, and red. Ghent Hybrids are tall plants, up to 8–10 ft. (2.5–3.0 m) high, and 6–8 ft. (1.8–2.5 m) wide. Plants are hardy in Zones 4b–8a.

Girard Hybrids
These hybrids were developed at Girard Nurseries principally from Knap Hill Hybrids. The goal was to establish mildew resistance, ease of propagation, and heat resistance. Flower color runs the full color range for deciduous azaleas, and some clones have double flowers. Plants are hardy in Zones 5a–8a. See also Girard Hybrids, p. 239.

Knap Hill Hybrids
Developed by Anthony Waterer in England in 1870 at the Knap Hill Nursery of Knap Hill, Woking, England. Knap Hill Hybrids have been used extensively in further hybridizing. The goal has been to improve the Ghent Hybrids by crossing with the Chinese azalea *R. molle* and several other species.
Knap Hill Hybrids are generally medium to large size, 4–10 ft. (1.2–3.0 m) high, and 4–6 ft. (1.2–1.8 m) wide. Flower colors are white, yellow, orange, pink, and red. Plants bloom mid to late midseason and are hardy in zones 5a–8a.
There are five subgroups of Knap Hill Azaleas—the Knap Hill, Exbury, Ilam, Slocock, and Windsor. The Exbury Hybrids are an extension of the Knap Hill Hybrids selected by Lionel de Rothschild of Exbury, Southampton, England. The Ilam Hybrids are an extension of the Knap Hill Hybrids by Edgar Stead of Ilam Estate, Christchurch, New Zealand. Ilam Hybrids have slightly larger flowers.

Leach Hybrids

Developed by David G. Leach of North Madison, Ohio, from cold hardy species and hybrids of North American deciduous azaleas. The Leach Hybrids are cold hardy to Zone 4b. Plants are medium to tall, 6–8 ft. (1.8–2.5 m) high, and 4–6 ft. (1.2–1.8 m) wide.

Mollis Hybrids

Originating in Belgium, the Mollis Hybrids are derived and selected from the Japanese azalea *R. japonicum* and the Chinese azalea *R. molle.*

Plants bloom mid to late season in colors of white, yellow, orange, pink, and red. Most plants are tall and upright to 8 ft. (2.5 m), and 6 ft. (1.8 m) wide. Mollis Hybrids are hardy in Zones 5b–8a.

Occidentale Hybrids

These hybrids of the "Western Azalea" *R. occidentale,* native to the west coast of North America, first originated in England and Belgium and later in Tacoma, Washington.

Occidentale Hybrids are tall plants, 8–10 ft. (2.5–3.0 m) in height. Flowers are fragrant, light in color with a yellow blotch, and appear in mid to late summer. Plants are hardy in Zones 7a–8b.

Rustica Flora Pleno Hybrids

Originating in Belgium, parentage of these hybrids is unknown. Plants are tall and upright, 6–8 ft. (1.8–2.5 m) high, and 5 ft. (1.5 m) wide. Plants are hardy in Zones 6b–8.

Slonecker Hybrids

Developed by Howard Slonecker from Knap Hill Hybrids. The goal was to produce deciduous azaleas adaped to the west coast of North America. Plants are 4–8 ft. (1.2–2.5 m) high and 3–5 ft. (0.9–1.5 m) wide. Slonecker Hybrids are hardy to Zones 5b–8a.

Weston Hybrids

Developed at Weston Nurseries of Hopkinton, Massachusetts, with the goal of improving cold hardiness. Plants are 6–8 ft. (1.8–2.5 m) high and 4–6b ft. (1.2–1.8 m) wide. Weston Hybrids are adapted to Zones 4b–8a.

Table 7. Deciduous Azalea Species

NAME	U.S.D.A. HARDINESS ZONES	HEIGHT IN 10 YEARS	FLOWER COLOR	FLOWERING SEASON	COMMENTS
R. alabamense	6b–9a	2–6ft. (0.6–1.8 m)	white	LM	stoloniferous; yellow blotch in flower
R. albrechtii	6b–8a	6–8 ft. (1.8–2.5 m)	purplish red	E	bell-shaped flowers; prefers woodlands
R. arborescens	5a–9a	to 15 ft. (4.5 m)	white	ML	yellow blotch in flower; fragrant
R. atlanticum	6a–9a	1–2 ft. (0.3–0.6 m)	white	M	syn. 'Coast Azalea'; flowers fragrant
R. austrinum	6b–10a	to 15 ft. (4.5 m)	pink and yellow	E	flowers fragrant; probably the yellow form is the original
R. bakeri	5b–8b	2–18 ft. (0.6–5.5 m)	red and orange	L	small, deep green leaves; 'Camp's Red' is a selected clone
R. calendulaceum	5b–8b	6–12 ft. (1.8–3.6 m)	yellow to red	L	syn. 'Flame Azalea'; wide color range; a tetroploid
R. canadense	3b–7a	3–4 ft. (0.9–1.2 m)	purplish pink	E	stoloniferous; prefers soils of low pH (4.5)
R. canescens	6b–10a	to 15 ft. (4.5 m)	white	M	sometimes stoloniferous; prefers moist woodlands
R. flammeum	6b–9a	2–10 ft. (0.6–3.0 m)	orange to red	E–M	syn. *R. speciosum*; stoloniferous
R. japonicum	5a–8b	4–6 ft. (1.2–1.8 m)	yellow, orange, and red	E–M	often confused with *R. molle*
R. luteum	6b–8a	to 12 ft. (3.6 m)	yellow	M	flowers fragrant; not widely grown in North America
R. molle	6b–8a	4–6 ft. (1.2–1.8 m)	yellow	E	erect growing; less cold hardy than *R. japonicum*
R. occidentale	7a–9b	6–15 ft. (1.8–4.5 m)	white, yellow, or pink	M	flowers fragrant; not heat tolerant
R. pentaphyllum	6b–8b	treelike	strong pink	E	slow to flower; white form also available
R. periclymenoides (nudiflorum)	4b–9a	4–6 ft. (1.2–1.8 m)	pale to deep pink	E–M	also a white form
R. prinophyllum (roseum)	4b–9a	6–15 ft. (1.8–4.5 m)	pink	M	syn. 'Pinkshell Azalea'; clove-scented flowers
R. prunifolium	7a–9b	6–15 ft. (1.8–4.5 m)	orange to red	VL	prefers partial shade
R. quiquefolium	6a–8b	small tree	white	E	5-whorled leaves often have reddish margin
R. schlippenbachii	5a–9a	10–15 ft. (3.0–4.5 m)	light purplish pink	VE	known as the Royal Azalea; prefers a slightly acid soil (pH 6.5)
R. serrulatum	7a–10a	to 15 ft. (4.5 m)	white	L	clove-scented flowers

Table 7. Deciduous Azalea Species (continued)

NAME	U.S.D.A. HARDINESS ZONES	HEIGHT IN 10 YEARS	FLOWER COLOR	FLOWERING SEASON	COMMENTS
R. vaseyi	5a–9a	to 15 ft. (4.5 m)	pink	E	white form also available
R. viscosum	4b–9a	3–15 ft. (0.9–4.5 m)	white	M–L	stoloniferous; flowers have a spicy fragrance

Table 8. Deciduous Azalea Hybrids

NAME	U.S.D.A. HARDINESS ZONES	HEIGHT IN 10 YEARS	FLOWER COLOR	FLOWERING SEASON	COMMENTS
'Annabella'	5a–8a	--	strong orange-yellow	--	Exbury Hybrid
'Aurora'	5b–8a	to 8 ft. (2.5 m)	orange	EM	more heat tolerant than Knap Hill Hybrids; Mollis Hybrid
'Beaulieu'	5a–8a	--	pink	M	orange blotch in flower; Knap Hill Hybrid
'Berryrose'	5a–8a	4 ft. (1.2 m)	vivid yellow	M	fragrant; Exbury Hybrid
'Bouquet de Flore'	5b–8a	to 10 ft. (3.0 m)	vivid red	L	yellow blotch, frilled flowers; Ghent Hybrid
'Brazil'	5a–8a	5 ft. (1.5 m)	reddish orange	M	frilled flowers; very dependable; Knap Hill Hybrid
'Bullfinch'	5a–8a	5 ft. (1.5 m)	deep red	LM	Knap Hill Hybrid
'Buttercup'	5a–8a	--	yellow	LM	Knap Hill Hybrid
'Buzzard'	5a–8a	--	pale yellow	M	flowers tinged pink, fragrant; Knap Hill Hybrid
'Cannon's Double'	5a–8a	--	yellowish white	M	double flowers, pink lobes; Exbury Hybrid
'Cecile'	5a–8a	5 ft. (1.5 m)	salmon, pink, and yellow	LM	orange-yellow blotch in flower; Exbury Hybrid
'Chetco'	6a–8a	4 ft. (1.2 m)	vivid yellow	M	Slonecker Hybrid
'Chicago'	5b–8a	to 10 ft. (3.0 m)	light reddish orange	M	Mollis Hybrid
'Coccinea Speciosa'	5b–8a	--	yellowish pink	LM	strong orange blotch in flower; Ghent Hybrid
'Corringe'	5b–8a	6–10 ft. (1.8–3.0 m)	pink	LM	flowers double; Ghent Hybrid

Table 8. Deciduous Azalea Hybrids (continued)

NAME	U.S.D.A. HARDINESS ZONES	HEIGHT IN 10 YEARS	FLOWER COLOR	FLOWERING SEASON	COMMENTS
'Crimson Tide'	6b–8a	--	red	--	flowers double; Inter-Group Hybrid, Girard Nurseries introduction
'Daviesi'	5b–8a	6–10 ft. (1.8–3.0 m)	pale yellow	L	Ghent Hybrid
'Delicatissima'	7a–9	--	yellowish white	M–L	yellow blotch in flower; Occidentale Hybrid
'Fireball'	5a–8a	--	fiery red	M	upright growth habit; Knap Hill Hybrid
'Fraserii'	--	3 ft. (0.9 m)	purplish pink	E	twiggy growth habit
'George Reynolds'	5a–8a	--	yellow	EM	Knap Hill Hybrid
'Gibraltar'	5a–8a	4 ft. (1.2 m)	vivid orange	M	very popular and easy to grow; Exbury Hybrid
'Ginger'	5a–8a	--	strong orange	--	Exbury Hybrid
'Golden Crest'	5a–8a	--	brilliant yellow	--	orange blotch in flower; Knap Hill Hybrid
'Golden Oriole'	5a–8a	--	brilliant yellow	EM	deep orange blotch in flower; Knap Hill Hybrid
'Golden Peace'	5a–8a	--	yellow	--	strong orange blotch in flower; Exbury Hybrid
'Golden Sunset'	5a–8a	--	vivid yellow	M	Knap Hill Hybrid
'Goldflakes'	5a–8a	4 ft. (1.2 m)	vivid yellow	EM	strong orange blotch in flower; Bovee Knap Hill Hybrid
'Homebush'	5a–8a	6 ft. (1.8 m)	rose pink	LM	semidouble flowers; Knap Hill Hybrid
'Ilam Copper Cloud'	5a–8a	--	orange	--	flowers frilled; Ilam Hybrid
'Ilam Red Letter'	5b–8a	--	reddish orange	M	Ilam Hybrid
'Ilam Red Velvet'	--	--	deep red	--	petals slightly turned back; Wells Hybrid
'Irene Koster'	7a–9	8 ft. (2.5 m)	white	M	flowers flushed pink, fragrant; Occidentale Hybrid
'Kathleen'	5a–8a	--	light orange	LM	darker blotch in flower; Exbury Hybrid
'Kilauea'	5a–8a	--	reddish orange	L	orange blotch in flower; Knap Hill Hybrid
'Klondyke'	5a–8a	--	strong orange	LM	orange-yellow blotch in flower; Exbury Hybrid
'Koster's Brilliant Red'	5b–8a	--	reddish orange	LM	Mollis Hybrid

Table 8. Deciduous Azalea Hybrids (continued)

NAME	U.S.D.A. HARDINESS ZONES	HEIGHT IN 10 YEARS	FLOWER COLOR	FLOWERING SEASON	COMMENTS
'Lemon Drop'	4a–8a	6 ft. (1.8 m)	vivid yellow	VL	fragrant; Weston Hybrid
'Magnifica'	7a–9a	8 ft. (2.5 m)	purplish red	LM	orange-yellow blotch in flower; Occidentale Hybrid
'Marina'	5a–8a	--	pale yellow	EM	deeper yellow blotch in flower; Exbury Hybrid
'Marion Merriman'	5a–8a	--	brilliant yellow	LM	vivid orange blotch in flower; Knap Hill Hybrid
'Mt. St. Helens'	--	--	pink	M	yellow and orange blotch in flower; Girard Hybrid
'My Mary'	5b–8a	--	light yellow	EM	fragrant; stoloniferous; Beasley Hybrid
'Narcissiflora'	5b–8a	6 ft. (1.8 m)	light yellow	LM	flowers double; Ghent Hybrid
'Norma'	--	--	reddish orange	LM	flowers edged deep pink; Rustica Flora Pleno Hybrid
Northern Lights Hybrids	4a–8a	--	--	--	group of extremely hardy hybrids developed at the University of Minnesota
'Old Gold'	5a–8a	--	light orange	LM	flower flushed pink; Exbury Hybrid
'Orangeade'	5a–8a	--	orange	LM	Knap Hill Hybrid
'Orient'	5a–8a	--	reddish orange	LM	orange blotch in flower; Exbury Hybrid
'Peachy Keen'	5b–8a	--	light pink	M	syn. 'Ilam Peachy Keen'; Ilam Hybrid
'Persian Melon'	5a–8a	--	orange-yellow	--	syn. 'Ilam Persian Melon'; large truss; Ilam Hybrid
'Persil'	5a–8a	--	white	M	pale yellow blotch in flower; Knap Hill Hybrid
'Prince Henri de Pays-Bas'	5a–8a	6–8 ft. (1.8–2.4 m)	strong orange	L	upright grower; Ghent Hybrid
'Raphael de Smet'	5a–8a	6 ft. (1.8 m)	white, edged pink	LM	upright growth habit; flowers double
'Royal Command'	5a–8a	--	vivid reddish orange	M–L	Exbury Hybrid
'Spek's Orange'	5a–8a	4 ft. (1.2 m)	red, tinged orange	--	orange blotch in flower; Mollis Hybrid
'Sunte Nectarine'	5a–8a	--	deep orange	M	yellow blotch in flower; Exbury Hybrid
'Superba'	7a–9	--	dark pink	--	orange blotch in frilled flowers; Occidentale Hybrid

Table 8. Deciduous Azalea Hybrids (continued)

NAME	U.S.D.A. HARDINESS ZONES	HEIGHT IN 10 YEARS	FLOWER COLOR	FLOWERING SEASON	COMMENTS
'Sylphides'	--	--	purplish pink	--	vivid yellow blotch; Knap Hill Hybrid
'Toucan'	--	--	pinkish white	LM	upright, open grower; Knap Hill Hybrid
'Tower Dainty'	5b–8a	--	pale pink	--	fragrant; Ghent Hybrid
'Unique'	5b–8a	6 ft. (1.8 m)	orange-yellow	LM	upright grower; Ghent Hybrid

Plant Listing by Flower Color

Includes all species/cultivars in Appendix A. Some species are listed under more than one flower color due to variations within that plant.

Rhododendron Species—Elepidote

PINK
R. *adenopodum*
R. *calophytum*
R. *catawbiense*
R. *degronianum*
R. *fortunei*
R. *makinoi*
R. *metternichii*
R. *orbiculare*
R. *oreodoxa*
R. *oreotrephes*
R. *ovatum*
R. *pachysanthum*
R. *pseudochrysanthum*
R. *rex*
R. *soulei*
R. *sutchuenense*
R. *vernicosum*
R. *williamsianum*
R. *zeylanicum*

RED
R. *arboreum*
R. *haematodes*
R. *houlstonii*
R. *smithii*
R. *thompsonii*
R. *zeylanicum*

WHITE
R. *aberconwayii*
R. *argyrophylum*
R. *brachycarpum*

R. *bureavii*
R. *campanulatum*
R. *catawbiense alba*
R. *decorum*
R. *fargesii*
R. *fictolacteum*
R. *hyperythrum*
R. *maximum*
R. *morii*
R. *ovatum*
R. *rex*
R. *roxieanum*
R. *sargentianum* Maricee
R. *uvarifolium*
R. *yakushimanum*

PURPLE
R. *ponticum*
R. *smirnowii*

YELLOW-ORANGE
R. *campylocarpum*
R. *dichroanthum*
R. *wardii*

Rhododendron Species—Lepidote

PINK
R. *carolinianum*
R. *chapmanii*
R. *ciliatum*
R. *cinnabarinum*
R. *ferrugineum*

R. *minus*
R. *mucronulatum*
R. *mucronulatum* Cornell Pink
 R. *racemosum*
R. *rubiginosum*
R. *yunnanense*

RED
R. *cinnabarinum*
R. *keleticum*

WHITE
R. *carolinianum*
R. *ciliatum*
R. *dauricum*
R. *ferrugineum*
R. *leucaspis*
R. *micranthum*
R. *minus*
R. *moupinense*
R. *racemosum*
R. *roxieanum*
R. *veitchianum*
R. *viscosum*
R. *yunnanense*

PURPLE
R. *augustinii*
R. *dauricum*
R. *fastigiatum*
R. *glomerulatum*
R. *hippophaeoides*
R. *impeditum*
R. *lapponicum*
R. *litangense*
R. *mucronulatum*
R. *oreotrephes*
R. *russatum*
R. *yungningense*

YELLOW-ORANGE
R. *burmanicum*
R. *cinnabarinum*
R. *concatenans*
R. *hanceanum*
R. *johnstoneanum*
R. *keiskei*
R. *lutescens*

Rhododendron Hybrids—Elepidote

PINK
'Alice'
'Anna Rose Whitney'
'Antoon van Welie'

'Apple Blossom'
'Bali'
'Bass River'
'Beauty of Littleworth'
'Ben Mosely'
'Bonnie Maid'
'Bosley-Dexter 1009'
'Bow Bells'
'Bravo'
'Brown Eyes'
'Cadis'
'Chesterland'
'Christmas Cheer'
'David Gable'
'Edith Pride'
'Golfer'
'Great Eastern'
'Jan Dekens'
'Janet Blair'
'Kate Waterer'
'Lem's Monarch'
'Maxecat'
'Mrs. C. S. Sargent'
'Mrs. Furnival'
'Mrs. G. W. Leak'
'Mrs. W. C. Slocok'
'Newburyport Belle'
'Parker's Pink'
'Party Pink'
'Pink Fondant'
'Pink Pearl'
'Pink Walloper'
'Platinum Pearl'
'Rocket'
'Rose Point'
'Roseum Pink'
'Ruby Bowman'
'Russell Harmon'
'Scintillation'
'Sham's Candy'
'Terrific'
'Todmorden'
'Tom Everett'
'Trude Webster'
'Van'
'Vernus'
'Wheatley'
'Wyandanch Pink'
'Yaku Duchess'
'Yaku King'
'Yaku Prince'
'Yaku Queen'

RED
'America'
'Baden Baden'
'Besse Howells'
'Britannia'
'Carmen'
'Damozel'
'Dr. H. C. Dresselhuys'
'Elizabeth'
'Elizabeth Hobbie'
'Francesca'
'Gi Gi'
'Glenda Farrell'
'Grace Seabrook'
'Halfdan Lem'
'Hallelujah'
'Holden'
'Humming Bird'
'Jean Marie de Montague'
'Markeeta's Flame'
'Markeeta's Prize'
'Nova Zembla'
'Redder Yet'
'Ruby Hart'
'Scarlet Wonder'
'Sham's Ruby'
'Shilsonii'
'Spring Parade'
'Taurus'
'Tony'
'Trilby'
'Vulcan'
'Vulcan's Flame'

ROSE
'Accomplishment'
'Albert Close'
'Atroflo'
'Cynthia'
'Dexter 974'
'English Roseum'
'Summer Rose'
'Winsome'

WHITE
'Album Elegans'
'Anna H. Hall'
'Beaufort'
'Belle Heller'
'Boule de Neige'
'Calsap'
'Catawbiense Album'
'Chionoides'
'County of York'

'Disca'
'Dr. Edward Lufton'
'Faggetter's Favorite'
'Fragrantissimum'
'Gomer Waterer'
'Helene Schiffner'
'Ice Cube'
'Joseph Paterno'
'Loder's White'
'Lodestar'
'Madame Masson'
'Minnie'
'Mrs. A. T. de La Mare'
'Mrs. E. C. Sterling'
'Mrs. Tom H. Lowinsky'
'Olympic Lady'
'Sappho'
'Sir Charles Lemon'
'Trinity'
'White Pearl'

PURPLE—LAVENDER—LILAC
'A. Bedford'
'Anah Kruschke'
'Blue Ensign'
'Blue Peter'
'Caroline'
'Catawbiense Boursault'
'Everestianum'
'Fastuosum Flore Pleno'
'Grierosplendor'
'Jonathan Shaw'
'Lee's Dark Purple'
'Maximum Roseum'
'Old Port'
'Olin O. Dobbs'
'Parson's Gloriosum'
'Purple Splendour'
'Roseum Elegans'
'Shawme Lake'
'Susan'

YELLOW—SALMON—CREAM
'Autumn Gold'
'Broughtonii Aureum'
'Buttermint'
'Carita'
'Champayne'
'Chikor'
'Crest' ('Hawk Crest')
'Damaris'
'Gladys'
'Golden Gala'
'Golden Star'

'Goldsworth Orange'
'Hello Dolly'
'Lem's Cameo'
'Marcia'
'Mary Belle'
'Medusa'
'Moonstone'
'Mrs. Betty Robinson'
'Odee Wright'
'Percy Wiseman'
'Ring of Fire'
'Rothenburg'
'September Song'
'Shamrock'
'Unique'
'Virginia Richards'

Rhododendron Hybrids—Lepidote

PINK
'Aglo'
'Alfred Wiacek'
'Alice Swift'
'April Blush'
'Balta'
'Bric-a-brac'
'Carolina Rose'
'Cilpiense'
'Donna Totten'
'Ethel Mae'
'Fairy Mary'
'Ginny Gee'
'Laurie'
'Llenroc'
'Myrtifolium'
'Olga Mezitt'
'Olive'
'Pikeland'
'Pink Diamond'
    ('Weston's Pink Diamond')
'Pink Drift'
'Pink Snowflakes'
'Pioneer'
'Pipit'
'P. J. M.'
'Rose Elf'
'Shrimp Pink'
'Spring Delight'
'Tiffany'
'Tom Koenig'
'Waltham'
'Wigeon'
'Wilsonii'
'Windbeam'

RED
'Jenny'

ROSE
'Barto Alpine'
'Conewago'
'Mucram'

WHITE
'April Gem'
'Arctic Pearl'
'Dora Amateis'
'Elsie Frye'
'Epoch'
'Forsterianum'
'Fragrantissimum'
'Hudson Bay'
'Laurie'
'Molly Fordham'
'My Lady'
'Peace'
'Pink Snowflakes'
'Small Gem'
'Snow Lady'
'Wyanoki'
'Yellow Eye'

PURPLE—LAVENDER—BLUE
'Blaney's Blue'
'Blue Bird'
'Blue Diamond'
'Blue Ridge'
'Blue Tit'
'Crater Lake'
'Early Bird'
'Fasia'
'Lanny's Pride'
'Malta'
'Mother Greer'
'Praecox'
'Purple Gem'
'Ramapo'
'Rose Marie'
'Sapphire'
'Senoria Meldon'
'Starry Night'
'Weston's Pink Diamond'

YELLOW—SALMON—CREAM
'Alison Johnstone'
'Chick'
'Chikor'
'Cream Crest'

'Curlew'
'Goldstrike'
'Lady Chamberlain'
'Lemon Mist'
'Mary Fleming'
'Patty Bee'
'Princess Anne'
'Saffron Queen'
'Spring Song'
'St. Judy'
'Yellow Hammer'

Evergreen Azalea Species

PINK
R. indicum
R. kaempferi
R. kiusianum
R. macrantha
R. serpyllifolium
R. simsii

RED
R. balsaminaeflorum
R. indicum
R. kiusianum
R. simsii

WHITE
R. indicum
R. kiusianum
R. mucronatum

PURPLE
R. kiusianum
R. macrosepalum
R. yedoense
R. yedoense var. poukhanense

ORANGE
R. macrantha
R. nakaharae
R. oldhamii

Evergreen Azalea Hybrids

PINK
'Amy'
'Anna Kehr'
'Big Joe'
'Blaauw's Pink'
'Cameo'
'Cavalier'
'Conversation Piece'
'Coral Bells' ('Kirin')
'Debonnaire'

'Diana'
'Dorothy Clark'
'Dream'
'Easter Parade'
'Eliza Hyatt'
'Eureka'
'Fascination'
'Fashion'
'Fedora'
'Flamingo'
'Forest Fire'
'Gaiety'
'Girard Border Gem'
'Girard Chiara'
'Girard Rose'
'Gumpo'
'Guy Yerkes'
'Hampton Beauty'
'Helena'
'Hino Pink'
'Hinomayo'
'Kathleen'
'Kirin'
'Lorna'
'Margaret Douglas'
'Maybelle'
'Mrs. Henry Schroeder'
'Mrs. Nancy Dipple'
'Nadine'
'Nancy of Robin Hill'
'Naomi'
'Parfait'
'Pink Pearl'
'Pink Ruffles'
'Pride's Pink'
'Rosebud'
'Springtime'
'Starlight'
'Vuyk's Rosyred'
'Yankee Doodle'

RED
'Addy Wery'
'Adelaine Pope'
'Aladdin'
'Amoenum'
'Beni Kirishima'
'Ben Morrison'
'Boudoir'
'Buccaneer'
'Caroline Gable'
'Christmas Cheer'
'Elizabeth Gable'

'Girard Scarlet'
'Glamour'
'Gumpo'
'Hershey's Red'
'Hino Crimson'
'Hinode Giri'
'Hino Red'
'James Gable'
'John Cairns'
'Modesty'
'Mother's Day'
'Red Red'
'Red Ruffles'
'Sakata Red'
'Sherwood Red'
'Stewartstonian'
'Sunglow'
'Surprise'
'Twenty Grand'
'Vuyks Scarlet'
'Wakaebisu'
'Ward's Ruby'

WHITE
'Adonis'
'Ben Morrison'
'Cascade' (Shammarello)
'Cloud Nine'
'Dayspring'
'Delaware Valley White'
'Desiree'
'Eikan'
'Everest'
'Festive'
'Gay'
'Glacier'
'Gumpo'
'Hardy Gardenia'
'Helen Curtis'
'H. H. Hume'
'Iro-Hayama'
'Iveryana'
'John Haerens'
'Martha Hitchcock'
'Moonbeam'
'Mrs. G. G. Gerbing'
'Palestrina'
'Polaris'
'Refrain'
'Roehr's Peggy Ann'
'Rose Greeley'
'Snow'
'Vespers'

'White Rosebud'

PURPLE
'Atlanta'
'Blue Danube'
'Corsage'
'Elsie Lee'
'Girard Fuschia'
'Herbert'
'Karens'
'Marjorie'
'Mildred May'
'Pink Pearce'
'Purple Splendour'
'Seneca'
'Sherwood Orchid'

ORANGE
'Alexander'
'Girard Hot Shot'
'Leo'
'Mary Dalton'
'Orange Beauty'

SALMON
'Louise Gable'

Deciduous Azalea Species

PINK
R. austrinum
R. canadense
R. occidentale
R. pentaphyllum
R. periclymenoides (nudiflorum)
R. prinophyllum (roseum)
R. schlippenbachii
R. vaseyi

RED
R. albrechtii
R. bakeri
R. calendulaceum
R. flammeum
R. japonicum
R. prunifolium

WHITE
R. alabamense
R. arborescens
R. atlanticum
R. canescens
R. occidentale
R. quinquefolium
R. schlippenbachii

R. *serrulatum*
R. *viscosum*

YELLOW
R. *austrinum*
R. *calendulaceum*
R. *japonicum*
R. *luteum*
R. *molle*
R. *occidentale*

ORANGE
R. *bakeri*
R. *calendulaceum*
R. *flammeum*
R. *japonicum*
R. *prunifolium*

Deciduous Azalea Hybrids

PINK
'Beaulieu'
'Cecile'
'Coccinea Speciosa'
'Corringe'
'Fraserii'
'Homebush'
'Mt. St. Helens'
'Peachy Keen'
'Superba'
'Sylphides'
'Toucan'
'Tower Dainty'

RED
'Bouquet de Flore'
'Bullfinch'
'Crimson Tide'
'Fireball'
'Ilam Red Velvet'
'Magnifica'

WHITE
'Cannon's Double'
'Delicatissima'
'Irene Koster'

'Persil'
'Raphael de Smet'

YELLOW
'Annabella'
'Berryrose'
'Buttercup'
'Buzzard'
'Chetco'
'Daviesi'
'George Reynolds'
'Golden Crest'
'Golden Oriole'
'Golden Peace'
'Golden Sunset'
'Goldflakes'
'Lemon Drop'
'Marina'
'Marion Merriman'
'My Mary'
'Narcissiflora'
'Persian Melon'
'Unique'

ORANGE
'Aurora'
'Brazil'
'Chicago'
'Gibraltar'
'Ginger'
'Ilam Copper Cloud'
'Ilam Red Letter'
'Kathleen'
'Kilauea'
'Klondyke'
'Koster's Brilliant Red'
'Norma'
'Old Gold'
'Orangeade'
'Orient'
'Prince Henri de Pays-Bas'
'Royal Command'
'Spek's Orange'
'Sunte Nectarine'

APPENDIX C: *Cold Tolerant Plants*

L = Lepidote   E = Elepidote

Rhododendrons: Flower Bud Hardy to −25°F (−32°C)

'Anna H. Hall'	E
'April Blush'	L
'Arctic Pearl'	L
'Balta'	L
'Bosley-Dexter 1009'	E
'Boule de Neige'	E
'Calsap'	E
R. carolinianum	L
R. catawbiense	E
'Catawbiense Album'	E
'Chesterland'	E
'Conewago'	L
R. dauricum	L
'Edith Pride'	E
'English Roseum'	E
R. hippophaeoides	E
R. lapponicum	E
'Malta'	L
'Maxecat'	E
'Maximum Roseum'	E
'Mrs. C. S. Sargent'	E
'Nova Zembla'	E
'Parson's Gloriosum'	E
'Pioneer'	L
'P. J. M.'	L
'Purple Gem'	L
'Redder Yet'	E
'Roseum Elegans'	E
'Roseum Pink'	E
'Russell Harmon'	E
'Terrific'	E
'Vernus'	E
'Windbeam'	L

Evergreen Azaleas: Flower Bud Hardy to −10°F (−23°C) and Colder

'Alexander'
'Cascade' (Shammarello)
'Corsage'
'Desiree'
'Eliza Hyatt'
'Elsie Lee'
'Girard Border Gem'
'Girard Chiara'
'Girard Fuschia'
'Girard Scarlet'
'Helen Curtis'
'Herbert'
'Hino Pink'
'Hino Red'
'James Gable'
'Karens'
'Marjorie'
'Maybelle'
'Palestrina'
'Parfait'

Glossary

Aerated Containing air, primarily oxygen. Usually used in reference to a soil trait as plant roots require oxygen.

Adventitious A type of bud that develops at a spot other than the leaf axils.

Anther The pollen bearing structure of the flower located at the top of the stamen. Common to seed plants.

ARS American Rhododendron Society.

Asexual A type of propagation other than sexual. For example, vegetative propagation is an asexual propagation method.

Azaleadron A plant resulting from cross pollination between an azalea and a rhododendron.

Backcrossing A hybridizing method in which a seedling is crossed (back) with one of its parents.

Cambium A cellular layer found between the xylem (wood) and phloem (bark). The cambium produces new cells.

CEC Cation Exchange Capacity. A measurement used in analyzing soil indicating the total number of exchangeable cations. Reflects the soil capacity to fix and hold nutrients as cations.

Chelated A mineral in soluble form.

Chlorosis A disease condition producing a yellowing of the foliage. Leaves fail to develop chlorophyll because of nutrient deficiencies or disease. Photosynthesis is reduced, causing a weakening of the plant. In extreme cases plant death occurs.

Corolla The petals of a flower.

Cultivar A particular clone or individual plant form identified by a specific name. Traditionally a contraction of "cultivated variety."

Dead-heading Removal of spent flowers to prevent seed set.

Deciduous A type of plant that loses its leaves at the end of the growing season.

Diploid Refers to chromosome count. A diploid plant has the normal number of chromosomes, one set from each parent. For *Rhododendron* this is 26 chromosomes.

Elepidote   One of two major classifications of rhododendron. Describes a type of rhododendron that lacks small scurfy scales and usually has large leaves.

Epiphyte   A type of plant that grows on another plant or object. Non-parasitic. Derives nutrients from air, rainwater, and organic matter without growing in the soil.

Ericaceae   The family of plants including rhododendrons and azaleas. Ericaceous plants grow best in acid soil conditions.

Flocculation   The clumping together of soil particles to form larger masses. Soil structure is improved by this process.

Fritted   Said of fertilizers having a protective surface which delays nutrient release into the soil. Time-released fertilizer.

Gravitational pull   The force exerted by gravity on the movement of soil water.

Hardening off   The process of adapting a new, tender plant to environmental differences. Involves lowering humidity from 100% to levels normally encountered outdoors and gradually introducing wind, sunlight, and temperature variations.

Heterogeneous   Differing in kind and exhibiting pronounced variability.

Hose-in-hose   A flower type with two rows of petals, one appearing inside the other.

Hybrid   A plant that represents the combined characteristics of its two parents. Typically heterogeneous.

Indumentum   A hairy or woolly texture exhibited on leaf and bud surfaces.

Ion   Electrified particles. *See* CEC.

Leach   Used in reference to fertilizer that is diluted and removed from the plant area by rain or irrigation water.

Lepidote   One of two major classifications of rhododendrons. Includes the scaly, small-leaved types.

Medium, media (plural)   Refers to growing mixture or mixtures with or without soil.

Microfoam   Trademarked name for a blanket used to insulate plant material during winter storage.

Mycorrhizae (plural)   Beneficial fungi living on the roots of rhododendrons.

Pathogenic   Used to describe any disease causing agent.

pH   A logarithmic scale used to measure effective hydrogen ions on a scale of 0–14. A rating of 7 is neutral; below 7 is acidic; above 7 is alkaline. Used in determining soil acidity or alkalinity.

Phloem   A plant tissue active in the transfer and storage of water and minerals. Comprises the outer layer or bark of stems.

Pistil   The flower part including ovary, style, and stigma.

Pollen sac   The pollen bearing part topping the anther.

Polyploid   A plant having greater than the normal number of chromosomes. *See* Diploid, Tetraploid.

RHS   Royal Horticultural Society, England.

Scion   A section of living material used in grafting to another plant. Typically a short piece of detached shoot containing several buds. When grafted to a rootstock, the scion supplies the upper portion to the newly grafted plant.

Seed leaves   The first set of leaves developed by a seedling. *See* True leaves.

Sepal   A modified leaf at the base of a flower. The outermost floral leaves.

Species   A group of plants exhibiting similar physical traits. These traits are passed on through sexual reproduction to the next generation.

Stigma   Female flower part that becomes receptive to pollen. The outermost portion of the pistil.

Stoloniferous   A type of plant that is capable of reproducing itself by sending stolons out from its base. New plants sprout from nodes or from buds at the stolon tip.

Style   Also called the pollen tube. Flower part between the ovary and stigma.

Tetraploid   Refers to chromosome count. A plant having twice the normal number of chromosomes. *See also* Diploid.

True leaves   The second set of leaves produced by a seedling. Usually indicates maturity of the seedling to transplant stage.

Xylem   Plant tissue located inside the cambium. The woody element of plant stems. Used chiefly in conducting water and minerals yet also serves as storage and support.

For Further Reading

Davidian, H. H. *Rhododendron Species, Volume I: Lepidotes.* Portland, Oregon: Timber Press, 1982.

Davidian, H. H. *Rhododendron Species, Volume II: Elepidotes (Arboreum—Lactaeum).* Portland, Oregon: Timber Press, 1989.

Davidian, H. H. *Rhododendron Species, Volume III: Elepidotes (Neriiflorum—Thomsonii).* Portland, Oregon: Timber Press, 1991.

Galle, Fred C. *Azaleas.* Portland, Oregon: Timber Press, 1987.

Greer, Harold E. *Greer's Guidebook to Available Rhododendrons.* Rev. ed. Eugene, Oregon: Offshoot Publications, 1987.

Kingdon-Ward, F. *Plant Hunters Paradise.* Toronto, London: Jonathan Cape Ltd., 1938.

Leach, David G. *Rhododendrons of the World.* New York: Charles Scribner's Sons, 1961.

Salley, Homer, and Harold Greer. *Rhododendron Hybrids.* 2d ed. Portland, Oregon: Timber Press, 1992.

Van Veen, Ted. *Rhododendrons in America.* 2d ed. Portland, Oregon: Binford & Mort, 1986.

West, Franklin H., et al. *Rhododendrons and Azaleas for Eastern North America.* Edited by Philip A. Livingston, Newtown Square, Pennsylvania: Harrowood Books, 1978.

Technical Papers

Neal, John W., Jr., and Larry W. Douglas. *Bionomics and Instar Determination of* Synanthedon rhododendri *(Lepidoptera: Sesiidae) on Rhododendron.* Beltsville, Maryland: U.S.D.A. Agricultural Research Service, 1984.

Neal, John W., Jr., and Larry W. Douglas. *Development, Oviposition Rate, Longevity, and Voltinism of* Stephanitis pyrioides *(Heteroptera: Tingidae), an Adventive Pest of Azalea, at Three Temperatures.* Beltsville, Maryland: U.S.D.A. Agricultural Research Service, 1988.

Plant Index: Rhododendrons

(L) = Lepidote; (E) = Elepidote. Species' names appear in italics. Hybrids or cultivars appear in roman type with single quotes. Named selections are listed by species.

18139 see: *R. vernicosum* 18139
R. aberconwayii (E) 51, 77, 213, 258
'A. Bedford' (E) 50, 53, 70, 219, 260
'Accomplishment' (E) 219, 260
R. adenopodum (E) 58, 213, 258
'Aglo' (L) 57, 231, 261
'Albert Close' (E) 54, 55, 58, 71, 81, 219, 261
'Album Elegans' (E) 62, 63, 219, 261
'Alfred Wiacek' (L) 56, 231, 261
'Alice' (E) 75, 219, 259
'Alice Swift' (L) 56, 62, 231, 261
'Alison Johnstone' (L) 77, 80, 231, 261
'Ambie' (L) 62
'America' (E) 50, 54, 55, 57, 194, 219, 260
'Anah Kruschke' (E) 50, 51, 52, 66, 219, 260; Fig. 17
'Anna H. Hall' (E) 55, 58, 60, 61, 63, 68, 72, 219, 261, 265; Fig. 18
'Anna Rose Whitney' (E) 50, 53, 58, 65, 67, 71, 73, 81, 219, 259; Fig. 19
'Antoon van Welie' (E) 52, 75, 219, 259
'Apple Blossom' (E) 54, 63, 219, 259; see also *Plant Index: Azaleas*
'April Blush' (L) 57, 231, 261, 265
'April Gem' (L) 61, 231, 261
R. arboreum (E) 75, 79, 213, 258
'Arctic Pearl' (L) 56, 57, 231, 261, 265
R. argyrophylum (E) 79, 213, 258
'Atroflo' (E) 61, 219, 261
R. augustinii (L) 18, 51, 52, 66, 67, 73, 78, 79, 81, 216, 259; Fig. 15
R. augustinii var. *chasmanthum* (L) 77
R. aureum (L) 193
R. aureum Wada (L) 192
'Autumn Gold' (E) 219

'Baden Baden' (E) 61, 219, 260
'Bali' (E) 55, 219, 259
'Ballet' (E) 68
'Balta' (L) 56, 60, 231, 261, 265
R. barbatum (E) 18
'Barto Alpine' (L) 67, 231, 261
'Bass River' (E) 220, 259
'Beaufort' (E) 71, 220, 260
'Beauty of Littleworth' (E) 81, 220, 259
'Belle Heller' (E) 50, 220, 260
'Ben Mosely' (E) 55, 71, 220, 259
'Besse Howells' (E) 54, 55, 60, 63, 71, 220, 260; Fig. 20
'Blaney's Blue' (L) 66, 231, 261
'Blue Bird' (L) 78, 231, 261
'Bluebird' see: 'Blue Bird'
'Blue Diamond' (L) 73, 78, 79, 231, 261
'Blue Ensign' (E) 58, 63, 73, 220, 260
'Blue Peter' (E) 72, 73, 75, 81, 82, 220, 260
'Blue Ridge' (L) 50, 231, 261
'Blue Tit' (L) 77, 78, 231, 261
'Bonnie Maid' (E) 61, 220, 259
'Bosely-Dexter 1009' (E) 63, 220, 259, 265
'Boule de Neige' (E) 54, 58, 60, 63, 64, 72, 220, 260, 265
'Bow Bells' (E) 73, 79, 81, 220, 259
R. brachycarpum (E) 54, 59, 82, 213, 258
'Bravo' (E) 55, 220, 259
'Bric-a-brac' (L) 52, 74, 231, 261; Fig. 34
'Britannia' (E) 75, 81, 220, 260
'Broughtonii' (E) 75
'Broughtonii Aureum' (E) 221, 260
'Brown Eyes' (E) 54, 221, 259
'Bud Flanagan' (E) 78
R. bureavii (E) 52, 60, 64, 79, 213, 258

271

R. burmanicaum (L) 51, 52, 216, 259
'Buttermint' (E) 61, 221, 260

'Cadis' (E) 60, 65, 72, 221, 259; Fig. 67
'California Blue' (L) 51
R. calophytum (E) 60, 66, 79, 81, 213, 258
'Calsap' (E) 55, 62, 82, 221, 260, 265
R. campanulatum (E) 18, 77, 213, 258
R. campylocarpum (E) 18, 193, 213, 258
R. campylogynum (E) 73
'Carita' (E) 221, 260
'Carita Inchmery' (E) 79
'Carmen' (E) 221, 260
'Carolina Rose' (L) 55, 62, 232, 261
'Caroline' (E) 50, 54, 57, 58, 70, 72, 82,
    105, 221, 260; Fig. 21
R. carolinianum (L) 52, 54, 55, 57, 58, 59,
    60, 63, 68, 70, 71, 72, 82, 89, 183,
    216, 258, 259, 265
R. catalgla (E) 63, 192
R. catawbiense (E) 18, 20, 31, 50, 52, 54, 55,
    57, 58, 63, 68, 70, 71, 82, 89, 150,
    183, 213, 258, 265; Fig. 9
R. catawbiense alba (E) 65, 213, 258
R. catawbiense insularis (E) 192
'Catawbiense Album' (E) 55, 57, 58, 60,
    61, 63, 68, 71, 72, 221, 260, 265;
    Figs. 22, 23
'Catawbiense Boursault' (E) 50, 55, 70,
    71, 221, 260
R. caucasicum (E) 18
'Champayne' (E) 50, 221, 260
R. chapmanii (L) 57, 58, 65, 70, 71, 192,
    216, 258
'Chesterland' (E) 68, 221, 259, 265
'Chick' (L) 80, 232, 261
'Chikor' (L) 61, 79, 232, 260, 261
'Chionoides' (E) 58, 61, 62, 65, 72, 221,
    260
'Christmas Cheer' (E) 78, 81, 221, 259
R. chrysanthum (E) 18
R. ciliatum (L) 79, 216, 258, 259
'Cilpinense'(L) 67, 79, 232, 261
R. cinnabarinum (L) 79, 216, 258, 259
'Clark's White' (E) 192, 193
R. compactum (L) 192
R. concatenans (L) 81, 216, 259
'Conewago' (L) 59, 61, 64, 69, 232, 261,
    265
'Conewago Improved' (L) 63
Cornell Pink see: *R. mucronulatum*
    Cornell Pink
'County of York' (E) 50, 70, 72, 82, 221,
    260; Figs. 24, 88
'Crater Lake' (L) 66, 232, 261

'Cream Crest' (L) 74, 232, 261
'Creeping Jenny' see: 'Jenny'
'Crest' see: 'Hawk Crest'
R. croceum (E) 19
'Cunningham's White' (E) 28, 151
'Curlew' (L) 74, 79, 80, 232, 262
'Cynthia' (E) 50, 65, 79, 81, 222, 260; Fig.
    84

R. dalhonsiae (L) 18
'Damaris' (E) 222, 260
'Damaris Logan' (E) 79
'Damozel' (E) 58, 222, 260
R. dauricum (L) 18, 54, 55, 58, 59, 63, 70,
    79, 81, 82, 192, 217, 259, 265
R. dauricum var. *album* (L) 82, 193, 222,
    229, 231
'David Gable' (E) 61, 70, 71, 222, 259
R. davidsonianum (L) 51, 52, 66, 73, 81
R. decorum (E) 66, 67, 70, 73, 79, 192, 213,
    258
R. degronianum (E) 60, 73, 213, 258
Delp Hybrids (L) 82, 233
'Dexter 974' (E) 64, 222, 260
Dexter's Hybrids (E) 61, 219, 220, 228,
    230
'Dexter's Pink' see: 'Apple Blossom'
R. dichroanthum 258
R. dichroanthum ssp. *scyphocalyx* (E) 51,
    213
'Disca' (E) 71, 222, 260
R. discolor (E) 19, 73, 192
'Dr. Edward Lufton' (E) 68, 222, 260
'Dr. H. C. Dresselhuys' (E) 70, 222, 260
'Donna Totten' (L) 53, 232, 261
'Dora Amateis' (L) 53, 54, 59, 60, 61, 62,
    66, 67, 69, 78, 79, 232, 261; Fig. 35

'Early Bird' (L) 50, 57, 71, 232, 261
'Edith Pride' (E) 55, 222, 259, 265
'Ed's Red' (E) Fig. 72
'Elizabeth' (E) 79, 81, 222, 260
'Elizabeth Hobbie' (E) 79, 222, 260
R. elliottii (E) 19
'Elsie Frye' (L) 52, 232, 261
'English Roseum' (E) 54, 55, 60, 70, 71,
    222, 260, 265; Fig. 25
'Epoch' (L) 62, 232, 261
'Essex Scarlet' (E) 192, 193
'Ethel Mae' (E) 62, 233, 261
'Everestianum' (E) 64, 71, 223, 260

'Faggetter's Favorite' (E) 73, 223, 260
'Fairy Mary' (L) 64, 233, 261
R. falconeri (E) 18

R. fargesii (E) 67, 77, 214, 258
'Fasia' (L) 82, 233, 261
R. fastigiatum (L) 60, 217, 259
'Fastuosum Flore Pleno' (E) 77, 223, 260
R. ferrugineum (L) 18, 59, 60, 82, 217, 258, 259
R. fictolacteum (E) 81, 214, 258
R. forrestii (E) 19
'Forsterianum' (L) 52, 233, 261
R. fortunei (E) 18, 50, 52, 55, 57, 58, 59, 60, 64, 66, 67, 68, 70, 71, 73, 88, 126, 192, 193, 214, 220, 223, 258; Fig. 10
'Fowle 19' see: 'Newburyport Belle'
'Fragrantissimum' (L) 51, 52, 75, 233, 260, 261
'Francesca' (E) 63, 223, 260

Gable Hybrids (E)(L) 239; see also *Plant Index: Azaleas*
'Gen. Schmidt' (E) 62
'Gi Gi' (E) 50, 64, 223, 260
'Ginny Gee' (L) 53, 62, 64, 66, 69, 72, 233, 261
'Gladys' (E) 77, 223, 260
'Glenda Farrell' (E) 223, 260
R. glomerulatum (L) 217, 259
'Gold Mohur' (E) 193
'Golden Gala' (E) 55, 223, 260
'Golden Star' (E) 61, 223, 260
'Goldstrike' (L) 233, 262
'Goldsworth Orange' (E) 77, 223, 261
'Golfer' (E) 67, 223, 259
'Gomer Waterer' (E) 50, 52, 61, 70, 73, 223, 260; Fig. 26
'Grace Seabrook' (E) 66, 223, 260
R. grande (E) 18
'Great Eastern' (E) 63, 223, 259
'Grierosplendour' (E) 50, 58, 223, 260
R. griersonianum (E) 192
Guyencourt Hybrids (L) 64

R. haematodes (E) 66, 79, 192, 193, 214, 258
'Halfdan Lem' (E) 52, 67, 224, 260
'Hallelujah' (E) 66, 73, 224, 260
R. hanceanum (L) 217, 259
'Hawk Crest' (E) 61, 78, 79, 222, 260
'Helene Schiffner' (E) 67, 224, 260
'Hello Dolly' (E) 61, 73, 224, 261
'Henry's Red' (E) 63
R. hippophaeoides (L) 54, 59, 66, 79, 82, 217, 259, 265
R. hirsutum (L) 18
R. hodgsonii (E) 18
'Holden' (E) 55, 71, 224, 260

'Hong Kong' (E) 62
'Hotei' (E) 78
R. houlstonii (E) 72, 214, 258
'Hudson Bay' (L) 57, 233, 261
'Humming Bird' (E) 80, 224, 260
R. hyperythrum (E) 192, 258
R. hyperythrum (Creech's Narrowleaf Form) (E) 58, 214

'Ice Cube' (E) 50, 54, 55, 56, 57, 58, 63, 71, 72, 224, 260; Fig. 27
'Ignatius Sargent' (E) 56
R. impeditum (L) 54, 59, 60, 63, 66, 73, 78, 217, 259

'Jan Dekens' (E) 81, 224, 259
'Janet Blair' (E) 50, 53, 54, 57, 58, 60, 61, 62, 63, 64, 68, 71, 72, 82, 224, 259; Fig. 28
'Jean Marie de Montague' (E) 51, 52, 60, 61, 65, 66, 70, 73, 79, 224, 260; Figs. 29, 84
'Jenny' (L) 62, 233, 261
R. johnstoneanum (L) 78, 217, 259
'Jonathan Shaw' (E) 224, 260
'Joseph Paterno' (E) 68, 224, 260

'Kate Waterer' (E) 50, 80, 224, 259
R. keiskei (L) 57, 58, 64, 66, 68, 70, 78, 192, 193, 217, 259
R. keiskei Yaku Fairy (L) 60, 192, 217
R. keleticum (L) 66, 217, 259
Ken Janeck see: *R. yakushimanum* Ken Janeck
K. Wada see: *R. yakushimanum* K. Wada
'King George' (E) 192

'Lady Chamberlain' (L) 80, 233, 262
'Lanny's Pride' (L) 50, 233, 261
R. lapponicum (L) 57, 217, 259, 265
'Laurie' (L) 53, 57, 60, 61, 233, 261
'Lavender Girl' (E) 77
'Lee's Dark Purple' (E) 54, 55, 56, 224, 260
'Lemon Ice' (E) 62
'Lemon Mist' (L) 51, 52, 233, 262
'Lem's Cameo' (E) 51, 73, 225, 261
'Lem's Monarch' (E) 73, 225, 259
'Letty Edwards' (E) 77
R. leucaspis (L) 19, 217, 259
R. litangense (L) 66, 217, 259
'Llenroc' (L) 57, 60, 61, 64, 233, 261
'Loder's White' (E) 51, 77, 80, 225, 260
'Lodestar' (E) 56, 59, 63, 72, 82, 225, 260
R. lutescens (L) 52, 78, 79, 81, 217, 259

R. macabeanum (E) 19
'Madame Masson' (E) 71, 225, 260
'Macopin (L) 56
R. makinoi (E) 52, 58, 60, 64, 70, 71, 214, 258; Fig. 11
'Malta' (L) 82, 233, 261, 265
'Malvatica' 240
'Marcia' (E) 80, 225, 261
Maricee see: *R. sargentianum* Maricee
'Markeeta's Flame' (E) 51, 225, 260
'Markeeta's Prize' (E) 52, 225, 260
'Mars' (E) 193, 194
'Mary Belle' (E) 52, 60, 61, 225, 261
'Mary Fleming' (L) 50, 53, 57, 59, 60, 61, 62, 64, 66, 69, 71, 72, 124, 234, 262; Fig. 36
'Maxecat' (E) 71, 225, 259
R. maximum (E) 18, 20, 50, 54, 57, 58, 63, 65, 68, 70, 71, 72, 82, 192, 214, 258; Fig. 12
'Maximum Roseum' (E) 50, 56, 57, 63, 71, 225, 260, 265
'May Day' (E) 79
'Medusa' (E) 67, 225, 261
Mehlquist Hybrids (L) 231
'Melanie Shaw' (E) 61
R. metternichii (E) 58, 64, 66, 70, 71, 72, 77, 82, 192, 193, 214, 258
'Mi Amor' (L) 51
R. micranthum (L) 57, 218, 259
'Minnie' (E) 71, 225, 260
Mist Maiden see: *R. yakushimanum* Mist Maiden
R. minus (L) 18, 50, 57, 58, 63, 68, 72, 192, 218, 259
'Molly Fordham' (L) 56, 61, 62, 234, 261
'Moonstone' (E) 81, 225, 261
R. morii (E) 79, 81, 214, 258
'Mother Greer' (E) 66, 234, 261
R. moupinense (L) 52, 218, 259
'Mr. W. R. Coe' (E) 53
'Mrs. A. T. de La Mare' (E) 77, 226, 260
'Mrs. Betty Robinson' (E) 67, 81, 226, 261
'Mrs. C. S. Sargent' (E) 60, 63, 226, 259, 265
'Mrs. E. C. Sterling' (E) 75, 226, 260
'Mrs. Furnival' (E) 50, 60, 73, 77, 226, 259
'Mrs. G. W. Leak' (E) 51, 78, 81, 226, 259
'Mrs. Tom H. Lowinsky' (E) 62, 77, 226, 260
'Mrs. W. C. Slocock' (E) 77, 226, 259
'Mucram' (L) 54, 234, 261
R. mucronulatum (L) 52, 57, 66, 67, 68, 72, 82, 192, 218, 259
R. mucronulatum Cornell Pink (L) 56, 59, 64, 232, 261
'My Lady' (L) 234, 261
'Myrtifolium' (L) 51, 234, 261

'Newburyport Belle' (E) 54, 55, 226, 259
'Nova Zembla' (E) 50, 53, 54, 56, 59, 60, 65, 68, 70, 72, 226, 260, 265; Fig. 30

'Odee Wright' (E) 226, 261
'Old Port' (E) 64, 226, 260
'Olga Mezitt' (L) 53, 56, 57, 59, 60, 61, 63, 64, 69, 72, 82, 234, 261
'Olin O. Dobbs' (E) 61, 226, 260
'Olive' (L) 234, 261
'Olympic Lady' (E) 81, 226, 260
R. orbiculare (E) 73, 79, 214, 258
R. oreodoxa (E) 67, 77, 79, 214, 258
R. oreotrephes (L) 67, 218, 258, 259
'Oudijks Favourite' (L) 78
R. ovatum (E) 72, 214, 258

R. pachysanthum (E) 60, 215, 258
'Parker's Pink' (E) 54, 55, 61, 64, 227, 259
'Parson's Gloriosum' (E) 63, 227, 260, 265
'Party Pink' (E) 56, 227, 259
'Patty Bee' (L) 61, 64, 66, 234, 262
'Peace' (L) 80, 234, 261
R. pemakoense (L) 19
'Percy Wiseman' (E) 227, 261
'Pikeland' (L) 53, 234, 261
'Pink Bonnet' (E) 69
'Pink Carolinianum' (L) 82
'Pink Diamond' see: 'Weston's Pink Diamond'
'Pink Drift' (L) 78, 79, 234, 261
'Pink Fondant' (E) 69, 227, 259
Pink Parasol see: *R. yakushimanum* Pink Parasol
'Pink Pearl' (E) 51, 78, 80, 81, 227, 259; Fig. 84
'Pink Sherbet' (E) 62
'Pink Snowflakes' (L) 51, 74, 234, 261
'Pink Touch' (E) 69
'Pink Twins' (E) 62
'Pink Walloper' (E) 52, 67, 227, 259
'Pioneer' (L) 50, 56, 60, 61, 82, 234, 261, 265
'Pipit' (L) 79, 235, 261
'P.J.M.' (L) 51, 53, 56, 57, 58, 59, 60, 61, 62, 63, 64, 66, 67, 69, 70, 71, 72, 73, 78, 82, 85, 89, 91, 124, 131, 149, 183, 235, 261, 265; Figs. 37, 78
'P.J.M. Elite' (L) 235
'Platinum Pearl' (E) 61, 227, 259

R. ponticum (E) 18, 51, 52, 78, 215, 258
'Praecox' (L) 78, 79, 80, 235, 261
Pride Hybrids (E) 222, 229
'Princess Anne' (L) 78, 235, 262
R. pseudochrysanthum (E) 60, 64, 66, 78, 79, 192, 258
R. pseudochrysanthum (Nelson's Form) 58, 215
'Purple Gem' (L) 61, 82, 89, 183, 235, 261, 265
'Purple Splendour' (E) 51, 61, 67, 227, 260; Fig. 31; see also *Plant Index: Azaleas*
'Purpureum Elegans' (E) 63

'Queen Nefertite' (E) 52

R. racemosum (L) 51, 59, 60, 64, 66, 67, 70, 78, 79, 192, 218, 259
'Ramapo' (L) 51, 52, 56, 60, 64, 66, 67, 74, 82, 235, 261; Fig. 38
'Redder Yet' (E) 69, 227, 260, 265
R. rex ssp. *rex* (E) 215, 258
'Ring of Fire' (E) 66, 227, 261
'Rocket' (E) 227, 259
'Rose Elf' (L) 67, 74, 235, 261
'Rose Marie' (L) 61, 235, 261
'Rose Point' (E) 73, 227, 259
'Roseum Elegans' (E) 57, 59, 65, 70, 81, 227, 260, 265
'Roseum Pink' (E) 56, 63, 71, 72, 227, 259, 265; Fig. 32
'Rothenburg' (E) 79, 228, 261
R. roxieanum (E) 64, 66, 79, 215, 258, 259
R. rubiginosum (L) 79, 218, 259
'Ruby Bowman' (E) 52, 65, 228, 259
'Ruby Hart' (E) 228, 260
R. russatum (L) 59, 60, 67, 77, 218, 259
'Russell Harmon' (E) 56, 63, 228, 259, 265

'Saffron Queen' (L) 51, 235, 262
'Sandwich Appleblossom' see: 'Apple Blossom'
'Sapphire' (L) 67, 79, 235, 261
'Sappho' (E) 53, 81, 221, 228, 260
R. sargentianum (L) 234
R. sargentianum Maricee (L) 74, 234, 261
'Scarlet Wonder' (E) 79, 228, 260
'Scintillation' (E) 50, 53, 57, 59, 60, 61, 63, 64, 65, 69, 70, 72, 82, 228, 259; Fig. 33
'Senoria Meldon' (L) 66, 235, 261
'September Song' (E) 66, 228, 261
'Seta' (L) 67, 80, 235

'Shamrock' (E) 228, 261
'Sham's Candy' (E) 62, 63, 228, 259
'Sham's Ruby' (E) 82, 228, 260
'Shawme Lake' (E) 63, 228, 260
'Shilsonii' (E) 79, 228, 260
'Shrimp Girl' see: 'Shrimp Pink'
'Shrimp Pink' (L) 56, 235, 261
'Sir Charles Lemon' (E) 228, 260
'Slippery Rock' (E) 56
'Small Gem' (L) 67, 236, 261
R. smirnowii (E) 60, 63, 77, 215, 258
R. smithii (E) 52, 215, 258
'Snow Lady' (L) 52, 74, 79, 236, 261; Fig. 39
R. soulei (E) 79, 215, 258
'Spring Delight' (L) 62, 236, 261
'Spring Parade' (E) 59, 62, 228, 260
'Spring Song' (L) 64, 236, 262
'St. Judy' (L) 77, 80, 236, 262
'Starry Night' (L) 61, 236, 261
R. strigillosum (E) 62; Fig. 14
'Summer Rose' (E) 57, 229, 260
'Summer Summit' (E) 62
'Susan' (E) 77, 81, 229, 260
R. sutchuenense (E) 66, 215, 258

'Taurus' (E) 61, 67, 229, 260
'Terrific' (E) 69, 229, 259, 265
R. thompsonii (E) 18, 79, 215, 258
'Tiffany' (L) 61, 236, 261
'Todmorden' (E) 229, 259
'Tom Everett' (E) 53, 64, 71, 229, 259
'Tom Koenig' (L) 53, 236, 261
'Tony' (E) 82, 229, 260
'Towhead' (L) 62
'Trilby' (E) 51, 229, 260
'Trinity' (E) 56, 229, 260
'Trude Webster' (E) 50, 51, 66, 75, 229, 259

'Unique' (E) 51, 61, 66, 67, 81, 229, 261
R. uvarifolium (E) 79, 215, 258

'Van' (E) 66, 229, 259
'Vanessa' (E) 78
R. veitchianum (L) 52, 218, 259
R. vernicosum (E) 72, 215, 258
R. vernicosum 18139 (E) 192, 215
'Vernus' (E) 56, 229, 259, 265
'Virginia Richards' (E) 73, 81, 229, 261
R. viscosum (L) 18, 71, 218, 259; Fig. 16
'Vulcan' (E) 50, 61, 64, 65, 230, 260
'Vulcan's Flame' (E) 61, 230, 260

'Waltham' (L) 56, 64, 236, 261

R. wardii (E) 19, 73, 77, 79, 193, 215, 258
R. wasonii (E) 79
'Weston's Pink Diamond' (L) 56, 61, 236, 261
'Wheatley' (E) 53, 60, 71, 72, 230, 259
'White Pearl' (E) 75, 230, 260
'White Surprise' (L) 61
'Wigeon' (L) 66, 236, 261
R. williamsianum (E) 19, 66, 67, 78, 81, 192, 193, 216, 258
'Wilsonii' (L) 82, 236, 261
'Windbeam' (L) 50, 53, 54, 56, 59, 60, 63, 64, 66, 70, 71, 72, 82, 236, 261, 265; Fig. 40
'Winsome' (E) 79, 230, 260
'Wongii' (L) 80
'Wyandanch Pink' (E) 82, 230, 259
'Wyanoki' (L) 63, 236, 261

'Yaku Duchess' (E) 62, 230, 259

Yaku Fairy see: *R. keiskei* Yaku Fairy
'Yaku King' (E) 62, 230, 259; Fig. 72
'Yaku Prince' (E) 57, 72, 230, 259
'Yaku Queen' (E) 62, 72, 230, 259
R. yakushimanum (E) 51, 52, 54, 55, 58, 59, 60, 62, 63, 64, 65, 66, 67, 68, 70, 71, 72, 73, 75, 77, 78, 79, 81, 82, 105, 160, 192, 193, 216, 230, 258; Fig. 13
R. yakushimanum K. Wada (E) 50, 59
R. yakushimanum Ken Janeck (E) 50, 59, 62, 63, 82, 216
R. yakushimanum Mist Maiden (E) 20, 63, 82, 85; Fig. 69
R. yakushimanum Pink Parasol (E) 216
'Yellow Eye' (L) 62, 237, 261
'Yellow Hammer' (L) 80, 237, 262
R. yungningense (L) 66, 218, 259
R. yunnanense (L) 52, 79, 218, 259

R. zeylanicum (E) 18, 51, 216, 258

Plant Index: Azaleas

(EV) = Evergreen; (D) = Deciduous. Species' names appear in italics. Hybrids or cultivars appear in roman type with single quotes. Named selections are listed by species.

'Apple Blossom' (D) 81; see also *Plant Index: Rhododendrons*
'Addy Wery' (EV) 77, 244, 262
'Adelaine Pope' (EV) 53, 244, 262
'Adonis' (EV) 81, 244, 262
R. alabamense (D) 22, 50, 53, 57, 253, 262
'Aladdin' (EV) 81, 244, 262
R. albrechtii (D) 22, 65, 67, 74, 77, 80, 253, 262; Fig. 41
'Alexander' (EV) 67, 244, 262, 265
'Ambrosia' (EV) 191
'Amoenum' (EV) 62, 68, 244, 262
R. amoenum see: *R. obtusum*
R. amogianum (D) 22
'Amy' (EV) 81, 244, 262
'Annabella' (D) 78, 254, 264
'Anna Kehr' (EV) 53, 191, 244, 262
'Apple Blossom' (D) 81
R. arborescens (D) 22, 50, 54, 57, 61, 64, 65, 67, 80, 81, 82, 251, 253, 263
'Atlanta' (EV) 63, 244, 262
R. atlanticum (D) 22, 50, 57, 66, 68, 73, 74, 77, 80, 82, 191, 251, 253, 263
'Aurora' (D) 56, 254, 264
R. austrinum (D) 22, 50, 53, 57, 74, 191, 253, 262, 264

Back Acres Hybrids (EV) 238, 245, 248
R. bakeri (D) 22, 50, 53, 55, 56, 57, 59, 61, 65, 68, 69, 70, 72, 73, 77, 80, 82, 251, 253, 263, 264; Fig. 42
R. balsaminaeflorum (EV) 65, 243, 262
Beasley Hybrids (D) 251, 256
'Beaulieu' (D) 73, 78, 254, 264
'Beaulieu Manor' see: 'Beaulieu'

Belgian Indian Hybrids (EV) 238, 240, 241
Beltsville Dwarfs (EV) 191
Beltsville Hybrids (EV) 246, 247
'Ben Morrison' (EV) 50, 65, 244, 262, 263; Fig. 53
'Beni Kirishima' (EV) 69, 244, 262
'Berryrose' (D) 71, 254, 264
'Betty Oliver' (D) 51
'Big Joe' (EV) 69, 244, 262
'Blaauw's Pink' (EV) 78, 244, 262
'Blue Danube' (EV) 68, 78, 244, 263
'Border Gem' (EV) 56
'Boudoir' (EV) 55, 56, 60, 63, 82, 244, 262
'Bouquet de Flore' (D) 69, 81, 254, 264
Bovee Knap Hill Hybrid (D) 255
'Brazil' (D) 59, 62, 64, 69, 71, 72, 73, 254, 264
'Buccaneer' (EV) 60, 244, 262
'Bullfinch' (D) 71, 254, 264
'Buttercup' (D) 56, 254, 264
'Buzzard' (D) 53, 254, 264

R. calendulaceum (D) 22, 51, 53, 54, 55, 57, 59, 60, 61, 65, 66, 69, 70, 72, 77, 81, 82, 251, 253, 263, 264; Fig. 43
'Cameo' (EV) 81, 244, 262
'Camp's Red' (D) 253
R. canadense (D) 22, 54, 64, 67, 68, 81, 82, 253, 263
R. canescens (D) 18, 22, 50, 51, 53, 57, 73, 253, 263
'Cannon's Double' (D) 57, 254, 264
Carla Hybrids (EV) 238, 244, 250
Carlson Hybrids (EV) 238–39, 250

'Caroline Gable' (EV) 244, 262
'Cascade' (Glenn Dale) (EV) 244
'Cascade' (Shammarello) (EV) 54, 63, 82,
    245, 263, 265
'Cavalier' (EV) 71, 245, 262
'Cecile' (D) 51, 56, 57, 60, 67, 69, 70, 72,
    80, 254, 264; Fig. 49
'Chetco' (D) 53, 68, 254, 264
'Chicago' (D) 80, 254, 264
'Chief Joseph' (D) 73
'Chinsoy' (EV) 66
Chisolm-Merritt Hybrids (EV) 239, 246
'Chojuho' (EV) 191
'Christmas Cheer' (EV) 81, 245, 262
'Cleopatra' (EV) 239
'Cloud Nine' (EV) 52, 245, 263
'Coast Azalea' see: R. atlanticum
'Coccinea' (D) 191
'Coccinea Speciosa' (D) 65, 77, 80, 81,
    254, 264
'Conversation Piece' (EV) 61, 68, 245,
    262
'Copper Cloud' (D) 65
'Coral Bells' see: 'Kirin'
'Corneille' (D) 65, 77
'Corringe' (D) 51, 254, 264
'Corsage' (EV) 54, 63, 70, 81, 82, 191, 245,
    263, 265
R. coryi (D) 22
'Cream Cup' (EV) 191
'Crimson Tide' (D) 55, 255, 264

David Leach Hybrids (D) 250, 252
'Daviesi' (D) 57, 60, 69, 77, 80, 255, 264
'Dayspring' (EV) 65, 245, 263
'Debonnaire' (EV) 53, 245, 262
'Delaware Valley White' (EV) 50, 55, 59,
    60, 65, 66, 69, 70, 72, 245, 263; Fig.
    55
'Delicatissima' (D) 78, 255, 264
'Desiree' (EV) 61, 245, 263, 265
'Diana' (EV) 81, 245, 262
'Dorothy Clark' (EV) 50, 245, 262
'Dorsett' (EV) 191
'Dr. Henry Schroeder' (EV) 57
'Dr. James Dippel' (EV) 191
'Dragon' (EV) 191
'Dream' (EV) 69, 72, 245, 262

'Easter Parade' (EV) 53, 245, 262
Eastern Fire see: R. kaempferi Eastern Fire
Eden Hybrids (EV) 239, 247
'Edna' (EV) 73
'Eikan' (EV) 74, 245, 263
'Eliza Hyatt' (EV) 57, 245, 262, 265

'Elizabeth Gable' (EV) 69, 81, 246, 262
'Elsie Lee' (EV) 56, 57, 70, 71, 72, 82, 191,
    246, 263, 265
R. eriocarpum see: R. tamurae
'Eureka' (EV) 61, 246, 262
'Everest' (EV) 68, 69, 74, 79, 246, 263
Exbury Hybrids (D) 66, 68, 82, 89, 183,
    248, 251, 254, 255, 256; Fig. 87

R. farrerae (D) 22
'Fascination' (EV) 50, 246, 262
'Fashion' (EV) 51, 246, 262
'Fedora' (EV) 54, 55, 60, 63, 73, 81, 246,
    262
'Festive' (EV) 51, 246, 263
'Fireball' (D) 56, 57, 65, 255, 264; Fig. 50
'Firefly' (EV) 238
'Flame Azalea' see: R. calendulaceum
'Flamingo' (EV) 71, 246, 262
R. flammeum (D) 22, 50, 51, 53, 253, 263,
    264
R. flavum (D) 18, 21
'Forest Fire' (EV) 65, 246, 262
'Fraserii' (D) 81, 255, 264
'Frostburg' (EV) 191

Gable Hybrids (EV) 239, 244, 245, 246,
    247, 248, 249, 250; see also Plant
    Index: Rhododendrons
'Gable's Tall Lavendar' (EV) 63
'Gaiety' (EV) 67, 246, 262
'Gardenia' (EV) 191
'Gay' (EV) 71, 246, 263
'George L. Tabor' (EV) 50, 51
'George Reynolds' (D) 61, 255, 264
'Geraldine' (EV) 54
Ghent Hybrids (D) 68, 82, 251, 254, 255,
    256, 257
'Gibraltar' (D) 51, 53, 56, 57, 59, 60, 62,
    64, 65, 67, 68, 69, 70, 71, 72, 73, 81,
    89, 183, 191, 255, 264; Fig. 51
'Ginger' (D) 62, 67, 73, 78, 255, 264
'Girard Border Gem' (EV) 59, 72, 191,
    246, 262, 265
'Girard Chiara' (EV) 59, 72, 246, 262, 265
'Girard Fuschia' (EV) 59, 246, 263, 265
'Girard Hot Shot' (EV) 61, 246, 263
Girard Hybrids (D)(EV) 239, 246, 256
'Girard Rose' (EV) 61, 246, 262
'Girard Scarlet' (EV) 80, 191, 246, 263,
    265
'Glacier' (EV) 53, 70, 71, 191, 247, 263
'Glamour' (EV) 52, 67, 73, 247, 263
Glenn Dale Hybrids (EV) 238, 239, 240,
    242, 244, 245, 246, 247, 248, 249,
    250

'Golden Crest' (D) 71, 255, 264
'Golden Eagle' (D) 62
'Golden Oriole' (D) 60, 64, 69, 78, 255, 264
'Golden Peace' (D) 57, 71, 255, 264
'Golden Sunset' (D) 64, 71, 255, 264
'Goldflakes' (D) 70, 255, 264
'Gumpo' (EV) 52, 66, 241, 247, 262, 263
'Guy Yerkes' (EV) 60, 66, 247, 262

'Hampton Beauty' (EV) 71, 247, 262
'Hardy Gardenia' (EV) 53, 247, 263
Harris Hybrids (EV) 240, 242
'Helen Curtis' (EV) 56, 57, 59, 71, 72, 247, 263, 265
'Helena' (EV) 247, 262
'Herbert' (EV) 54, 59, 60, 69, 70, 72, 82, 191, 247, 263, 265; Fig. 56
Hershey Hybrids (EV) 240, 247; Fig. 76
'Hershey's Red' (EV) 67, 70, 71, 247, 263; Fig. 57
'H. H. Hume' (EV) 50, 80, 247, 263
'Hino Crimson' (EV) 60, 63, 67, 68, 70, 71, 73, 74, 80, 81, 89, 183, 191, 247, 263; Fig. 58
'Hino Pink' (EV) 57, 247, 262, 265
'Hino Red' (EV) 56, 57, 59, 72, 247, 263, 265
'Hinode Giri' (EV) 51, 77, 81, 89, 183, 247, 263
'Hinomayo' (EV) 77, 78, 80, 81, 247, 262
'Homebush' (D) 51, 56, 57, 59, 60, 64, 65, 67, 68, 69, 72, 73, 74, 77, 80, 191, 255, 264; Fig. 52
'Hot Shot' (EV) 56, 191
H. R. Schroeder Hybrids (EV) 242, 245, 249

'Ilam Copper Cloud' (D) 255, 264
Ilam Hybrids (D) 251, 255, 256
'Ilam Peachy Keen' see: 'Peachy Keen'
'Ilam Persian Melon' see: 'Persian Melon'
'Ilam Red Letter' (D) 51, 191, 255, 264
'Ilam Red Velvet' (D) 255, 264
'Ima-shojo' see: 'Christmas Cheer'
'Indian Summer' (EV) 191
'Indica' see: *R. simsii*
'Indica Alba' (EV) 238
R. indica alba (EV) 245
R. indicum (EV) 21, 67, 68, 73, 241, 243, 262
R. indicum Balsaminiflorum (EV) 57, 243
'Inspiration' (D) 73
Inter-Group Hybrids (EV) 255

'Irene Koster' (D) 74, 81, 255, 264
'Iro-Hayama' (EV) 77, 78, 247, 263
'Iveryana' (EV) 52, 247, 263

'J. Jennings' (D) 191
'James Gable' (EV) 59, 69, 73, 81, 248, 263, 265
Jane Abbott Hybrids (EV) 60
R. japonicum (D) 22, 60, 67, 81, 82, 251, 252, 253, 263, 264
'Jean Haerens' see: 'John Haerens'
'Jeanne' (EV) 191
'John Cairns' (EV) 78, 81, 248, 263
'John Haerens' (EV) 52, 248, 263

Kaempferi Hybrids (EV) 240, 241, 244, 246, 248, 249, 250
R. kaempferi (EV) 20, 21, 57, 59, 60, 64, 65, 68, 69, 72, 74, 77, 81, 82, 238, 239, 240, 242, 243, 262
R. kaempferi Eastern Fire (EV) 80
'Karens' (EV) 82, 248, 263, 265
'Kathleen' (D) 56, 59, 67, 73, 74, 82, 255
'Kathleen' (Gable) (EV) 248
'Kathleen' (Glenn Dale) (EV) 248
Kehr Hybrids (EV) 240, 244, 250
Kerrigan Hybrids (EV) 240, 245, 246, 250
'Kilauea' (D) 255, 264
'Kirin' (EV) 51, 52, 70, 71, 78, 245, 248, 262; Fig. 54
R. kiusianum (EV) 21, 52, 54, 57, 59, 60, 61, 65, 67, 68, 69, 73, 74, 77, 79, 82, 191, 240, 243, 262
R. kiusianum var. *album* (EV) 60
R. kiusianum Komo Kulshan (EV) 55, 57
R. kiusianum SH-RBF (EV) 61
'Klondyke' (D) 51, 53, 56, 57, 59, 60, 62, 69, 70, 71, 72, 74, 191, 255, 264
Knap Hill Hybrids (D) 68, 82, 251, 252, 254, 255, 256, 257
'Knap Hill Red' (D) 191
R. komiyamae (EV) 21
'Koster's Brilliant Red' (D) 81, 255, 264
R. kurume (EV) 188
Kurume Hybrids (EV) 238, 239, 240, 241, 244, 245, 247, 248, 249, 250

Leach Hybrids see: David Leach Hybrids
'Ledifolia Alba' (EV) 238
'Lemon Drop' (D) 64, 256, 264
'Leo' (EV) 78, 248, 263
Leonard Frisbee see: *R. occidentale* Leonard Frisbee
'Lhetco' (D) 67
'Life' (D) 51

Linwood Hybrids (EV) 241, 247
'Lorna' (EV) 60, 248, 262
'Louise Gable' (EV) 59, 61, 69, 73, 81, 191, 248, 263; Fig. 59
R. luteum (D) 22, 65, 67, 68, 69, 74, 79, 80, 82, 251, 253, 264; Fig. 44

'Macrantha' see: *R. indicum*
R. macrantha (EV) 66, 74, 243, 262
R. macrosepalum (EV) 21, 53, 65, 243, 262
'Magnifica' (D) 80, 256, 264
'Malvatica' (EV) 240
'Margaret Douglas' (EV) 50, 51, 65, 248, 262
R. mariesii (D) 22
Mariko see: *R. nakaharae* Mariko
'Marina' (D) 68, 256, 264
'Marion Merriman' (D) 77, 256, 264
'Marjorie' (EV) 54, 248, 263, 265
'Martha Hitchcock' (EV) 74, 191, 248, 263
'Mary Dalton' (EV) 61, 248, 263
'Maxwell' (EV) 238
'Maybelle' (EV) 56, 59, 248, 262, 265
R. microphyton (EV) 21
'Mildred Mae' (EV) 68, 248, 263
'Mizu no Yuma Buki' (EV) 191
'Modesty' (EV) 66, 248, 263
R. molle (D) 18, 22, 251, 252, 253, 264
R. mollis (D) 77
Mollis Hybrids (D) 68, 252, 254, 255, 256
'Moonbeam' (EV) 66, 249, 263
Mossholder-Bristow Hybrids (EV) 241, 245
'Mother's Day' (EV) 56, 60, 68, 73, 78, 80, 191, 249, 263
'Mrs. G. G. Gerbing' (EV) 50, 53, 249, 263
'Mrs. Henry Schroeder' (EV) 57, 249, 262
'Mrs. Nancy Dipple' (EV) 57, 249, 262
Mt. 7 Stars see: *R. nakaharae* Mt. 7 Stars
'Mt. St. Helens' (D) 56, 57, 61, 62, 256, 264
R. mucronatum (EV) 21, 77, 80, 81, 191, 238, 243, 262
'My Mary' (D) 53, 61, 256, 264
'Myogi' (EV) 191

'Nadine' (EV) 54, 241, 249, 262
R. nakaharae (EV) 21, 53, 57, 60, 65, 67, 68, 73, 77, 90, 241, 243, 262
R. nakaharae Mariko (EV) 79
R. nakaharae Mt. 7 Stars (EV) 80
'Nancy of Robin Hill' (EV) 53, 61, 65, 249, 262
'Naomi' (EV) 78, 249, 262

'Narcissiflora' (D) 59, 65, 69, 72, 74, 78, 80, 81, 191, 256, 264
R. nipponicum (D) 22
'Norma' (D) 80, 191, 256, 264
North Tisbury Hybrids (EV) 241, 244
Northern Lights Hybrids (D) 56, 256
R. nudiflorum see: *R. periclymenoides*
R. nudipes (D) 22

R. oblongifolium (D) 22
R. obtusum (EV) 18, 21, 57, 67, 68, 77, 79, 244
Occidentale Hybrids (D) 252, 255, 256
R. occidentale (D) 21, 22, 67, 68, 73, 74, 77, 79, 81, 252, 253, 263, 264
R. occidentale Leonard Frisbee (D) 80
'Old Gold' (D) 53, 56, 59, 69, 74, 78, 256, 264
R. oldhamii (EV) 21, 53, 68, 243, 262
'Opal' (EV) 191
'Orange Beauty' (EV) 65, 81, 249, 263
'Orangeade' (D) 51, 53, 256, 264
'Orient' (D) 71, 256, 264
R. otakumii (EV) 21
'Oxydol' (D) 56, 69, 72, 80, 81

'Palestrina' (EV) 60, 63, 74, 78, 80, 81, 249, 263, 265
'Parfait' (EV) 53, 249, 262, 265
'Peachy Keen' (D) 53, 256, 264
'Peggy Ann' (EV) 71
R. pentaphyllum (D) 22, 65, 81, 253, 263
Pericat Hybrids (EV) 241, 247
R. periclymenoides (D) 18, 22, 53, 54, 56, 59, 65, 66, 67, 68, 69, 70, 81, 82, 251, 253, 263; Fig. 45
'Persian Melon' (D) 61, 256, 264
'Persil' (D) 56, 77, 191, 256, 264
'Pink Drift' (EV) 73
'Pink Pearce' (EV) 249, 263
'Pink Pearl' (EV) 51, 66, 249, 262
'Pink Ruffles' (EV) 50, 51, 249, 262
'Pinkshell Azalea' see: *R. prinophyllum*
'Polar Bear' (EV) 191
'Polaris' (EV) 69, 249, 263
'Polypetalum' (EV) 67
R. poukhanense (EV) 56, 59, 60, 64, 69, 72, 77, 81, 82, 239, 242; Fig. 48
Pride Hybrids (EV) 55, 241, 248, 249
'Pride's Pink' (EV) 82, 249, 262
'Pride's Pride' (EV) 64
'Pride's White' (EV) 64
'Primrose' (D) 53
'Prince Henri de Pays-Bas' (D) 77, 256, 264

'Princess Royal' (D) 52, 68
R. prinophyllum (D) 22, 53, 56, 57, 60, 62, 64, 70, 72, 74, 82, 253, 263
R. prunifolium (D) 22, 50, 51, 53, 55, 57, 59, 61, 64, 69, 81, 89, 183, 191, 253, 263, 264
'Purple Splendour' (EV) 56, 67, 68, 73, 81, 82, 249, 263; Fig. 60; see also *Plant Index: Rhododendrons*

'Queen Emma' (D) 64
R. quinquefolium (D) 22, 77, 253, 263

'Raphael de Smet' (D) 77, 256, 264
'Red Red' (EV) 56, 72, 249, 263
'Red Ruffles' (EV) 51, 249, 263
'Red Velvet' (D) 72
'Refrain' (EV) 52, 249, 263
'Renne' (D) 52, 68, 69
R. repens (EV) 21
R. reticulatum (D) 22
Robin Hill Hybrids (EV) 241, 242, 245, 249
'Roehr's Peggy Ann' (EV) 249, 263
'Rose Greeley' (EV) 59, 72, 78, 191, 250, 263; Fig. 77
'Rosebud' (EV) 59, 60, 68, 69, 70, 73, 74, 78, 79, 80, 81, 82, 191, 250, 262; Fig. 61
R. roseum see: *R. prinophyllum*
'Royal Command' (D) 78, 256, 264
R. rubropilosum (EV) 21
'Rufus' (D) 55
Rustica Flora Pleno Hybrids (D) 252, 256
Rutherford Hybrids (EV) 238, 241, 249

'Sakata Red' (EV) 81, 250, 263
R. sanctum (D) 22
R. sataense (EV) 21, 240
'Satan' (D) 64
Satsuki Hybrids (EV) 241–42, 245, 247
R. scabrum (EV) 21
R. schlippenbachii (D) 59, 60, 61, 64, 65, 67, 68, 69, 72, 73, 74, 77, 80, 81, 82, 89, 183, 253, 263; Fig. 46
'Scott Gartrell' (EV) 191
'Seneca' (EV) 74, 250, 263
R. serpyllifolium (EV) 21, 53, 65, 243, 262
R. serpyllifolium var. *albiflorum* (EV) 21
R. serrulatum (D) 22, 50, 57, 253, 264
SH-RBF see: *R. kiusianum* SH-RBF
Shammarello Hybrids (EV) 242, 245, 246, 247, 248, 249
'Sherwood Orchid' (EV) 52, 63, 67, 74, 250, 263

'Sherwood Red' (EV) 50, 52, 74, 250, 263; Fig. 62
R. simsii (EV) 17, 21, 68, 238, 243, 262
Slocock Hybrids (D) 251, 254
Slonecker Hybrids (D) 252
'Snow' (EV) 51, 238, 250, 263
Southern Indian Hybrids (EV) 242, 247, 249
R. speciosum see: *R. flammeum*
'Spek's Orange' (D) 77, 256, 264
'Springtime' (EV) 54, 56, 59, 60, 69, 72, 91, 250, 262; Fig. 63
'Starlight' (Kerrigan) (EV) 52, 250, 262
'Starlight' (Carlson) (EV) 250
'Stewartstonian' (EV) 57, 59, 60, 65, 67, 68, 69, 70, 72, 81, 250, 263; Fig. 64
'Strawberry Ice' (D) 56, 59, 69, 72, 74
'Sun Chariot' (D) 52, 57
'Sunglow' (EV) 53, 250, 263
'Sunte Nectarine' (D) 78, 256, 264
'Superba' (D) 77, 256, 264
'Surprise' (EV) 61, 65, 250, 263
'Sylphides' (D) 74, 257, 264

R. tamurae (EV) 21, 241
'Tang' (D) 56
'Tangelo' (D) 67
R. tashiroi (EV) 21
'Tonga' (D) 56
R. tosaense (EV) 21
'Toucan' (D) 59, 64, 69, 70, 71, 72, 257, 264
'Tower Dainty' (D) 80, 257, 264
R. tschonoskii (EV) 21
R. tsusiophyllum (EV) 21
'Tunis' (D) 57
'Twenty Grand' (EV) 68, 250, 263

'Unique' (D) 77, 257, 264

R. vaseyi (D) 22, 51, 54, 55, 56, 60, 61, 64, 65, 68, 70, 72, 74, 77, 80, 81, 82, 254, 263; Fig. 47
R. vaseyi var. *alba* (D) 61, 74
'Vespers' (EV) 66, 250, 263
R. viscosum (D) 22, 50, 53, 60, 64, 69, 77, 80, 81, 82, 251, 254, 264
Vuyk Hybrids (EV) 242, 249, 250
'Vuyk's Rosyred' (EV) 79, 250, 262
'Vuyk's Scarlet' (EV) 67, 78, 80, 191, 250, 263

'Wakaebisu' (EV) 66, 250, 263
'Ward's Ruby' (EV) 81, 191, 250, 263
'Washington State Centennial' (D) 67

Wells Hybrids (D) 255
Weston Hybrids (D) 252, 256
'White Lights' (D) 67
'White Rosebud' (EV) 71, 250, 263
'White Swan' (D) 56
'Wilhelmina Vuyk' see: 'Palestrina'
'Windsor Appleblossom' (D) 61
'Windsor Buttercup' (D) 53, 61

Windsor Hybrids (D) 251

'Yankee Doodle' (EV) 56, 250, 262
R. yedoense (EV) 21, 67, 81, 243, 262
R. yedoense var. *poukhanense* (EV) 21, 191, 243, 262
'Yellow Pom Pom' (D) 55

Subject Index

Acclimation 47
Acid soil 24
Aftercare 142
Air drainage 38
Air temperature 38
Aluminum sulfate 27
Azalea Hybrid groups 238

Backcrossing 199
Bark split 132
Bonsai 89
Bud moth 131

Care in the landscape 105
Cleft graft 153
Climate 42, 48
   rainfall 45
   temperature 44
Cold frame 167
Companion plants 90
   bulbs 91
   ground covers 91
   trees and shrubs 90
   wild flowers 91
Container growing 177
Cuttings 149
   hardening off 141
   aftercare 142

Dead-heading 115
Disease control 119
Diseases 119, 120
   armillaria root rot 122
   blight 123
   bud blast 125
   dieback 122
   leaf gall 125
   leaf rust 125
   petal blight 124
   powdery mildew 123

   root rot 120
   twig blight 122
Division 147

Elepidote 13

Ferrous sulfate 26
Fertilizer 96, 108
Field growing 165
Flower show 201
   committees 202
   entry rules 208
   evaluation 210
   judging 209
   preparing trusses 204
   show classes 206
   types of shows 202

Garden sanitation 119
Good Doer plant lists 47, 213
Good Doer plants 47
Grafting 151
Green graft 157

Hardening off 141
History 13–21
Hybridizing 187
   collecting seed 196
   goals 189
   growing seedlings 159
   history 188
   methods 195, 198
   parent selection 190
   pollination 195
   research 189
   selecting superior seedlings
      200

Insects 126
   bud moth 131

lace bug 126
leaf miner 128
midge 127
mite 127
rhododendron borer 128
scale 128
stem borer 129
thrip 127
weevil 130
white fly 127
Ions 26
Iron 112
Iron deficiency 112
Iron sulfate 26

Lace bug 126
Landscaping 83
    accent plants 85
    border plantings 87
    color 84
    companion plants 90
    container growing 89
    foundation planting 90
    group planting 86
    natural screens 87
    spacing 86, 88
    specimen plants 85
    woodland planting 87
Leaf miner 128
Lepidote 13
Light 31

Media 139, 181
Midge 127
Minerals 37
Minor elements 111
Mites 127
Mulches 33
Mulching 107, 175

Nearing Frame 164
Nitrogen 36, 109
Nursery 165
    container growing 177
    field growing 165
Nutritional needs 36, 108
Nutritional deficiencies 108
    minor elements 111
    nitrogen 109
    phosphorus 110
    potassium 110

Organic matter 33
Origin—azaleas 21
Overwintering 183

Peat moss 29, 34
Pests 126; *see also* Insects
pH 24
Phosphorus 110, 136
Pollination 195
Potassium 110, 136
Physiological problems 132
    bark split 132
    foliage damage 132
    stem canker 132
    sunscald 132
Plant explorers 18, 19
Plant protection 100
Plant selection 46
Propagation 135
    deciduous azaleas 146–48
    evergreen azaleas 139, 143
    rhododendrons 149, 151–53,
        157–59
Pruning 113, 169
Purchasing plants 46

Quality rating 41

Rhododendron borer 128
Root cuttings 148
Root killing temperatures 89
Root pruning 118

Saddle graft 152
Selection of plants 41
Shade 23, 31
Side graft 153
Site 23
Soil amendments 34
Soil drainage 28
Soil pH 24
Soil structure 29
Soil temperature 35, 120
Species 19
Sphagnum moss 29, 34
Stem borer 129
Stem canker 132
Stem cuttings 146
Sulfur 27
Sunscald 132

Thrip 127
Tissue culture 148
Transplanting 93–103
    aftercare 100
    best time 93
    fertilizer use 96
    large plants 105
    preparation 94

procedure 97

Watering 105
Weeds 112, 172

Weevils 130
White fly 127
Wind 37
Windbreak 37, 87

Corrections

page 18. 1803 *Rhododendron caucasicum* from Europe, *R. obtusum* from Asia, and *R. minus* from North America

page 20. First sentence to read, Species tend to propagate "true" from seed with a range of variability among seedlings, some species exhibiting wider variability than others. Second sentence of third paragraph to read, . . . this can lead to much debate whether such plants are of individual species or of hybrid origin.

page 22. Japan. *Rhododendron amagianum* is the correct spelling

page 26. Third sentence to read, Since lime moves through the soil very slowly it is best to incorporate it into the soil before planting (surface application to landscape plants is effective, however, because rhododendrons have feeder roots near the soil surface).

page 28. First sentences to read, . . . it is not recommended in large amounts for rhododendrons. *Rhododendron* is rather tolerant of aluminum but can be damaged by excess aluminum in the soil.

page 29. Last sentences to read, Sandy soils benefit greatly from the moisture-retentive qualities of sphagnum peat moss, but that rots quickly. Use about 25% sphagnum peat moss and 75% fine pine bark to make up the organic amendments incorporated into sandy soils.

pages 41 ff. In Chapter Three (and elsewhere), please read "hybrid" in most instances where the word "cultivar" appears as the intent is to address selection of all *Rhododendron* entities, whether they be taxa (species, subspecies, etc.), named or unnamed selections of taxa, and named or unnamed hybrids of known or unknown parentage.

page 50. 'Champagne' is the correct spelling

page 91. Wild Flowers: lady's slipper (*Cypripedium* spp.)

page 95. First sentence of third paragraph to read, Incorporate decayed pine bark . . . .

page 98. Width shown in Fig. 90 is 4 ft.

page 99. Last sentence of second paragraph to read, . . . roots will quickly extend into such media, but it is still necessary to spread the roots when transplanting.

page 161. Fig. 109: After about three months the seedlings are ready for transplanting.

page 191. Mildew Resistance: 'Coccinea', 'J. Jennings', 'Persil', *R. speciosum*

page 193. Last sentence of second paragraph to read, Similar research reveals that the species capable of dwarfing or developing compact offspring among the nonscaly rhododendrons include *R. yakushimanum* and *R. williamsianum*.

page 195. Add sentence to 5: If stored for more than one week add a desiccant such as silica gel.

page 253. Table 7: *R. pentaphyllum* to 4 ft. (1.2 m), *R. quinquefolium* to 3 ft. (0.9 m)